THE WORLD'S MOST
MYSTERIOUS MURDERS

THE WORLD'S MOST MYSTERIOUS MURDERS

by

LIONEL AND PATRICIA FANTHORPE

A HOUNSLOW BOOK
A MEMBER OF THE DUNDURN GROUP
TORONTO • OXFORD

Publisher: Anthony Hawke
Copy-Editor: Lloyd Davis
Design: James M. Hart
Printer: Transcontinental

National Library of Canada Cataloguing in Publication Data
Fanthorpe, R. Lionel
The world's most mysterious murders / Lionel and Patricia Fanthorpe.

Includes bibliographical references.
ISBN 1-55002-439-6

1. Murder. I. Fanthorpe, Patricia II. Title.

HV6505.F35 2003   364.15'23   C2003-901078-3

1   2   3   4   5   07   06   05   04   03

Canadä

We acknowledge the support of the Canada Council for the Arts and the Ontario Arts Council for our publishing program. We also acknowledge the financial support of the Government of Canada through the Book Publishing Industry Development Program and The Association for the Export of Canadian Books, and the Government of Ontario through the Ontario Book Publishers Tax Credit program, and the Ontario Media Development Corporation's Ontario Book Initiative.

Care has been taken to trace the ownership of copyright material used in this book. The author and the publisher welcome any information enabling them to rectify any references or credit in subsequent editions.

J. Kirk Howard, President

Printed and bound in Canada.⊕
Printed on recycled paper.
www.dundurn.com

Dundurn Press	Dundurn Press	Dundurn Press
8 Market Street	73 Lime Walk	2250 Military Road
Suite 200	Headington, Oxford,	Tonawanda NY
Toronto, Ontario, Canada	England	U.S.A. 14150
M5E 1M6	OX3 7AD	

THE WORLD'S MOST
MYSTERIOUS MURDERS

TABLE OF CONTENTS

FOREWORD
by Canon Stanley Mogford, M.A.

M urders are a fact of life. They have always been happening, and they no doubt always will. Motives may vary but are common to murders all down the centuries and all over the world.

One persistent motive is greed. Someone possesses what another wants. Abel in the Book of Genesis had his Lord's affection, and Cain resented it. Greed has led to countless murders, sometimes even for the most trivial of gains. George Joseph Smith, the infamous murderer of the "brides in the bath," did it all for a return that by any standard was paltry beyond belief. Greed has created much havoc and tragedy.

Another underlying motive is hatred. Hatreds begin slowly but, if allowed to persist, grow to be all-consuming. One of Tolstoy's great short stories is called "A Spark Neglected Burns the Whole House." Hatred drives one neighbour to take a shotgun to another or pour petrol into his house to set it on fire. Hatred takes many forms, all of them harmful. Passion turns some to murder. The last sad lady to be hanged for murder in Britain, Ruth Ellis, was so tormented by her seemingly cruel lover that she gave way to the demons inside her and blasted him to death. She never sought to excuse herself for what she had done and, perhaps more than anything else, her execution led to a public aversion to all such hangings.

Fear of discovery seems yet another recurrent reason to kill. The need to suppress a secret has driven many to unspeakable crimes. The courts and the police are often frustrated by witnesses who know what has happened and yet are fearful of speaking against those who intimidate them. Psychotic murders are harder to analyze. They often seem motiveless, but their origins lie somewhere in the recesses of a diseased or troubled mind. Those weak and bullied and solitary, who see themselves as victims, sometimes look for victims whom they can, in turn, torture, bully or kill.

All these motives, and others like them, we shall find in the murder cases Lionel and Patricia Fanthorpe have compiled for us. They have selected widely from very early years to those fresh in the memory, and from many countries: Africa, the Bahamas, Britain, Canada, Egypt and many others. Murderers span every boundary and are from every age. The old writer of the Book of Ecclesiastes was surely, sadly, all too close to the truth in Chapter 1, Verse 9: "That which hath been is that which shall be; and that which hath been done is that which shall be done: and there is no new thing under the sun."

As in all the Fanthorpes' other books, their treatment has been meticulous and non-judgmental. Every situation is carefully outlined for us, introducing us to the victims, the perpetrators and witnesses. The motives are analyzed. Occasionally the authors challenge us with ideas of their own — logical and supported by evidence, but which some readers may find hard to accept. Can it really be true that Brutus was not one of the group of conspirators and that the famous words "Et tu, Brute" can bear a totally different interpretation? What will readers make of the idea that Thomas Becket was mistaken for another in Canterbury, and the wrong man murdered? At least they stimulate thought, stir up the "little grey cells," as Agatha Christie's well-known detective Hercule Poirot used to say.

Some of us have long been immersed in detective fiction. We have been brought up to enjoy the skills of Miss Marple, Allenby, Morse, Frost, Sherlock Holmes and a host of others. All such books have one thing in common: they introduce us to a murder, then to the clues that are unearthed, to the families involved and the witnesses, ending in a dramatic denouement and the identity of the murderer. In real life, it is by no means so easy. People fall under suspicion, as Lord Dudley did in the death of his wife, Amy Robsart, but there is now no way to prove it. Others, like Jack the Ripper, commit crime after crime, then seemingly disappear and are never traced and punished. The cases we have in this book are fact, not fiction; some are resolved, but others are likely to remain a mystery for all time.

The World's Most Mysterious Murders is a fascinating book. The characters are interesting, as are the days and circumstances in which they lived. Hearts and minds are probed for motives. We are grateful to the authors for their skill in selection, their powers of description and the fertility of their imagination. The book deserves a wide readership and, no doubt, will receive it.

Stanley Mogford, M.A.
February 2003

(The authors are deeply grateful to Canon Mogford, who is widely acknowledged to be one of the finest academic scholars in Wales.)

1

WITH MURDER IN MIND

Murder can be defined clearly and simply as the act of deliberately killing another human being, but the peripheries of that basic definition are not as clear and straightforward as its core. At what stage, for instance, does a developing fetus become a human being in the legal or moral sense? Is it human from the moment of its conception? If an assault on a pregnant woman results in the death of her unborn child — while the woman herself survives — is her attacker guilty of murder? If the life-support system of an apparently comatose trauma victim is deliberately unplugged, is that murder? If someone in unspeakable, chronic pain and discomfort begs to be released from unbearable suffering, is it murder to grant their desperate request?

And where does the sanity of the perpetrator come into the equation? How sane or rational does the killer have to be in order to be capable of a deliberate act in the sense that most of us would understand the word "deliberate"? If a mentally ill person is convinced that some innocuous passer-by is actually an alien monster cunningly disguised as a human being, and if that mentally ill person then kills what he believes to be a dangerous disguised alien, can he be said to have deliberately killed a human being? Questions of this sort are not easy to answer.

But if, for the sake of the argument, we assume that the murderer is sane, and that the victim is truly human by any criteria, we can begin to research not only the act of murder, but its widely varied motivations.

The human body is a strange, dynamic, biochemical paradox. There are occasions when it can survive situations that would kill a gorilla, a crocodile or the biggest armour-plated dinosaur. There are other times when the lightest blow, the smallest incision or the mildest toxin will bring it to a sudden, permanent halt. The act of murder can be performed with solid, liquid or gaseous poisons; with lethal injections of seemingly harmless air; with a smoothly delivered, scientific blow to the head from a martial artist; or with a powerful, spine-shattering neck-wrench from an unarmed combat expert. "Accidents" can be arranged by tampering with automobile brakes or placing logs across railway tracks. Victims can be strangled with silken cords, or weighted down with cement, an anchor or heavy chains and sent to sleep with the fishes. Heads can be severed. Arteries can be slit open with razors. Painful death can be heralded with heavy clubs and knuckle-dusters. Ever since the discovery of gunpowder — and its more sophisticated explosive descendants — guns and bombs have been used as murder weapons. Lasers can kill as surely as they can heal. Electricity can light the way to the afterlife just as surely as it can power a kitchen stove. Murderers have been known to incinerate their victims, to put pillows over their faces and lie on them, to run them over with cars, or to tie them to railway tracks just before a heavy locomotive rattles downhill towards them. The list is practically endless. Any fool can kill: it takes a genius to preserve life.

Motives for murder are almost as varied as the means of committing the act. Professional hit men (and women) are motivated by the fee offered for their services. For them, the act itself is largely devoid of emotion, as it would be for a butcher in an abattoir.

The genuine psychotic murderer has been defined in the memorable words of the experts of the Farmington Trust Research Unit as "a moral cripple." According to their authoritative findings, there are three classes of morality. Those in their first category, the psychotic personality, are able to distinguish between "good" and "bad," but only in the way that the rest of us distinguish between round and square, left and right, green and red, high and low. Psychotics feel no revulsion against what the rest of us see as cruel, wrong and inhuman; neither do they experience any emotional satisfaction in connection with goodness and kindness.

The second Farmington category, and the one to which most people can safely be assigned, is the authoritarian moralist. This grouping consists of good, honest folks who have taken a holy book, an inspirational spiritual leader or an idealistic set of political or philosophical teachings as their moral and ethical authority. They know perfectly well when they have failed to live up to those standards set by Christ, Buddha, Mohammed or Confucius, which they have striven to follow, and they experience strong emotions over these failures. They feel guilty, they are penitent, they vow to do better and keep closer to their leader — or their rule book — in the future. Being human, they inevitably fail again, but they do keep trying to adhere to their principles. When such a man or woman is driven by desperate circumstances to contemplate — or even commit — murder, it is always against their own high source of moral authority. They are emotionally restrained by the knowledge that murder contravenes the code by which they try to live. When they do occasionally break that code, their feelings of remorse and failure frequently drive them to confess.

The third Farmington category, those regarded as having the highest moral standards of all, are the autonomous moral thinkers. These are people who have the highest concern for others, and are strongly emotional over ethical and moral behaviour. They differ from the authoritarian moralists, however, by being their own gurus. No book of rules for them, no matter how holy or inspired its authors are reputed to be. Autonomous moral thinkers are prepared to back their own clear moral judgments against even the most celebrated and venerable traditional standards. They know what is right and wrong. They are deeply, emotionally involved with what is good and what is evil, but they reserve the right to evaluate every situation according to its individual merits. Christ's teaching about the Hebrew Sabbath law illustrates this autonomous moral thinking to perfection. The old Sabbath law was good. Millennia ago, it was originally intended to provide a much-needed day of rest for servants and domestic draft animals. In the hands of the ancient authoritarian moralists, however, provisions for not working on the Sabbath became reduced to an absurdity. It was even wrong in their eyes to heal on the Sabbath. Jesus, of course, throughout his earthly ministry, healed anyone who came to him for help on any day of the week. He declared boldly, "The Sabbath was made for man — not man for the Sabbath." He backed his own moral judgment against the traditional view of the day. This is precisely what the autonomous moral thinker always does.

An autonomous moral thinker might even come around to the decision that killing a particularly odious and venomous character was morally acceptable. This moral dilemma is illustrated in our short story "An Old-Fashioned Priest," originally published in the Spring 1995 issue of *Beyond* magazine:

> The interior of St. David's was almost dark, although the sanctuary lamp gleamed faintly.
>
> The familiar, bearish bulk of Father Hughes moved slowly from the confessional towards the sacristy. He stretched his great arms until the knotted muscle of his huge shoulders threatened the seams of the old black cassock. He yawned inaudibly, and felt in his pocket for the sacristy key.
>
> "Father?" The whisper slid through the darkness like an invisible scorpion. Hughes looked around, seeing no one at first. Then a slight, shadowy form approached from the far side of the church. The confessional box lay between them.
>
> "Am I too late?"
>
> Hughes shook his great shaggy head. "Never too late, my son; I've not turned a penitent away in twenty years. I won't make you the first."
>
> "The seal is still the seal, Father?"
>
> "With me, my son, yes. I'm an old-fashioned priest."
>
> The whisper grew more confidential still. "I have your solemn word, Father? Whatever I tell you will never reach the police?"
>
> "You have my word."
>
> The preliminaries over, Hughes settled back to listen. As the urgent whispering went on, he felt ice and fire contending for possession of his spine. His normally deep, relaxed breathing quickened. A pulse throbbed in his neck. Beads of sweat formed on the broad forehead. The hideously sick serial killer's confession continued.
>
> "... there'll be others, Father. I have to go on with it ..."

In twenty years of dredging the depths of human misery, in twenty years of patient counselling and forgiveness, Hughes had heard nothing like it … nothing that came within a thousand leagues of it.

Suddenly the whisper changed. Now it was toxic with mockery.

"It will destroy you, too, Father. You'll have to keep your sacred word, your priestly promise. You can't turn me in, can you? You are impaled on the horns of an impossible dilemma, a dilemma of my crafting. Take me to the police, and lose your integrity forever. Let me go, then read tomorrow's papers and know that you could have prevented that child's death."

Hughes took a breath so deep that it seemed to turn the church into one vast, stone vacuum. He moved very deliberately to the other side of the confessional. His great, square jaw was clamped shut. The grey eyes glinted like steel. The big, muscular hands moved ruthlessly in the darkness. There was a sickening crack like dead wood snapping in a hurricane.

"Your penance is death," said Hughes in a voice of terrible quietness, "and — as I told you — I am an old-fashioned priest."

Whether Father Hughes was right or wrong can form the subject of endless moral debates.

So, the professional killer is motivated by money. The psychotic kills because of a total absence of moral and ethical emotional imperatives to prevent it. The autonomous moral thinker, like Hughes in the story, may choose to kill because he, or she, judges it to be the lesser of two evils. Other motives include vengeance, jealousy, greed, assassination for religious or political reasons, silencing a witness, or eliminating a blackmailer.

The mind of the murderer contains both motives and methods. In the most mysterious murders of all, method and motive remain shrouded in secrecy. In some extreme cases, there are mysterious disappearances in which the body is never recovered. In others, it is the murderer who vanishes without trace — as Bela Kiss seems to have done after World War I.

2

THE MURDER OF PHARAOH TUTANKHAMUN

Co-author Lionel has a distant link with Howard Carter, who discovered Tutankhamun's tomb in November of 1922. Lionel attended Hamond's Grammar School in Swaffham, Norfolk, England, during the 1940s. His woodworking teacher at that time was a brilliant artist and craftsman named Harry Carter — Howard Carter's cousin.

The mystery of Tutankhamun — and his subsequent murder — begins with the young Pharaoh as a somewhat shadowy figure in the annals of twentieth-century Egyptology. He was known to have belonged to the Eighteenth Dynasty — but the Egyptian dynasties themselves need a certain amount of clarification in order to see them relative to one another on a longer time scale. Circa 3400 BC, Menes managed to unite the old Northern and Southern Kingdoms. The First, Second and Third Dynasties, which followed his work, were technically referred to as Thinite and Memphite. The Fourth, Fifth and Sixth Dynasties were also Memphite, and these first six dynasties together lasted through the reigns of fifteen Pharaohs, not counting Menes himself. The Sixth Dynasty ended with the death of Pharaoh Mereme II in 2476 BC and the Seventh

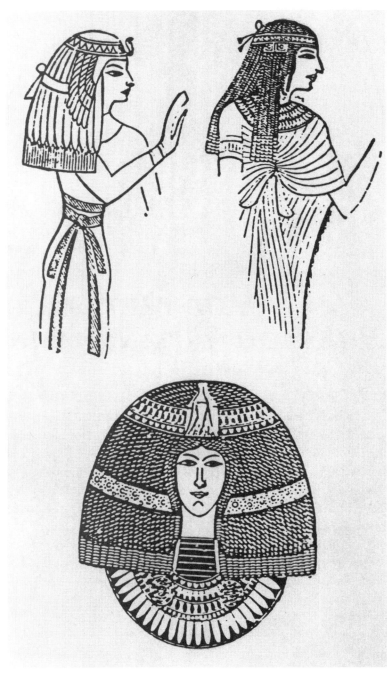

Egyptians from the time of the murdered Pharaoh Tutankhamun.

and Eighth Dynasties which followed him are generally regarded by Egyptologists as the Age of Misrule. Then came the Middle Kingdom under the Ninth and Tenth Heracleopolitan Dynasties. This was followed by the Eleventh and Twelfth Theban Dynasties, whose last ruler was the Princess Sebeknefrure in 1788 BC. At this point the Hyksos (Shepherd Kings) came onto the Egyptian scene, and ran things throughout the Thirteenth to Seventeenth Dynasties. The story of Joseph and the famous "technicolour dreamcoat" is almost certainly set in this period. As Hyksos power ended in 1580 BC, Egypt began the period referred to as the New Kingdom. This incorporated the Eighteenth Dynasty, to which Tutankhamun belonged, and which is referred to as a Diospolite Dynasty. The Nineteenth and Twentieth Dynasties were also Diospolite — and they ended in 1090 BC with the arrival of the Tarite Dynasty.

It is odd that Tutankhamun's name does not appear in company with Akhenaten and Ay in the classic list of the Amarna Kings recorded at Abydos and Karnak. Tutankhamun's parentage — and even his true identity — are still shrouded in mystery: his precise origin is as uncertain as the identity of his murderer. There is evidence that he was raised at Amarna, and probably in the North Palace there. What sort of childhood would he have had? A strange one by twenty-first-century standards!

If his mother was Kiya, a secondary wife of Akhenaten, she probably died giving birth to him. Other theories of his parentage suggest that he was the son of Amenophis III and his chief wife Tyi, or his secondary wife Meritre. It is probable that the young prince was surrounded by tragic family deaths during his formative years. For example, Nefertiti, his stepmother, died during his early childhood, as did one of his stepsisters. Before she married Tutankhamun, his elder sister Ankhesepaaten had apparently had at least one daughter by her father, Akhenaten. To add to the general controversy and family mystery, she is sometimes recorded as being Tutankhamun's niece rather than his sister.

Akhenaten was unique among all the Pharaohs — not only those of his own Eighteenth Dynasty. Convinced that he was the living personification of the supreme god of the Egyptian pantheon, Amen-Re, he did his best to liquidate the other — lesser — deities. This naturally infuriated the powerful, wealthy priests who served them and depended upon public allegiance to them for their position and livelihood. The inescapable nexus between religious belief, social position and income was by no means unique to ancient Egyptian society: St. Paul encountered major difficulties in Ephesus when the local silversmiths (who made a good living out of selling statuettes of the goddess Diana) realized that this new Christian faith that Paul was advocating would be decidedly bad for trade.

The Egyptian pantheon is a complex one, and the perpetual name-changing that accompanies it makes matters more difficult. The god Aten was originally the disk of the sun. It seems that during most of the Middle Kingdom, Aten was at best a rather obscure local deity worshipped in the area around Heliopolis. His rise to prominence in the Egyptian pantheon was entirely the work of the Pharaoh known to most Egyptologists as Amen-hetep IV, who changed his name to Akhenaten — meaning "the Glory of Aten." When the Hyksos were overcome and the Theban monarchy was established at the start of the Eighteenth Dynasty, Amen, the local deity of Thebes, took over as chief god of Egypt and was worshipped as Amen-Ra, or Amen-Re.

Any analysis of the murder of Tutankhamun must look carefully at the disgruntled priests of Akhenaten's era. In the earliest times, the great Egyptian lords and provincial rulers had also acted as chief priests in their particular territories. This gave them a combined role as both religious and feudal leaders. Under their control, numerous assistant priests were delegated to do most of the actual religious work. Over the centuries, this fairly relaxed system was changed to a much more formal and rigorous organization. These modifications made it essential for the priesthood to become a specialized group of skilled professionals with their own exclusive expertise. Many leading Egyptologists have argued that in spite of this rigorous specialization, the priesthood and the laity were never separated in quite the same way that they were in some other socio-religious systems.

Priests were often referred to as hen neter, meaning "Servant of the God." They were also called uab, which meant "pure." Senior priests were often given special titles relating to their functions, such as khorp hemtiu, which translates as "Leader of the Skilled Craftspeople." Others were known as ur ma, which means "the Great Seer" or "the Great One Who Has Visions." Other sacerdotal titles included "Commander of the Military," which was used at Mendes and made its holder sound rather like an ancient Egyptian precursor of the fearless Templar warrior-priests. At Thebes, a senior priest rejoiced in the title of "First Prophet of Amen." The subset of priests who concentrated on ritual and liturgy was usually known as kheri-heb.

Some responsibility for Akhenaten's obsession with Aten is thought to lie with Tyi, who was probably his mother. She is thought by some pioneering Egyptologists — including the redoubtable Lewis Spence (1874–1955), author of *Ancient Egyptian Myths and Legends* — to have been Chief of the Royal Wives at the time and a fanatical devotee of Aten. Was she, in fact, Akhenaten's mother? And did she influence her son to venerate her favourite god above all the others? Spence seems to be on the right track here.

There is substantial evidence that when Akhenaten (Amen-hetep IV) ascended the throne, he assumed the title of "'High Priest of Ra-Heru-Akhti," otherwise recorded as "Chief Priest of Ra-Heru-Khuti, the Excellent One of the Meeting of Earth and Sky, in the Name of Shu, Who Is in Aten." Any Pharaoh who could devise a title like that for himself deserves his unique place in ancient history!

At the start of his reign, Akhenaten seems to have worshipped both Amen and Aten with commendable impartiality. He also built a vast obelisk at Thebes to glorify Ra-Harmachis. Shortly afterwards it became inescapably clear that Akhenaten intended to put the worship of Aten ahead of everything else. The priests of Amen, drawn from the wealthiest and most powerful Egyptian families, were not impressed. The followers of Amen-Ra and the followers of Aten became engaged in a titanic socio-religious struggle for power and ascendancy. Akhenaten responded to this situation by building a new city at Tel-el-Amarna in Middle Egypt. He and his supporters used it as their citadel during the struggle, and named it Akhet-Aten.

Within the bitter soil of this socio-religious battle, the seeds of Tutankhamun's murder may well have been sown.

A careful forensic investigation of the tomb as it was when Howard Carter and Lord Carnarvon entered it reveals a number of curious and intriguing clues: the burial had apparently been carried out rapidly. The sarcophagus and its lid did not match properly; there were messy splashes of paint on the floor which whoever prepared the tomb had not bothered to clean. The tomb itself seems surprisingly small — inadequate for a Pharaoh, seen by his people as the incarnation of a god. It was this lack of ostentation that helped keep it safe from grave robbers for so many centuries. The badly matched lid, the minimal tomb size and the careless paint splashes all add up to one thing: this was never meant to be Pharaoh's tomb in the first place. The whole scenario shouts of hasty improvisation.

In 1925, Professor Douglas Derry, an anatomist from Cairo University, performed an autopsy on Tutankhamun. The dead Pharaoh lay inside the third of three concentric coffins that were glued together with a resinous adhesive that stubbornly defied the best efforts of Howard Carter and Professor Derry to open and separate them. To make matters worse, Tutankhamun himself was firmly glued to the base of the innermost coffin, making him almost inaccessible to the postmortem investigators. The body had to be dismembered before they could remove it — a process that hardly made it easy to determine the cause of death. Derry did, however, pay particular attention to a strange mark on Tutankhamun's face, not far from his left ear. Could it have been an arrow wound?

In 1969, a further examination of Tutankhamun's body was made by Professor R. G. Harrison, who was then on the staff of the University of Liverpool. Relying on X-ray evidence, Harrison found that Tutankhamun's sternum was missing, as were numerous ribs. Had the young Pharaoh met with a serious accident? A fall from his horse, or from a chariot? Harrison's X-rays revealed two other startling details. There was a small, loose bone fragment inside the skull. There was also a curious dark area at the base of the skull. What might those things mean? They might have happened at the time of the hypothetical accident that damaged Tutankhamun's ribs and sternum. They might have been inflicted by a heavy, blunt instrument, such as a war club or a metal bar. If the young Pharaoh had not died in an accidental fall, had someone assassinated him? Another possibility that needs to be considered carefully is that the embalmers accidentally dislodged a small piece of bone from inside the skull while they were pulling Tutankhamun's brain down through his nose in the customary way. If this is the true explanation for the tiny bone fragment, it is further evidence of the undignified and unusual haste with which Tutankhamun was prepared for burial.

Returning to the chronic hostilities between Akhenaten and the displaced priests of the deities he had demoted in favour of Aten, is it possible to find sacerdotal motives for the murder of Tutankhamun? Discoveries were made in the tomb of Akhenaten's security chief which suggested that there had been at least two priestly attempts to assassinate Akhenaten. These attempts were foiled by the highly efficient security chief, who subsequently arranged for the accounts to be engraved, for his posthumous honour, in his own tomb. These carvings included details of the arrest and torture of the conspirators. Plenty of extra reasons there for the displaced priests to hate Akhenaten — but why kill Tutankhamun so many years later?

Tutankhamun was only nine years old when he became Pharaoh. He was physically weak and his mind must have been seriously confused and disturbed as a result of his traumatic childhood. The priests found him ideal clay for their socio-political hands to work. We can see him clearly responding to priestly pressure, and the famous Restoration Stela is swiftly erected in his name at Karnak. The inscription on it repudiates Akhenaten and restores the old, traditional forms of polytheistic worship: exactly what the priests have required of him. As time passes, however, the malleable boy-Pharaoh grows into an independent young adult. He has a sister-wife now, and there are two dead fetuses buried with him. He is no longer the pliable, tractable, manipulable boy. He wants to be as powerful as Akhenaten was. He no longer wishes to live in fear of the priestly politicians — he wishes to inspire fear in them. Is he not the latest incarnation of the supreme god Aten?

The priests understand this change in him only too clearly. The memory of Akhenaten and his dreaded security staff is still vivid — summary arrests and torture are not easily forgotten. A cloaked, masked figure steps from the sinister shadows behind the young Pharaoh as he walks, leaning heavily on his stick. The heavy club descends on the fragile royal skull. Just to make sure, a sharp iron spike resembling an arrowhead is thrust through the cheek, high up near the left ear. It penetrates the brain. It loosens a fragment of bone inside the skull. Tutankhamun is dead. Now he must be disposed of as if he had never existed.

But the priestly manipulators are not the only suspects: there are at least four others. Tutankhamun's sister-wife, Ankhesenamun, might have been disappointed with him as a husband. If we think of the Cleopatra story, it becomes clear that Egyptian royal ladies had their own personal power and ambition. Was it her hand that secretly struck him down? There is evidence that the dead daughters in the tomb with Tutankhamun both had genetic defects. Did Ankhesenamun simply want him out of the way so that she could have a fresh, healthy husband who could provide heirs to their dynasty?

Field Marshal Horemheb, commander of the armies of Egypt, is another prime suspect. Why serve an inexperienced boy young enough to be your son, when you can get rid of him and take command yourself? It would not have been the first military coup in history. The pattern is a familiar one. We can almost imagine them walking through a dark, lonely corridor in a remote wing of the palace. Horemheb is pretending that he has important, confidential information for the young Pharaoh's ears alone. He is a powerfully built, professional soldier: the heavy war club comes down just once. With his kind of muscle, Horemheb does not need to strike twice. With his loyal officers and the Egyptian army to back him, no one questions his claim to the throne.

Treasurer Maya, and Ay, the Grand Vizier, are also possible suspects.

Maya had worked miracles to restore Egypt to financial stability — and even prosperity — after the financial and economic debacle that had characterized Akhenaten's disastrous reign. He had no motive to kill Tutankhamun other than to preserve the financial achievements for which he had worked so hard and so skillfully. There is also evidence that he was genuinely fond of Tutankhamun, that he was heartbroken by the young Pharaoh's death, and that he was responsible for a beautiful and sincere inscription saying, in effect, that it had been a real pleasure to work for such a good master. There is no proof that he wasn't involved in the murder, but he seems an unlikely conspirator.

Ay was, by all accounts, a politician's politician. He could smell the direction of the slightest social breeze, the gentlest tides of public opinion, and immediately turn his own ship of state in that direction. The most damning evidence against Ay is that he was the man who performed the all-important ceremony of the opening of the mouth at Tutankhamun's funeral ritual: the man who did that part of the ceremony was supposed to be the next Pharaoh. As the most skillful of all Tutankhamun's spin-doctors, Ay had the most to lose if the clay boy-Pharaoh hardened into a strong, ceramic adult ruler with real opinions and real power. There was also the tantalizing prospect of marriage to the beautiful and nubile young widow, Ankhesenamun. Ay was old enough to be her grandfather: life was sliding relentlessly past him. He might never get such a good opportunity again. Murdering Tutankhamun would give him a beautiful young bride and the unlimited power of Pharaoh. But even though the young man was far from strong, did Ay — a desk-bound politician, not a powerful soldier like Horemheb — have the physical strength to do the deed? Making a mess of the assassination would have been the end of everything. It was a risk he could not afford to take. He would have needed help. His crafty, politically astute brain could recognize his need of allies, and of one ally in particular:

Horemheb. The deal might have raced through his mind: offer Horemheb the succession in return for killing Tutankhamun.

There is further curious evidence in the form of a letter, supposedly written by Ankhesenamun, to the king of the powerful Hittites — among Egypt's most virulent enemies at that time. If the letter is genuine, and it really is from the desperate young widow, Ankhesenamun is begging the Hittite king to send one of his sons to marry her to save her from being forced into a marriage with Ay, whom she hates, fears and strongly suspects of her husband's murder. It is significant that Ankhesenamun disappears shortly afterwards. She apparently fades from Egyptian history as if — like Tutankhamun — she had never existed at all.

There are no certainties. The murder of Tutankhamun remains one of the great mysteries of history, but the most likely solution is a conspiracy between the military muscle of Horemheb and the serpentine mind of Ay.

3

THE MYSTERY OF THE JULIUS CAESAR MURDER PLOT

We're all familiar with Shakespeare's historical play which deals with the story of Caesar's murder. As far as can be ascertained at this distance in time, Shakespeare follows the actual events with a reasonable degree of accuracy.

Ranking alongside Alexander the Great and Genghis Khan, Gaius Julius Caesar was one of the most effective and influential military and political leaders of all time. He was one of the pioneers who established the mighty Roman Empire; he was undeniably one of the most powerful men in history. So what went wrong — and why?

To understand the reasons for his tragic and untimely death, we need to know all we can about the man himself — and his background. Caesar had an uncle named Marius, who was a notable military reformer and a leading light in the group known as the Populares. While Caesar was still very young, Uncle Marius had influenced him considerably, and the boy grew up to become a popular and successful people's champion. Thanks to his awesome powers of leadership, he became consul in 59 BC, and went on to achieve the rank of perpetual dictator. Like all outstandingly powerful and ambitious men, Caesar had a talent for acquiring and extending his influence in numerous directions simultaneously. So great was his lasting impact on the world that his name, Caesar, lives on in the German form kaiser, the Slavonic tsar and the Arabic qaysar.

Caesar's gens — or clan — name, Julia, was, after the Roman custom, Julius or Iulius; and because he was born in the month known to the Romans as Quintilis, it was renamed July in his honour. The Caesares seem to have been the only surviving patrician family in the gens Julia, but by Julius's time patrician blood was no longer much of an advantage. It could actually prove to be something of a hindrance, as patricians were banned from the powerful political office of tribune of the Plebeians. Many of the ancient, noble Roman families claimed to be able to trace their ancestry all the way back to a god, or goddess, and the Julii Caesares were no exception: their founder was none other than the beautiful and passionate goddess Venus.

Roman political ambition was directed towards the consulship — with elevation to the post of censor afterwards. Such rank was vitally important because Rome itself was vitally important internationally. After smashing Carthage in the Second Punic War (218–201 BC), Rome became the leading power in the lands around the Mediterranean. The governor of a Roman province — someone like Pontius Pilate at the time of Jesus, for example — had extensive opportunities to exploit and plunder his region: opportunities that could make a greedy and unscrupulous man immensely rich and powerful. The wealth of the Mediterranean was also absorbed by the Roman Equites, or knights, who made their money from tax-farming. This was an iniquitous system under which the top man with tax rights to an entire province would sell off subsidiary rights to different parts of it to various tax collectors, who would in turn sell off ever smaller districts — always at a substantial profit for the tax-farmers and to the great disadvantage of the taxpaying public. While Roman nobles, governors and Equites lived on the fat of the conquered lands, the Roman peasantry that made up the core of the legions had been disadvantaged by the aftermath of the Second Punic War — even though Rome had been victorious. From about 130 BC onwards, there were several revolutionary and reactionary fracases that led inevitably to one type of military dictatorship or another.

There are disagreements among scholars about the precise date of Julius Caesar's birth, but July 12 in 100 BC seems to meet with general

Roman Senator from the time of
Julius Caesar.

acceptance. His father, Gaius, died when Julius was only sixteen, but his mother, Aurelia, and his uncle Marius more than made up for the loss.

As in modern democracies, political ambition called for substantial financial resources. Caesar did not have them, but with a character and personality like his, a political career was as natural as air to an eagle or salt water to a shark. Right from the start, Caesar went flat out for a political office of some kind. It is always difficult to make a fair assessment of another human being's true motives, but fairness and objectivity lead to a favourable evaluation of Caesar's aims and objectives. He was not solely concerned with the power and prestige that accompanied political success in the Rome of his day: he genuinely wanted to improve the Greek and Roman Mediterranean world, and he knew that power was an essential prerequisite of change.

As his career progressed and his experience and understanding of politics increased he came to understand that the degree of power he would need would have to be monarchical, or very close to it. Caesar's crossing of the Rubicon in 49 BC has made its way into the lexicon as a metaphor for any act of irreversible commitment. It was that momentous and decisive act which was the turning point in Caesar's career, and the unmistakable danger signal to his opponents that he was the leading contender for monarchical power.

Thirty-five years prior to his momentous action at the Rubicon, Caesar had married Cornelia, daughter of Lucius Cornelius Cinna. Cinna had been one of the co-revolutionaries with Caesar's uncle and mentor,

Marius. It was unfortunate for Caesar that Sulla returned from the eastern parts of the empire in 83 BC, led a successful reaction against the revolutionaries and promptly ordered Caesar to divorce his lovely young bride because of her father's out-of-favour politics. Caesar, to his eternal credit, told Sulla to go to hell and stuck loyally to Cornelia whatever the consequences. A man who is prepared to put everything on the line, including his life, for the sake of the woman he loves is a man worth following.

Prudently, however, Caesar left Rome and went first to Asia, then Cilicia, on military service.

After Sulla died, four years later in 78 BC, Caesar promptly returned to Rome and launched his political career as a prosecuting lawyer. In this role he targeted Dolabella, one of the late Sulla's leading counterrevolutionary faction. Caesar lost the case and left for Rhodes to improve his oratorical skills by studying there with Molon, who enjoyed a worldwide reputation as a professor of oratory.

The fact that pirates were able to practise their nefarious trade in the Mediterranean at all was an indication of the slipshod and slovenly state of Roman control of the area. It was one of the many things that Caesar was so anxious to improve once he had achieved the necessary power. The pirates, however, made an error very similar to that of a spider with a hornet in its web. Caesar raised the ransom, went home, organized an overwhelmingly powerful naval task force, captured the pirates and crucified them all. The message began to spread: you cross Gaius Julius Caesar at your peril. In order to fully understand this dimension of Caesar's character, it is important to appreciate that he dealt with those pirates solely in his capacity as a private Roman citizen. He held no state office of any kind at that time. In 74 BC, when Mithradates VI of Pontus made the strategical error of attacking Rome, Caesar promptly raised a very effective private army with which to fight him.

Caesar became consul in 59 BC despite great opposition. He built the First Triumvirate with Pompey and Crassus and went on to conquer Gaul. His famous visit to Britain in 55 BC was almost a casual spinoff from his highly successful foray into Gaul.

Caesar's sequence of decisive, far-flung conquests set the seal of military genius on this amazing man. His intelligence was matched only by his incredible energy and stamina. He swam as powerfully as an Olympic medallist, and few men would have matched him in hand-to-hand combat: armed with a good sword and shield and with his back to a stout wall,

Caesar would have shown his cowardly assassins that he was no soft target. Like the great medieval East Anglian hero, Hereward, or the fearless Alamo warrior Jim Bowie, Caesar would have gone down surrounded by the corpses of his attackers.

His amazing strength and brilliant leadership qualities were demonstrated at their finest in his defeat of Vercingetorix, the able and charismatic Arvernian leader of the amalgamated Gauls. The substantial sums of money that Caesar looted from his conquest of Gaul were put to effective use back in Rome, where he hired political agents to do the necessary wheeling and dealing.

Caesar's amazing success in Gaul put a severe strain on the dubious diplomatic glue that held the precarious triumvirate together. Pompey was jealous of Caesar and Crassus was deeply unhappy about Pompey. They made a repair-of-relationships pact at Luca in 56 BC, under which it was agreed that Caesar's official provincial commands should go on for a further five years, while Pompey was granted a five-year command in Spain and Crassus got Syria. Crassus didn't hold Syria for long: his Roman forces were annihilated by the Parthians in 54 BC.

Various underhanded machinations carried out by Caesar's enemies in the senate led to a civil war, and Pompey's growing jealousy of Caesar inevitably put the two leaders on opposite sides. Caesar drove Pompey's forces out of Italy, then beat him in Spain. Following a further defeat at Caesar's hands at Pharsalus on August 9, 48 BC, Pompey retreated to Egypt, where one of King Ptolemy's officers assassinated him. Caesar spent the winter in Alexandria, making the most of his golden opportunities with the delicious young Queen Cleopatra.

Caesar's next minor campaign was the swift and decisive destruction of the upstart King Pharnaces, son of Mithradates VI of Pontus — whom Caesar had dealt with years before. Pharnaces fared even less well than his unsuccessful father had done. Caesar wrote off this skirmish with the memorable "Veni, vidi, vici." ("I came, I saw, I conquered.")

Caesar returned to Rome with the title of dictator, but left almost immediately for Africa, where his opponents were gathering against him. He put them down at Thapsus and sped back to Rome once more. He had scarcely had a moment to breathe the air of his native city before trouble in Pompey's old province of Spain took him to Munda, where he again put down the rebels with his customary vigour and skill. For the next few months he worked hard on his lifelong ambition of improving the Greco-

Julius Caesar

Roman world that he loved so much, and which caused him so much grief and anguish. In 44 BC, on March 15 (the infamous Ides of March), he was cut down by a group of conspirators in the senate house.

The great unanswered questions associated with the murder of one of the finest leaders in the whole of history are: Who really did it? And why? The conventional answers are a long way short of the truth, but what strange truths underlay Caesar's assassination?

The anguished cry of "Et tu, Brute" is almost parallel to Christ's poignant words to Judas Iscariot in Gethsemane. The man to whom they were directed, Marcus Junius Brutus, was a former enemy. Caesar, magnanimous beyond the boundaries of wisdom, had forgiven Brutus for his former hostility and had come to trust him. Indeed, there is considerable mileage in the theory that Brutus was Caesar's illegitimate son. He might well have been, for Caesar's mighty sexual appetites were well known and widely reported. The delectable Cleopatra was by no means his only attractive partner.

Were the hands of two or three outraged husbands, fathers and brothers among those holding the daggers that brought Caesar down?

The second motive was the neurotic fear and jealousy that so many less successful politicians would inevitably feel in the presence of a charismatic colossus like Caesar. It is almost as though the confidence and charisma radiating from such a great leader were so tangible that they struck ordinary people like a physical blow. The pride of lesser men who recognized their own inferiority in the light of that greatness would suffer wounds that stung harder than they could bear. Because Caesar's greatness was such a vast challenge to their smallness, they had to bring that greatness down into the dust of death.

The third theory is perhaps the most intriguing of all. It depends upon the validity of the theory that Brutus was Caesar's illegitimate son, that both men knew it, and that they felt deep affection for each other accordingly. The horror of the Ides of March, according to this theory, was a covert plan that went horrendously wrong. Brutus, completely loyal to Caesar, was to go undercover to flush out the most dangerous and strident of Caesar's enemies by pretending to be one of them. Then, when the would-be assassins gathered to kill Caesar, Brutus would spring to his father's defence, pass him a spare sword, and together they would destroy the conspirators their plot had revealed.

Neither could have had the faintest inkling in advance that there would be so many potential assassins. They had counted on no more than a half-dozen opponents at the worst; there were, in fact, ten times that number. This revelation puts an entirely different construction on "Et tu, Brute." Realizing that he, himself, was doomed, Caesar's lightning-fast tactical and strategical brain worked at its highest speed to save his son, Brutus. "Et tu, Brute" did not mean the anguished reproach of "Even you, Brutus?" It meant "And you, Brutus! Pretend to be one of them, boy. Your only chance for life is to stab me. Make them think you really are with them."

And so, characteristically and with the greatest and noblest love and generosity, Caesar dies hoping that he has saved his beloved son.

4

WHO KILLED KING WILLIAM RUFUS?

William II, known as Rufus — either because of his red hair, his ruddy complexion, or both — was killed by an arrow while hunting in the New Forest on August 2, 1100. The actual situation of that arrow adds to the mystery of the king's death. One account of the fatal injury describes how William fell from his horse onto the arrow, which snapped off a few inches clear of his chest. The fall not only snapped the shaft, but drove its lower section right through his rib cage and deep into his body, so piercing his heart. If that were indeed the case, death would have been almost instantaneous. A modern forensic scientist, however, would have been less than convinced. If Rufus had been wearing the customary short, thick, leather hunting coat of the period, an arrow might not have penetrated very far through it. If, as another account suggests, the arrow was deflected by an oak tree and hit Rufus as a ricochet, it would have lost a lot of its initial momentum and been even less likely to penetrate to a fatal extent. Human bone is very tough. Human ribs are as flexible, as resilient and as resistant to penetration as good quality marine plywood. Only if the arrow had been heavy enough and fast enough to pierce a stout leather hunting jerkin, and then found a precise spot between two of the King's ribs, would it have been likely to go in so far — or to do so much damage. However, if Rufus had tumbled from his horse with only a shallow flesh wound, and had, furthermore, fallen backwards — which is what a rider tends to do if struck from the front — what would the assassin have done? Running from his place of concealment, he seizes a heavy stone from the forest floor, snaps off the feathered end of the shaft, and drives the stump into William like a vampire hunter disposing of Dracula's Uncle Fang. Rufus's killer then rolls the corpse facedown to create the impression that it was the fall that drove home the fatal arrow stump.

Working on the scenario that Rufus's death was not accidental, but that he was the victim of an assassin, who killed him, and why? A brief survey of William the Norman's genealogical tree is an essential preliminary to understanding his son's murder. William the Conqueror was the son of Robert "the Devil" (Robert II), Duke of Normandy, who was himself the son of Duke Richard II, son of Duke Richard the Fearless (Richard I). William the Conqueror's mother was Herlève de Falaise, and her father was Fulbert "the Tanner" de Falaise. William's more distant ancestors were of Viking stock.

The Conqueror's wife was Matilda of Flanders, who was descended from Alfred the Great on one side and French royalty on the other. She predeceased her husband, dying at Calvados in 1083. The Conqueror himself died on September 9, 1087.

Traditionally, the New Forest had a curse on it as far as the Conqueror's family were concerned:

> William's Forest is William's bane:
> There shall the sons of his house be slain.

William I's son Richard died young in the New Forest, some while before Rufus met his strange end there. The Conqueror's other sons were Robert, known as "Curthose" because of his short legs, and Henry, who went on to become King Henry I after Rufus's sudden and convenient death — making Henry (variously known to historians as Beauclerc and "the Lion of Justice") a prime suspect for instigating Rufus's murder.

Although Rufus seems to have been William the Conqueror's favourite son, he was never given any responsibility for government until he ascended the throne after William's death. Rufus was crowned in Westminster on September 26, 1087 — just fifteen days after William's funeral.

Early chroniclers described Rufus unflatteringly. There was nothing of the smart, upright military bearing about Rufus that there had been about his father. He was bullnecked. His shoulders sloped in a pronounced way. He was very much overweight. His gait was awkward and clumsy. He was depicted as longhaired and clean shaven, with strong, rather coarse features. His stutter was so pronounced that he frequently became inarticulate; on the occasions when he could talk coherently he combined blasphemy with cruel, derisive wit. His courtiers were said to be greedy parasites — miniatures of their unpleasant monarch. He was generally regarded as godless, foul-tempered and possessing the sexual appetites and moral standards of a vigorous young billy goat. As most of these early chroniclers were closely connected with the church and saw everything from a narrow ecclesiastical point of view, they were unlikely to recall any of Rufus's good points — even supposing that he had had any.

He died unmarried, and with no acknowledged issue.

Rufus may simply have been irreligious, or it might have gone much deeper than that — an idea that forms the basis for one of the more intriguing theories attached to his death. Was the church's vigorous disapproval based on the persistent rumours that William Rufus was a secret pagan who had gone back to the Norse gods of his remote Viking ancestors? Or did the church suspect that he had become a leading light — perhaps even the fabled Red King — of another ancient pagan fertility cult? Details of the specific role of the Red King in the various fertility rituals tend to differ from one locality to another, and from one ancient tradition to another. In essence, the Red King — representing the male principle, rather as Baal did in the worship of Baal and Astarte (or Ashtoreth) in early Canaan — was encouraged to indulge in every possible pleasure for the four seasons before his sacrificial death. His redness may have been intended to symbolize the sacred blood he was destined to shed, the same sacred blood with which the Earth was fertilized and renewed.

Those accounts of Rufus's murder that postulate his willingness to play the role of the sacrificial Red King seem to overlook the considerable body of historical evidence pointing to his dominance, his selfishness, his greed and his determination to have his own way in almost every situation. There is little or no evidence suggesting that he would ever have considered sacrificing himself for the good of his people and the sufficiency of their harvest! Provided that what mattered in the minds of the believers was simply the Red King's death in the right place at the right time for the ritual fertility magic to work, then it was irrelevant whether or not William Rufus was willing.

Suspect number one, therefore, appears to be an unknown adherent of the harvest sacrifice fertility cult. He lurks in thick New Forest undergrowth on that early August day. The corn is in the fields. If the harvest is to succeed, the Red King must die. The unsuspecting Rufus rides slowly into range. An arrow flies. The rest is history.

A possible shred of supporting evidence for Rufus's involvement with a ritualistic fertility cult was his cryptic remark to nervous courtiers when the ship in which they were crossing the English Channel ran into a heavy storm and looked as if it might sink at any moment. "Have no fear! Kings never drown!" shouted Rufus above the roar of wind and waves. What inspired that confidence that he would die in some other way? Was he, perhaps, already committed to a magical, sacrificial death in the New Forest?

The area over which William the Conqueror created the New Forest had originally been predominantly Jutish, and had been called Ytene, which means "belonging to the Jutes." The Jutes were a Germanic tribe who had occupied large areas of Hampshire, Kent and the Isle of Wight after their arrival on the heels of the retreating Romans in the fifth century. All of that changed in 1079, when the Conqueror decided that he wanted a hunting ground close to his headquarters at Winchester. Was it perhaps a disgruntled and resentful Jute who killed William II because this bad-tempered Norman tyrant's father had displaced his own proud Jutish ancestors?

Rufus's arrogance and dominating cruelty may have provided his killer with a slightly different motive: personal revenge. Had he taken what he wanted, autocratically and imperiously, from the wrong peasant? Had he raped the wrong blacksmith's wife or daughter? Burnt down the wrong hovel? Punished the wrong family for daring to touch the royal deer that had their precious sanctuary in the New Forest? Sent his vicious tax collectors to an impoverished village once too often? Was it a victim's brother, husband, lover or son who hid patiently among the New Forest trees? Did personal hatred string the great yew bow? Did family vengeance sharpen the fatal arrow?

Rufus was not exactly popular among his own kith and kin. His formidable uncle, Bishop Odo of Bayeaux, organized a revolt against him with the assistance of Rufus's brother Robert, Duke of Normandy. They were, however, no match for the ferocious Rufus. Their revolt was soon put down — although, uncharacteristically, Rufus allowed them to retain their titles. Having sorted out his domestic troubles, Rufus defeated Malcolm III of Scotland and replaced him with the obedient and compliant Edgar Aetheling. The blood on the royal sword from the battles in Scotland had barely had time to dry before Rufus sorted out the Duke of Northumberland. When his unpopular brother Robert more or less mortgaged Normandy to Rufus and left on a crusade, William II was more or less in control of all the original territories that had once owed allegiance to his valiant father, William I.

Other reasons for the church's hatred of Rufus included his treatment of the saintly Archbishop Anselm, whom Rufus had forced into exile. Pompous, bureaucratic senior clerics who dared to criticize him were met with the contempt that many of them undoubtedly deserved, and Rufus's cutting sarcasm did nothing to endear him to them. Money was the main problem, however, as far as the irritated clergy were concerned. Rufus had evolved an ingenious technique of failing to appoint replacements when important church positions became vacant, and then quietly diverting the money that would have been due to the holders into the royal coffers. In this, he can almost be viewed as a precursor of Henry VIII and his treatment of the monasteries more than four centuries later.

If Hell hath no fury like a woman scorned, neither can it match the pious fury of an ardent church office-seeker deprived of his hoped-for promotion by a fat, greedy, blasphemous king. Was the lurking bowman concealed in the forest a frustrated clergyman, longing to fill one of the lucrative offices that William II was carefully holding in abeyance? William meets the fatal arrow. The homicidal clergyman meets his archbishop and discusses his long-overdue promotion.

The best-known story of William II's untimely departure centres on Walter Tirel (often rendered Tyrell), who was the Lord of Poix and reputedly a loyal friend of Rufus. A hunting party, of which Rufus was the instigator, set out on the bright, sunlit summer morning of August 2, 1100. The semi-official version told of how the huntsmen had separated and spread out as they continued their pursuit of the New Forest deer and of how Rufus and Tirel went together. A deer duly appeared, and Rufus called to Tirel to shoot it. One variation says that the arrow went wild, glanced off an oak and took Rufus fatally in the chest. Another omits the intermediate oak tree. Both versions report that the horrified Tirel — fearing that he would be charged with deliberately causing the king's death — galloped away as fast as he could and took ship for Normandy.

This popular story goes on to relate how the dead, or dying, Rufus was eventually found by a group of peasants, who took him away in a cart. In an age when forensic medicine did not exist, it is tempting to wonder whether the unpopular king had become separated from Tirel and been brought down by a group of vengeful New Forest peasants, still seething with resentment over what had been done to them when the New Forest was created as a Royal Norman hunting zone. Seeing the hated Rufus entirely without companions or protectors, the opportunistic peasants attack him and thrust one of his own hunting arrows into his chest. A wild tale about how they had found him there would be easy enough to concoct and spread. Other disgruntled peasants would be quick to aver that the murder group could not possibly have done it as they had been together all the time with scores of their fellow labourers. So why would Tirel make a bolt for it? Had one or other of the peasants seen him in the middle distance and shouted something to the effect that he was the man who had fired the fatal arrow? Uncertain of who would be believed, and anxious to get clear in case the peasants decided to silence him, too, Tirel gallops to safety.

Alternatively, had Rufus caught them killing one of his precious deer? The foul-tempered king roars abuse at the hungry peasantry. He threatens torture — maiming, mutilation, branding, even hanging. If you're going to be killed unpleasantly anyway, why not take the king with you? They go for him, drag him from his horse, and kill him. Tirel is in the background, unable to help, fearful of being killed as a dangerous witness. He decides on flight. Why does he say nothing afterwards? What Norman nobleman could ever hold his head up again if he has to admit, "I saw these ruffians attacking my friend the king, and instead of riding in like a loyal and gallant Norman warrior to rescue him, I fled in terror in case they did the same to me!" Does that explain Tirel's precipitous flight and his subsequent curious silence? The popular — entirely fictional — version of the stray arrow, fired by accident (and not in anger) by an innocent but careless Tirel, begins to spread. Tirel is all too happy to go along with it. A Norman nobleman can live with the reputation of being careless and reckless — he cannot live with the reputation of being a disloyal coward. Bad enough to have fled from a doughty warrior, or overwhelming odds, on the field of honour; but to flee from peasants, leaving your king to die, would have been insuperable.

Further strange complications muddy the waters: Walter Tirel was known to his contemporaries as an experienced and proficient archer. He was too experienced a hand to have loosed off a wild, dangerous shot — especially in the king's vicinity. There is evidence that an abbot named Suger, who was a close friend of Tirel, protected and sheltered him after he left England. Tirel is also alleged to have given very interesting testimony to his abbot friend:

> "I was not even in that part of the New Forest when the King was killed. I never saw him at all that day."

Truth seems to have died with Rufus: if not the fast-retreating Walter Tirel, then who?

Suspicion falls on Henry, William II's younger brother and a very strong contender for the English throne. Henry was with the hunting party that day. There is evidence that he did nothing to organize a pursuit of Rufus's killer — could that indicate complicity? Furthermore, Henry left immediately for London to be crowned as King Henry I — barely three days after Rufus's abrupt end in the New Forest. Was brotherly love a little thin between William the Conqueror's sons?

His brother Robert, as well as his brother Henry, had understandable reasons for wanting to get rid of Rufus, but they were not alone. There were Anglo-Saxons in plenty who still bitterly resented the loss of Harold and their own royal line. To them, one unwelcome Norman king was as expendable as another. There were also a number of powerful, influential and unscrupulous Normans who preferred Robert, and who — even without Robert's express sanction — would willingly have given fate a hand in arranging for William II to join his fierce Viking ancestors in Valhalla.

William's death remains one of the most mysterious in history. Was he the sacrificial Red King of the ancient fertility rite? Was his death revenge for one of his many brutal acts of cruelty? Did an infuriated church leader kill the godless king who had failed to promote him — under the delusion that in removing Rufus he was doing the will of God? Was William II murdered on secret orders from Henry, or from the aristocratic Norman supporters of Robert Curthose? Did deer-poaching peasants conclude that if the infuriated Red King was going to have them mutilated and hanged anyway, they might as well send him on ahead? Or — unlikely as it seems — did Walter Tirel simply have a genuine accident during the adrenaline-bolstered hunt on that fateful August day?

5

THE MYSTERY OF
THOMAS BECKET

One of the greatest mysteries associated with Thomas Becket, born on December 21, 1118, is the true identity of his mother. Romantic myths and legends can sometimes conceal historical truths and are always worth open-minded investigation. Thomas's father, Gilbert Becket, was said to have fought in the Crusades. During one battle he was taken prisoner by the Saracens, and while in captivity fell in love with a beautiful and courageous Saracen girl who helped him escape. Circumstances of war forced the very reluctant Gilbert to take ship for England before she was able to reach him, but her love, courage and determination were so strong that she ran away from her family, converted to Christianity for Gilbert's sake, sold all her jewels to pay for her passage and followed him on the next available vessel. This would almost certainly have been part of the mighty Templar fleet, where she would have been fully protected and treated with great respect. The fearless girl knew almost no English other than the names Gilbert Becket and Cheapside. But this was enough: she found him, they were joyfully reunited, they married and eventually became the proud and loving parents of Thomas, the future Archbishop of Canterbury — and possible murder victim.

This legend of his mother's origin could be true, but serious academic historians are divided on the subject. Dr. Giles, M. Thierry, Froude and Michelet tend to accept it as genuine. Canon Robertson, a scholarly Becket biographer, disagrees. On balance, we think there may well be some truth in it, and Thomas's own remarkably forceful character provides ancillary evidence of his having inherited interesting and strongly positive genes. The kind of girl who would have had the courage to change her religion, sell everything she owned, risk the perils of the sea and venture boldly to an unknown land with barely three words of her English lover's language to guide her, would have been an outstanding human being. The son of such a mother would have been more than a match for an arrogant king.

A second legend, as strange as the possible origins of Becket's mother, concerns a mysterious semi-secret exhumation of his bones. Cecil Humphery-Smith was interviewed by Christopher Morgan and Andrew Alderson for an excellent article of theirs which appeared in the *Sunday Times* on June 22, 1997. Cecil told the researchers that when he was only fourteen years old, during World War II, his godfather Canon Julian Bickersteth told him what — in his opinion — had really happened to Becket's bones. Becket was made a saint in 1173, barely three years after his mysterious murder. His elaborate tomb in the cathedral at Canterbury became a great centre of pilgrimage for nearly four centuries. This tomb was the work of two superb craftsmen: Elyas of Dereham in Norfolk and Walter of Colchester. They were given unlimited means for the shrine's construction, and it was covered with gold and jewels. One account maintains that there were gems larger than goose eggs embedded in the gold.

During the course of his attack on the Roman church — and its saints — Henry VIII gave orders in 1538 for Becket's bones to be burned and their ashes scattered, and for his shrine to be destroyed. The rhetorical question is posed: Who would have dared defy Henry VIII and his ruthless henchman Thomas Cromwell?

The history of the famous Nanteos Cup — believed by many to be the Holy Grail itself — indicates that the awesome king and Cromwell, his grim hatchet man, were not too powerful to be defied occasionally. Before Abbot Whiting of Glastonbury was murdered at Henry's behest, he sent seven of his fearless young monks from Glastonbury to Strata Florida in

Wales — taking with them the famous sacred cup that legend had linked with Joseph of Arimathea. This cup eventually passed into the safekeeping of the noble Powell family of Nanteos, who protected it for more than four centuries. When the last of the Powells died, the cup passed to a niece of theirs, mother of the present guardian. Whether that ancient, sacred cup really came from Palestine with St. Joseph in the first century, or whether it was simply an ancient sacred vessel used by the holy people of Glastonbury, many well-documented healing miracles are associated with it. Just as Whiting's fearless men thwarted Henry's rapacious greed at Glastonbury, so, according to Humphery-Smith's evidence, the commissioners acting for Cromwell and the king were apparently thwarted by the Canterbury clergy in the 1530s.

Cecil reported that his godfather, Bickersteth, had told him that he had been one of four men who shared the secret of an exhumation of Becket's bones during or immediately after World War II. Debris from an earlier air raid was thought to have given them the cover they needed to open a semi-secret grave, which they had been led to believe might contain Becket's bones — placed there for safekeeping by the sixteenth-century cathedral staff, who knew well in advance that Henry VIII's commissioners were coming to pay them an unwelcome visit. Some nondescript bones were then placed in Becket's shrine for Cromwell's minions to destroy — the saint's real remains having been concealed and camouflaged by being placed in what looked like just any other ordinary grave. There was known to have been an exhumation of what were believed to have been Becket's bones on January 23, 1888. That episode was well attested and recorded, and the remains were duly measured, photographed and examined by Dr. W. Pugin Thornton. There was also a semi-official, semi-secret exhumation on July 18, 1949 — but Humphery's evidence seems to point to the possibility of yet another, more secret, exhumation at around the same date — or a few years earlier.

Bickersteth, Canon John Shirley and two others were said to have opened this mysterious grave and examined its contents. Humphery-Smith reported that Bickersteth had told him that they had found the bones of an unusually tall man (Archbishop Thomas Becket was said to have been almost two metres tall), fragments of episcopal robes and Becket's signet-ring seal. When Canon Shirley died, his ashes were laid to rest in St. Mary Magdalene's Chapel, and a light, funded by his bequest, burns there perpetually. Those who share Cecil's belief in the secret of the moved bones believe that the eternal flame is there to honour the murdered archbishop rather than merely to commemorate Canon Shirley, good man though he was.

There is another possible explanation for the mysterious twentieth-century episode of the four secretive senior clerics who believed that they had found Becket's bones in that mysterious, anonymous tomb: perhaps it was not Becket who fell victim to the four murderous knights. Let's consider this possible scenario: if Becket's bones were not in Becket's tomb, perhaps someone else was slaughtered by the drunken assassins who lurched into Canterbury Cathedral on that fatal December 29 in 1170. What if some other priest, or senior member of the cathedral staff, was standing where the conspirators expected to find their victim? What if this same loyal senior Becket supporter had deliberately allowed the assassins to think that he was the archbishop?

In Bernard Shaw's brilliant play *The Devil's Disciple*, the hero quite deliberately allows himself to be arrested by troops who have mistaken him for the local minister of religion, who is actually a fearless militia leader — along the lines of Paul Revere — in the struggle for independence. There is no safer escape route than mistaken identity, especially if it can be combined with encouraging one's enemies to convince themselves that one is dead. Becket, a genuine hero from head to toe, would never have knowingly allowed one of his loyal supporters to die in his place. Suppose, however, that Becket wasn't there at the fateful moment. By the time Thomas knows what has happened, it is far too late to do anything about it. His loyal friend and supporter is dead, his blood and brains still spreading across the cathedral floor. If Becket doesn't seize his opportunity and escape now, his friend will have made the supreme sacrifice for nothing. Suppose that only a tiny handful of Becket's closest circle know the truth: the real archbishop is spirited away to safety overseas — perhaps even back to his semi-legendary mother's homeland in the Middle East. Henry's assassins are not likely to investigate as far afield as that.

There are even possibilities of Templar involvement. Suppose that a tall, powerful, athletic, middle-aged knight, known only as Thomas the Templar, takes an honourable place alongside his warrior-priest brethren. He distinguishes himself in more than one battle, and as a Brother Templar of the utmost integrity. Only the Grand Master and a small inner core of Knight Commanders know his amazing secret. When he finally dies — almost certainly killed in action — his loyal brethren faithfully pre-

Knaresborough Castle. Did Becket's killers find refuge here?

serve his body according to twelfth-century Templar tradition, and take his remains, in secret, back to Canterbury. The truth, known to an inner core of high-ranking Templars, is also entrusted to a few loyal clergymen at Canterbury. Under the cloak of anonymity, Thomas, the Templar hero — alias Archbishop Becket — is laid to rest in an ordinary grave. The secret is kept faithfully and well, and passed down very discreetly and cautiously through the years.

What Henry VIII's commissioners desecrate and ruin nearly four hundred years later are merely an elaborate shrine and the bones of the man Henry II's assassins had mistaken for Archbishop Becket in 1170. It could have happened that way — or it could have been a quick ecclesiastical sleight of hand that took place during the 1530s. If either scenario is historically factual, then the bones of the real archbishop are still there in Canterbury Cathedral, honoured by the undying flame of the red lamp of martyrdom that wise old Canon Shirley provided. If those bones could be DNA-tested, they might be found to contain genetic patterns that indicate a mother of Middle Eastern origin.

There is a fascinating contemporary poem, "Vie Saint Thomas," written in French by Garnier, a poet from Pont-Sainte-Maxence. It seems to

View from the river by Knaresborough Castle, where Becket's murderers may have taken refuge.

have been begun in 1173 and completed in 1175. The whole consists of some six thousand lines, and line 956 contains a very interesting piece of evidence connecting Becket to the Knights Templar. Garnier writes of how Sir Richard of Hastings, Master of the Temple, and his companion, a man named Hostes, did their utmost to bring about an honourable reconciliation between Becket and Henry II. Garnier's words make it abundantly clear that these two senior Templars were held in very high esteem by the other knights and nobles assembled at the time.

Even if it was not Becket himself who was slain on that fateful December 29, 1170, the murder mystery remains: four assassins broke into Canterbury Cathedral that night and killed somebody. Who sent them, and why?

Reliable historical accounts name the four assassins as Reginald FitzUrse, Richard le Breton, Hugh de Morville and William de Tracy. A

6

EDWARD II — BORN 1284, CROWNED 1307, KILLED 1327

The great mystery surrounding the supposed murder of King Edward II hinges on whether the agonized screams heard from Berkeley Castle in 1327 were part of an elaborate escape plan, or whether Edward actually died there in indescribable pain.

Edward II's father, Edward I, reigned from 1272 until 1307. He was known as "the Hammer of the Scots" because of his harsh, brutal suppression of his northern neighbours. By contrast, he was also referred to by some historians as "the English Justinian" — a reference to his founding of the English Parliament. Edward II, also known as Edward of Caernarvon — who was, incidentally, the first member of an English royal family to hold the title Prince of Wales — failed utterly to live up to his father's formidable legacy. He married Isabella, daughter of Philip IV of France in 1308, and they had a son who grew up to become Edward III, but it seemed that Edward II's sexual preferences were for his close male companions, Piers Gaveston and the young Despenser. He generously bestowed wealth and titles on his favourites — to the extreme annoyance of the established English barons, who began to plot his downfall.

Berkeley Castle, where Edward II supposedly died.

Historians record that Edward II preferred the "pleasures and extremes" of life to ruling, guarding, governing and guiding his people. A ruler can be forgiven much — and usually is — if his adventures in war lead to conquest and success. Edward, however, more or less lost everything — including his credibility — at Bannockburn on June 24, 1314.

Historians differ slightly in their accounts of that great Scottish victory led by Robert the Bruce. However, there is wide agreement that a small force of exceptionally valiant and effective knights turned up providentially to aid Bruce's army by destroying the cream of the English archers who had been deployed to take out Bruce's cavalry — just as the bowmen of Gwent would take out the French cavalry a century later at Agincourt. With the English bowmen destroyed, the Scots had victory within their grasp. That grasp tightened significantly when an English knight named Henry de Bohun tried to earn his plinth in the Hall of Fame by skewering Robert the Bruce. As Henry thundered towards the fearless Scot, Bruce moved nimbly under and away from the lethal spear point, wheeled swiftly, and shattered de Bohun's helmet and skull with his battle-axe. So powerfully effective was the blow that Bruce's axe handle splintered as well. There were no further attempts to challenge Robert the Bruce in one-on-one combat that day.

Berkeley Castle, where Edward II supposedly died.

Who were those mysterious knights who aided Bruce so effectively at Bannockburn? In 1307, the odious and treacherous Philip le Bel, Philip IV of France, had attempted to destroy the noble Order of the Templars. Admittedly, he did them serious damage, but the indomitable Templars were not wiped out. And as of 1314, they have yet to be. Some found refuge and hospitality in Scotland and the surrounding islands. These unparalleled warrior-priests were now more than happy to show their gratitude and loyalty to gallant hosts who had helped them when they were at their nadir. Another of their motives for helping the Scots to defeat Edward so decisively was the fact that his queen, Isabella, was the daughter of their perfidious archenemy, Philip le Bel.

The barons drew together to force Edward under their control in the hope of preventing the worst of his errors and excesses. Their efforts were at least partially successful. Isabella, however, soon allied herself with Roger de Mortimer, the ruthless leader of the barons, and joined in the invasion from France that resoundingly defeated Edward and the Despensers. The latter were promptly executed with a degree of cruelty and savagery that seemed excessive even by the brutal standards of their day. Edward was compelled to abdicate in favour of his young son, who became Edward III.

Edward II's prison room in Berkeley Castle, where he supposedly died.

In 1327, Edward II was imprisoned in Berkeley Castle. Sir Thomas, Lord Berkeley, was reinforced by Sir John Maltravers, and the two of them were responsible for keeping watch over the deposed king. Lord Berkeley was called away in September 1327, and Sir Thomas Gourney, along with William Ogle, took on the duties of guarding the former monarch. The courtiers and staff at Berkeley were aroused by hideous screams, which were alleged to have been emitted by Edward as he died in agony from appalling internal burns. If the traditional version is to be believed, an expert executioner had been secretly brought in from Europe and commissioned to kill Edward in such a way that there would be no external marks to show how he had died. Some reports allege that a hollow tube — one version says it was a small brass trumpet, such as heralds might use — was inserted into Edward's anus and rectum, and a red-hot poker was then guided up through it, fatally burning several of the royal victim's internal organs. Some accounts also allege that the supposed secret European executioner was immediately struck down with a sword by one of the disgusted barons who had hired him in the first place! That blow might have been struck out of enlightened self-interest: as long as such a man lived, there was always the chance that he could operate on his former employers if the balance of power shifted again.

Ogle and Gourney were accused of the murder and fled. Ogle's fate remains unknown, but Sir Thomas Gourney was captured in Spain and directed back to England. There is evidence, however, that he died in France on his way home. Maltravers, who was suspected of regicide, was never brought to book for any complicity in the death of Edward II, but was executed elsewhere for a different crime.

Meanwhile, it was obviously in Roger Mortimer's mind to kill Edward II's son, the boy king Edward III, at the first opportunity. He would then make the necessary arrangements to marry Isabella, who was already his mistress, and proclaim himself King Roger I. Fortunately for the boy king, who was wise beyond his years, he had a troop of loyal and trustworthy soldiers who obeyed him rather than the dangerously ambitious Mortimer — who was not the only member of his family to try to take the English throne! Leading his soldiers through a secret passage, young Edward III arrested Mortimer in Nottingham Castle in October 1330. He was promptly sentenced to death and executed at Tyburn in London. The boy king had been very ably supported in this venture by a loyal old captain of guards who had known him since he was a baby and had an almost paternal affection for him. When co-author Lionel's well-known TV series "Castles of Horror/Bloody Towers" aired, he played the part of this powerful old captain — and accidentally broke the hinges of an ancient castle door in the process of rushing in to deal with Mortimer to save his young master's life!

Three mysteries surround the horror that allegedly took place in Berkeley Castle on that fateful night when the horrendous screams were heard. First, was it really ex–King Edward II who died there, or had some hapless servant who bore a good enough likeness to the ex-monarch been sacrificed in his place? If so, was that the reason the barons killed the imported executioner? If a cunning escape for the former king had been planned, secrecy was of the essence. Secondly, if it was really Edward of Caernarvon who died there in such appalling circumstances, who killed him? Mortimer and Isabel are not above suspicion — at least as those who gave the lethal orders, even if not as parties to the horror in the castle. Thirdly, if Edward was spirited away from Berkeley, as some sources report, what became of him? It is alleged by one or two researchers that a letter written by an old priest in France was sent to King Edward III several years after the Berkeley episode. The letter said that the former monarch had lived there secretly for several years as a pious, but comfortable, religious recluse — a hermit almost — and had finally slipped away naturally and peacefully.

7

WHO — OR WHAT — KILLED THE PRINCES IN THE TOWER?

During the late summer or early autumn of 1483, twelve-year-old Edward V and his ten-year-old brother, Richard of York, disappeared. They were the sons of Edward IV, and in order to understand the political and social background to the fate of the young princes it is necessary to consider their father and his times. Edward IV was significantly bigger and stronger than the average man of his time, being well over six feet tall. He had an insatiable sexual drive and had been involved with numerous royal mistresses before marrying Elizabeth Woodville. She became the mother of the two young princes, while Edward's extramarital adventures continued unabated. Apart from his frequent infidelities, he seems to have been a fair-minded, friendly, benign ruler, popular with his people — at least at the start of his reign. The other side of his character, however, was ruthless and direct. After defeating Henry VI, Edward arranged for Henry's heir, the young Prince of Wales, to be assassinated. There is also a considerable body of evidence to suggest that Edward arranged for feeble and ineffectual old Henry VI (yet another hapless prisoner in the Tower!) to go to a better world rather earlier than if nature had

The Tower of London. The murdered princes were hidden here.

been allowed to take its normal course. Edward also executed his own rebellious younger brother, George, for treason.

Germane to the mystery of the disappearing princes was their father's habit of luring his lady friends into bed by promising to marry them afterwards. Fifteenth-century law and custom decreed that such a promise of marriage — especially when made in the presence of a reputable witness — was as legally binding as marriage itself. The giving of such a promise would make any subsequent marriage to another partner null and void — practically the same as bigamy. In order to enjoy sex with Eleanor Butler (one of his many conquests), Edward had promised to marry her, and — very significantly — Bishop Stillington was a witness to the king's words. This promise to Eleanor was made some years before Edward married Elizabeth Woodville. It was on these grounds that Richard III declared the two young princes to be illegitimate, and this illegitimacy clouds the whole issue of their mysterious disappearance. If they had no legal claim to the throne, why on Earth did Richard arrange to have them killed? Wasn't there more risk involved in a conspicuous double murder than in simply granting the boys minor titles and giving them some land? In that way, Richard would have been perceived as the generous, humane benefactor of his brother's bastard children. This would have increased his popularity with the people at large, and even endeared him to the powerful Woodvilles.

Unless Richard had planned to carry out the murders himself in the dead of night, when there were no witnesses — hardly likely in the heavily guarded Tower — he would have needed unscrupulous henchmen to do the deed for him. The problem with unscrupulous henchmen is that their talents can very easily be purchased by the opposition — and Richard was a wily enough politician to know that. Whatever else he was, Richard III was not a fool: why couldn't he see that the success of the illegitimacy charge made murder an unnecessary risk?

Throughout the whole of his elder brother's reign, Richard had served as a loyal soldier and administrator. Accordingly, Edward had appointed Richard as protector in case he himself died before his elder son became old enough to rule. Edward, who had grown immensely and unhealthily fat in middle life, died at the age of only forty-four on April 9, 1483. At the end of May, his sons were taken to the Tower of London by their kind, protective and affectionate Uncle Richard — who promptly disqualified them from the succession because of their illegitimacy. Uncle Protector

The Tower of London. The murdered princes were hidden here.

then claimed the throne for himself as Richard III. Two years later, in 1485, he was killed at the Battle of Bosworth Field, and Henry Tudor, the victor, was proclaimed King Henry VII.

Historians normally split into two main schools of thought concerning the disappearance of the hapless young princes. Traditionally, it was accepted that they had been butchered, and their bodies disposed of on Richard's orders. Revisionist historians, however, argued that Richard wasn't such a bad guy after all; it was just that his reputation had been destroyed by the Tudor propagandists. Several other sinister possibilities are well worth analyzing.

Shakespeare also played a very significant part in the destruction of Richard III's reputation. His theatrical Richard delivers a soliloquy that includes the line, "I am determined to prove a villain." Brilliant as he was in other fields, Shakespeare was not an academic historian. He relied on somewhat dubious works written by Hollinshed and Hall, who had in turn based their writings on Sir Thomas More's biography of Richard III. The evidence against Richard is much less substantial than the propaganda directed against him. Sir Thomas More said he was a hunchback with a withered arm. Although some portraits — and they may well have been altered — show him with one shoulder higher than the other, painters who lived at the time and would have seen Richard show him without any deformity at all. Contemporary reports of his fighting skill, strength and stamina make it unlikely that he was physically challenged in any way.

The Tudor propagandists also accused Richard of murdering his wife Anne, who died young in 1484 — but a great many people died young in the fifteenth century, and there is evidence that the royal pair were genuinely fond of each other and travelled everywhere together. Richard was accused of wanting to get rid of Anne so that he could marry his niece, Elizabeth, the eldest daughter of his late brother, Edward IV, in order to strengthen his grip on the throne and prevent her from marrying Henry Tudor — to whom she had been promised by her mother, Elizabeth Woodville. As things turned out, Elizabeth's promise was eventually kept!

This Henry Tudor had only the slenderest of claims to the English throne. He was the son of Owen Tudor, whose only grip on the succession was his marriage to the widow of Henry V. Nevertheless, Henry Tudor was powerfully supported by the Duke of Buckingham and Bishop Morton. The former had once been one of Richard's staunchest supporters, but had left him either because he was revolted by the murder of the young princes, or because Richard had promised him rewards that never materialized.

Another school of thought regards Buckingham as the boys' murderer in order to safeguard the throne for his new master, Henry Tudor. Tantalizing questions surround him, one of which centres on the fate of Sir James Tyrell. Was this Tyrell a descendant, or relative, of Tyrell the huntsman, who had been linked to the death of King William Rufus in the New Forest? Having allegedly obtained a confession from Tyrell regarding the murders of the boys, Henry Tudor silenced him in the time-honoured way with axe and block — before he could retract it, or say anything contradictory about their deaths.

Yet the mystery surrounding James Tyrell's character is as great as any in history. The young princes had to all intents and purposes vanished in 1483. James Tyrell was born about 1445, the eldest son of Walter Tyrell, who owned Gipping Hall near Stowmarket in Suffolk. Walter had been executed in 1462 for treason against Edward IV. Records show that in late summer of 1483 — around the date that the boys vanished — James Tyrell was definitely in London. Had Richard III sent for him to assassinate the unfortunate princes? From 1483 until 1501, Tyrell's career went

The Tower of London. The murdered princes were hidden here.

moderately well, despite his family's allegiance to the "wrong" side during the Wars of the Roses. In 1501, however, Tyrell made the politically fatal mistake of harbouring the Yorkist heir Edmund de la Pole, Earl of Suffolk. Edmund had fled to the fortress of Guisnes in France to escape from Henry VII's attentions — and James Tyrell was at that time in charge of Guisnes. On May 16, 1502, James Tyrell was beheaded.

A famous historical record, *The Great Chronicle of London*, was written around 1512. On pages 236–237 it suggests that, although Sir James Tyrell was blamed for the murder of the princes, another — unnamed — hand was actually responsible. A scholar named Polydore Vergil wrote *Anglica Historia* at roughly the same time. Vergil reported that the boys were not dead, but had been "conveyed secretly away, and obscurely concealed in some distant region …"

A whole new scenario now unfolds around the mysterious — and probably gravely misjudged — James Tyrell. Suppose that, far from murdering the helpless young princes, James spirited them safely away — first to the family seat at Gipping, and then over the Channel to Guisnes, where he protected them. What if, after revealing his Yorkist sympathies by protecting Edmund de la Pole, Tyrell's protection of the missing princes is suspected by Henry VII? A false confession to their murder doubly ensures

Tyrell's own death — but safeguards the fugitive princes from any pursuit by Henry VII. At this distance in time it is difficult to judge whether James Tyrell was a brutal murderer or a protective hero who sacrificed himself to keep the refugee princes safe and hidden somewhere in France.

One of Henry Tudor's earliest acts after his victory at Bosworth was to repeal Richard's "Titulus Regius" law that had made Edward IV's boys by Elizabeth Woodville illegitimate. This repeal meant that the missing (or murdered) Edward V had been a genuine king of England, after all, so his sister Elizabeth — Henry Tudor's future queen — was also a legitimate royal descendant of Edward IV.

Their marriage united the Houses of Lancaster and York, thus ending the Wars of the Roses. But was it Henry Tudor who murdered the missing princes because they posed a threat to his throne after being legitimized? Was Tyrell's forced confession and rapid execution the watertight defence Henry Tudor needed against any possible accusation that he had killed the boys? How could he possibly have harmed them when Tyrell had made it plain that they were already dead, and that he had done it?

In 1674 — 191 years after the young princes had mysteriously disappeared — a wooden chest containing what were assumed to be the remains of the uncrowned boy king, Edward V, and his younger brother, Richard, Duke of York, was discovered in the Tower of London. Workmen were labouring in the White Tower, replacing the decaying staircase that served the Chapel of St. John the Evangelist. Large stones and rubble were strewn all around. When the workmen reached the floor of the basement, beneath the crumbling stairs, they were surprised to find more loose stones there instead of the solid paving they had expected. As they pulled these loose stones out of the way, they encountered the lid of a large wooden box. One of the men opened the lid and — showing great daring — put his hand inside to feel for the contents. Perhaps he had been hoping to find coins or jewels hidden there. What he actually pulled out was a human arm bone. Within an hour, the men were looking at what seemed to be bones comprising two small human skeletons.

Charles II was king at the time, and he ordered the royal surgeon to examine the bones. As a result of the doctor's work, Charles accepted that the skeletons were those of the two missing princes. Their remains were kept in the Chapel of the White Tower for four years, then placed in a small marble casket and solemnly interred in Westminster Abbey. At the service, the archbishop said the prayers, and the king gave a short address:

> It is right and meet that we commend the bones of these young princes to a place of final rest. Their fates at the order of Richard III grieves us, and though almost two centuries have passed, the vile deeds of that villain shall ne'er be forgotten.

Charles then made the sign of the cross and led the dignified little procession out of Westminster Abbey.

It seems that in 1728, an antiquary named Thomas Hearne found out that some bones alleged to be those of one or both of the missing princes in the Tower had been sent to the Ashmolean Museum in Oxford, and that the redoubtable Ashmole himself had arranged for their transfer. In 1933, during the final years of George V's reign, Lawrence E. Tanner was the Keeper of the Monuments of Westminster Abbey. Accompanied by William Wright, president of the Anatomical Society of Great Britain, Tanner examined the bones. To their very great surprise, along with portions of two human skeletons, they found a quantity of assorted animal bones. Could these have been put in two centuries earlier to fill the gaps when the alleged transfer to the Ashmolean took place? Modern carbon dating and DNA testing of those bones would throw a great deal of light on the mystery of the missing princes.

It is widely assumed to this day that Edward and Richard were brutally murdered on the orders of their wicked uncle, Richard III, but before making him the subject of a homicide investigation, it needs to be remembered that plague and a thousand other natural causes might have been responsible for the boys' deaths. If the princes had succumbed to natural causes of some sort, the question arises as to why the facts were not immediately made public. It would have been very convenient for Richard III to display their bodies in honourable royal state and to have an eminent court physician announce publicly that the princes had died of the ague, the plague, or some other widely known terminal malady all too common in the fifteenth century. Richard's official line might not have been universally believed, but even allowing for the embryonic state of forensic medicine in his time, there would have been some visible signs on the

Richard III. Did he really kill the princes in the Tower?

bodies to go into the court physician's report. Politically, from Richard's angle, a partially believed, natural-causes report would have been vastly preferable to no report at all.

An embarrassing disappearance was far more likely to raise questions. Where were the boys? Why had no one seen them for several months? Had they been murdered and their bodies concealed somewhere in — or under — the grim old Tower of London? Had they been spirited away abroad?

Natural causes are not impossible — but they are not very probable. If, then, the boys were murdered, who are the suspects?

First and foremost is Richard III, himself, but the case against him weakens the more closely it is examined.

Then there is the possibility that Henry Tudor killed the boys — or had them killed. Being married to their sister was a slender enough claim to the throne, if the real Edward V put in an appearance and asked his brother-in-law for his kingdom back.

Margaret Tudor, Countess of Richmond and Derby, was Henry Tudor's mother, and was fanatically loyal to her son; she may have been behind the murder of the boys in the Tower in order to protect Henry's throne — and he, himself, might never have realized what a fearsome crime his devoted mother had instigated on his behalf. The case of Queen Jezebel and King Ahab in the Old Testament has certain parallels here: a very powerful and dedicated woman can be capable of almost anything to benefit those she loves. Livia, wife of Augustus Caesar, provides another example. She almost certainly poisoned anyone who stood in her way — or in his!

Not entirely free of suspicion, despite his senior position in the church, was Morton, Bishop of Ely and London. His cunning brain had devised the tax collector's insidious weapon known as Morton's Fork: if a man being assessed for tax spent lavishly and lived conspicuously well, Morton argued that he could well afford to pay taxes. If a man lived a frugal and austere life with none of the trappings of wealth, Morton argued that he must have saved a great deal and so could well afford to pay taxes. A mind capable of thinking up that forerunner of the modern-day Catch-22 was also devious enough coldly to calculate whether killing the princes in the Tower, or spiriting them away to exile in France, would best serve his own interests and the interests of his party.

Neither does Henry Stafford, the Duke of Buckingham, escape the relentless spotlight that picks out the most likely suspects. Buckingham, a descendant of Edward III, was not without some ambition of his own towards his ancestor's throne. The princes were as much in his way as Richard's. At least one theory of the tragedy has Buckingham leading his murderous henchmen to the Tower and commanding Robert Brackenbury to admit them. According to this version of events, Buckingham also ordered Brackenbury to go away until dawn — and take his own servants as well as the princes' attendants away for the night. As soon as the coast was clear, Buckingham sent in his hired killers with instructions to do their work swiftly and silently, and to hide the bodies effectively. As a final inducement to them, he made it clear that if the princes did not die in accordance with his precise instructions — they most certainly would!

How do the two serious challenges to Henry VII's claim to the throne shed extra light on the mystery of the princes in the Tower? One challenge to Henry came from the followers of Perkin Warbeck and the other from the followers of Lambert Simnel. Both of these claimants were supposed to be the princes in the Tower. Both attempts failed. Did they fail because a few prominent and powerful people — including Henry himself — either knew for certain that the boys were long since dead and buried safely under a basement floor in the Tower, or that they were very much alive and well and living quietly in exile?

The mystery of the vanishing princes was inextricably involved with the social and political turmoil during the Wars of the Roses, also known as the Cousins' War. It happened because most of the children of Edward III and Queen Phillipa lived long enough to become ambitious adults. Unfortunately, Edward, the Black Prince (so called either because of the colour of his armour or because of his violent temper) died before his father. This left only the boy king Richard II. The lad was deposed in 1399 and died — not without a little surreptitious help! — in 1400.

Some historians and investigators of the young princes' tragedy would argue that the court of England in the fifteenth century contained too many royal egos who could never agree on which of them should be the next monarch. Conversely, whoever won the crown could never feel safe with so many equally royal rivals arguing their various causes and breeding prolifically. A dangerous game of musical thrones developed: a violent free-for-all with the English crown as the prize for the last man standing. Considering the ferocity of the competition, it is rather surprising that this turned out to be Henry Tudor. But whether he disposed of the young princes, or merely sent them into permanent exile, remains one of the intriguing open questions of history.

8

TRAGIC AMY ROBSART: DID SHE FALL — OR WAS SHE PUSHED?

Amy Robsart, Lady Dudley, was the only legitimate child of Sir John Robsart, Lord of the Manor of Siderstern (spellings vary) in Norfolk. Amy's mother was Elizabeth Appleyard, widow of Roger Appleyard, lord of the manor of Stanfield. He had died in 1530 after siring four children. Elizabeth's maiden name before marrying Roger had been Scott, and her father, John, had lived at Camberwell in Surrey. Elizabeth died in 1549, the year that Kett's Rebellion shook Norfolk.

This rebellion — which was, in a nutshell, against the Enclosure Acts, which deprived the poor of the common land on which they depended — was one of the most significant events in Norfolk history, and as such became the subject of one of co-author Lionel's televised ballads in the 1960s:

> Bob Kett, he was a Wymondham man,
> A Norfolk yeoman bold,
> Who fought against oppression
> In the gallant days of old.

Four hundred years and more have passed,
But England won't forget
The valiant stand for freedom
That was made by Robert Kett.

'Twas in the sunshine of July
In fifteen forty-nine,
Folk crowded into Wymondham
To pray at Becket's Shrine.

They tore down all the fences
Around the Common Land.
With Robert and with William Kett
They swore to make their stand.

Beneath a mighty oak tree
On the road to Hetherset,
They listened to the stirring words
Of dauntless Robert Kett.

He marched them close by Norwich Wall;
They camped on Mousehold Down.
King's herald came to warn them —
But the Ketts attacked the town.

Their cannon roared and thundered
As they battered down the wall.
The rebels stormed the city —
And by dusk they'd won it all.

Northampton marched to Norwich
With fourteen hundred men.
The angry rebels fought them off
Across the Palace Plain.

Earl Warwick rode from London
Upon an August day.
His foreign troops were ruthless
And the Norfolk lads gave way.

His cavalry pursued them
And cut the farm boys down.
Bob Kett was hanged in Norwich —
And Will in Wymondham town.

Twelve months after her mother's death in the year of the Kett Brothers' rebellion, teenaged Amy (who had been born in 1532) married Robert Dudley, who was destined to become the Earl of Leicester, on June 5, 1550. Lord Robsart and Lord Dudley (Robert's father) both conferred land and property on the young couple, and the opening years of their marriage — spent in Norfolk — seemed to have been happy enough.

The ambitious young Robert Dudley, however, soon became deeply involved in local politics, and was constable of Castle Rising in Norfolk, as well as the county's member of Parliament. Disaster struck with the death of the sickly young King Edward VI on July 6, 1553. Robert misjudged the situation badly and helped his father and brothers to put his sister-in-law, the hapless little Lady Jane Grey, on the throne. Her reign lasted only for a few desperate, precarious days and ended with her death at the hands of the headsman — and Robert Dudley's imprisonment in the Tower to await a similar fate. Surprisingly, Robert was pardoned and released on October 18, 1554, the faithful Amy having visited him regularly while he was confined.

Robert's great personal charm and undoubted ability subsequently landed him a senior post in the English army as master of ordnance during the battles in Picardy, where his brother Henry was killed in action. As a reward for their military service, the Dudleys were restored to their inheritance.

Robert Dudley's insatiable ambition made him something of a political weathercock. His allegiance was as flexible as his conscience. Like the famous Rhinestone Cowboy in the song, Dudley was prepared to do "a lot of compromising on the road to his horizon." It was clear at one point that he had found favour with Catholic King Philip of Spain during Queen Mary's reign in England, yet as soon as the Catholic Mary was dead and the Protestant Elizabeth had become queen, Robert cashed in on his former close friendship with her when she had been a girl. He was appointed Master of Horse, installed as a Knight of the Garter with the lieutenancy of Windsor Castle.

Kett's Oak, Norfolk, England, from the days of murdered Amy Robsart.

Elizabeth was apparently infatuated with Dudley, and made no secret of it.

There were powerful Spanish pressures to marry Elizabeth off to Archduke Charles. Dudley's links with the queen greatly upset the Duke of Norfolk, who favoured her marriage to Charles. Norfolk, and the two Spanish ambassadors during that period, de Feria and de Quadra, all seemed to be of the opinion that both Dudley and Elizabeth ought to be assassinated as soon as could be conveniently arranged.

During that politically volatile summer of 1560, Anne Dowe of Brentford went to prison — as did several others — for gossiping about Elizabeth's alleged pregnancy. All the contemporary salacious rumours said that Dudley was responsible. On January 22, 1561, Francis Bacon was born — ostensibly the son of Lady Bacon, wife of Sir Nicholas Bacon, the loyal and trustworthy keeper of Queen Elizabeth's Royal Seal. Historians have argued for centuries as to whether baby Francis was really

Elizabeth's son by Dudley. Another remotely possible hypothesis even suggested that bold Francis Drake — Elizabeth's toy boy! — was the young father. The Bacons were fanatical Protestants, as well as fanatical devotees of their queen. They would have been more than willing to smuggle the infant into their own home, swear it was theirs, and keep Elizabeth's secret safe forever.

It was almost at the end of that politically volatile summer, on September 8, 1560 — while rumours of her husband's responsibility for the queen's pregnancy were swarming like angry bees — that Amy Robsart was found at the foot of the stairs with a broken neck. Other accounts added a skull fracture. Had she fallen accidentally? Had she jumped suicidally? Or had a brutal assassin hurled her down deliberately? In Sir Walter Scott's semi-fictional account, the main villain is Varney, who allegedly set a booby trap for her. Most serious academic historians, however, regard Varney as totally innocent and uninvolved.

For some unknown reason, Dudley had persuaded Amy to go and stay with his agent — Anthony Forster, the member of Parliament for Abingdon, who rented Cumnor Place near Oxford. On the fatal day, Dudley himself was with the queen at Windsor, and instead of rushing straight to Cumnor he asked Sir Thomas Blount — a distant relative — to make the necessary investigations for him.

Mrs. Pinto had been Amy's maid. She gave evidence that she had heard her mistress praying desperately for deliverance from some unspecified stress and anxiety. This gave rise to a suspicion of suicide, and there were some reasons to believe that tragic Amy had been desperately worried about the possibility of having breast cancer. Medical knowledge in the sixteenth century was riddled with uncertainties and superstitions, but breast cancer had been known — and given primitive attempts at treatment — since the time of Galen, the classical medical pioneer. In his view, the physical condition was linked with melancholia, or depression. If sixteenth-century diagnosis were more advanced than we usually give it credit for today, and if Amy was chronically depressed by Dudley's earlier infidelities and his current involvement with Elizabeth, might Amy's death have been suicide after all? She never went to court with Robert Dudley, and never appeared with him in public. Was that because she was chronically ill?

After her body was found at the foot of the stairs, the jury brought in a verdict of accidental death, although there were allegations that Dudley had either bribed or threatened the jurors. He was not present at the inquest; nor did he attend Amy's funeral. Both these absences seem extremely odd. Do they mean anything?

If Amy was thrown down the stairs, who did it, and who gave the orders?

Dudley himself is the prime suspect, with Anthony Forster, his loyal agent, a close second. Queen Elizabeth, however, was not without her own powerful secret operatives, who would have been more than capable of murdering Amy and making their getaway afterwards.

Yet perhaps that apparently fatal staircase had nothing at all to do with Amy's tragic death — other than as a cunning piece of camouflage and stage setting. What if Dudley's scheme to get her to Cumnor Place was because of that prominent, steep and dangerous staircase? Suppose he, or one of his minions, had actually killed her elsewhere by breaking her neck, and her body had then been taken swiftly and secretly to Cumnor to be arranged convincingly at the foot of the stairs?

Robert Dudley, Earl of Leicester, was cunning and unscrupulous — even less worthy of trust than Hamlet's two student "friends," Rosencrantz and Guildenstern. After Amy's death, Dudley's career did nothing to enhance his reputation: he married Lady Sheffield, then — bigamously — also married Lettice Knollys, the widow of Walter Devereux, Earl of Essex. The rumour mill promptly went into overdrive and actually linked Dudley with the death of Devereux as well — but Elizabeth seems to have been unbelievably forgiving towards him.

In 1585, she put him in charge of the military expedition to the Netherlands: it was conspicuously unsuccessful and in 1587 he was removed because of his incompetence. Despite that debacle in the Low Countries, Dudley was subsequently made commander of the forces assembled to oppose the Spanish Armada in 1588 — fortunately for those under his command, he died later that year.

9

WHO KILLED THE BABES IN THE WOOD?

Wayland Wood lies just to the south of a small Norfolk market town called Watton. It has an interesting bronze town sign that depicts an oak tree with two young children resting below it. The name Watton may possibly derive from the old local name for a hare that was thought to have been called "Watt" or "Wat." Below the figure of a leaping hare on the town sign is a large barrel, or "tun," so that the symbols represent the phonetic elements of the town's name. The name of the wood that once contained the great oak of legend is also interesting and historically controversial. One school of thought associates it with wailing — a miserable sound indicating pain, or grief — so that it was the Wood of Sadness where the lost children died. Local ghost stories refer to glimpses of the wraiths of the two tiny, lost children, wandering alone and frightened in the dark wood. The wailing sound may also have been associated with the uncanny noise of the wind in the trees.

Other theories link the ancient deciduous forest with Wayland Smith, or Vulcan — the blacksmith of the old pagan gods, sometimes called Vuland. Wayland Smith is also linked with crossroads, where smiths traditionally built their forges. In some of the old myths these sites were protected by legendary divinities such as Hermes, or mighty, benign magicians like King Arthur's Merlin.

Wayland Wood has long been associated with one of the old broadside ballads, "The Children in the Wood, or the Norfolk Gentlemen's Last Will and Testament," first published in 1595 by Thomas Millington of Norwich. It tells the popular children's story of the two unlucky babes killed on the orders of their wicked uncle. There are a great many versions of the story dating from different eras, and there may even be parallels with much older tales such as the legend of Romulus and Remus (the founders of Rome), abandoned babies who were saved by a she-wolf. Old ballads, legends and traditional folktales sometimes merge and blend. There is even a version of the Babes in the Wood story that involves another woodland hero, Robin Hood; in it, he and his Merry Men rescue the lost children and give the wicked uncle his just deserts.

The best-known version of the story tells how a wealthy landowner and his wife died more or less simultaneously, leaving two tiny children: a three-year-old boy and his two-year-old sister, Jane. The dying parents had begged the husband's brother to care for the toddlers and to make sure that they eventually got their inheritance: £300 a year for life for the boy, and £500 for the girl when she married. A very unwise codicil to the will stipulated that if the children died before they grew up, the uncle got the lot!

Any streetwise student of human nature would have recognized this naïve arrangement as tantamount to putting a hungry wolf in charge of two lambs. It says something for the wicked uncle's ethics that he held off for a whole year before rapacity overcame his vestigial scruples. With his conscience dying quietly in a soundproof recess, somewhere among the muffled regions of his mind, he decided to send the children to join their parents. His wife (like the ogre's wife in Jack and the Beanstalk) was an altogether nicer person than he was. She had grown very fond of the children, and the wicked uncle had to think up some careful subterfuge to account for their forthcoming disappearance. The ruse he finally came up with was that he had a rich friend in London who would be able to give the children a much better chance in life than rural Norfolk could offer them. This friend could eventually introduce them to all the right people, generally assist with their education and so on. The unsuspecting aunt gave her consent, and the wicked uncle then hired a couple of local heavies, ostensibly to escort the children to London. He had, of course, paid these two rough and ready rural hit men to dispose of the children on the way and hide their bodies deep in Wayland Wood.

Even those governed by the worst of human nature occasionally exhibit some redeeming features; the episode of the penitent thief dying beside Christ at the crucifixion provides a classic example. The less cruel of the two criminals decided that, hard man though he was, he couldn't kill two tiny children. He quarrelled with his companion over it, they fought, and the more villainous of the two was killed. The survivor led the children into the woods and abandoned them, under the pretence that he was going to buy some food for them and would very soon return. The pathetic youngsters wandered for hours, trying to find blackberries to ease their desperate hunger. Finally, overcome by the cold, they sank down under a sturdy old oak tree and died there. Hence the oak sheltering the children on the Watton town sign. If there were ripe blackberries in the wood, it gives a fair indication of the season at which the tragedy happened.

At this juncture in the folktale, some kindly, caring robins cover the tiny bodies with oak leaves from the great tree. It should be pointed out that the oak is at the centre of magical and religious symbolism, and was particularly sacred to the druids. Are there grim traces of deep folk memories lurking in the ancient roots of this story? Were two Stone Age children (a boy and a girl) once sacrificed in Wayland Wood as part of an old fertility ritual? Is it the wailing of their heartbroken parents from millennia ago that lingers on in the wood's strange name? Did the blackberry stains represent the children's sacrificial blood? The words of the old ballad sum up this part of the story:

> The pretty babes, with hand in hand,
> Went wandering up and down,
> But never more could see the man
> Approaching from the town;
> Their pretty lips with black-berries
> Were all besmear'd and dyed,
> And when they saw the darksome night,
> They sat them down and cryed.
> Thus wandered these poor innocents,
> Till death did end their grief.
> In one another's arms they died,
> As wanting due relief.

No burial this pretty pair
Of any man receives,
Till Robin-redbreast piously
Did cover them with leaves.

According to folklore, Nemesis inevitably overtook the wicked uncle. He was met by one disaster after another, similar to those that befell Job in the biblical story: his barns caught fire repeatedly, destroying all that he had harvested; his cattle were stricken with mysterious illnesses and died; the soil on his estate lost its fertility. Despite their father's evil character, his own two sons remained loyal and loving: they attempted to recoup the family losses by embarking on an Elizabethan treasure-hunting adventure at sea. Both boys were drowned. Within the magically significant seven years found in so many folktales, the chain of disasters was complete: the wicked uncle died in abject misery in the squalor of a sixteenth-century debtors' prison.

The marginally more merciful of the two hired hit men, who had left the children to starve in Wayland Wood rather than kill them outright, was later caught and tried for another, unconnected offence. He confessed to his part in the children's deaths before the hangman sent him to join them.

But what is the historical connection between the Wayland Wood area and the story of the murdered children?

Griston Old Hall in Norfolk was once the property of the famous de Grey family, who, perhaps, had links with the Knights Templar during the twelfth and thirteenth centuries. It is possible that a certain Sir Vernon de Grey of Griston Manor was also a Templar. His adored wife Elizabeth was said to have died of the plague while trying courageously to nurse villagers on their estate who had become ill. According to the story, Vernon had gone out to the Holy Land hoping to die in battle and join her. He eventually got his wish, but not before distinguishing himself with great courage and chivalry in many fights.

In 1562, Sir Thomas de Grey died, and his seven-year-old son, also called Thomas, was made a ward of Queen Elizabeth I. As was customary in those days of arranged marriages aimed at safeguarding landed interests, it was decided that the boy would marry Elizabeth Drury, the daughter of another local Norfolk landowner.

Young Thomas had an uncle, Robert — the stereotypical wicked uncle of the folk story — who was a Catholic recusant in this era of Elizabethan Protestantism. He stood to inherit if young Thomas died before coming of age.

Life was fragile enough from natural causes in the sixteenth century, and death — rather than divorce — was then the chief breaker of families. Young Thomas's mother had predeceased her husband, and Sir Thomas had married again before he died. His widow, young Thomas's stepmother, had remarried and was now the wife of Sir Christopher Heydon of Baconsthorpe, a staunch Protestant. The Heydons invited young Thomas to stay with them. He never came home again. Whether in Baconsthorpe Hall, or on the journey back to Griston, the boy died. Because of the religious controversy that bitterly divided Protestants and Catholics at that time, anti-Catholic sentiments prompted the suspicion that Robert was responsible for his young nephew's death. Rumours of the wicked uncle's foul play were strengthened when he tried to claim the child-widow's dowry as well as the de Grey wealth that had rightfully been young Thomas's.

Because the secretive, sinister shadows of Wayland Wood lay nearby, the rumours of the boy's murder soon incorporated the silent darkness of the remoter parts of the forest as their setting. Robert was repeatedly fined and imprisoned for being a recusant, and when he died in 1601, he owed £1,780 in fines — the equivalent of about £200,000 at today's values. (Source: http://eh.net/hmit/ppowerbp/.)

Another interesting piece of Norfolk evidence records that the oldest of the local people who were still around in the 1870s remembered seeing wood carvings in Griston Hall depicting scenes from the story.

Lightning brought down a massive old Wayland oak in 1879; it was said to have been the very tree under which the hapless Babes in the Wood of the traditional folktale died.

When co-author Lionel was working with Anglia Television and BBC-TV's Look East programs in the 1960s, he wrote a Babes in the Wood ballad, based on the factual, historical version of the episode.

> Sir Thomas de Grey lay a-dying,
> His brother stood close by his bed.
> "Take care of my son for me, Robert,"
> And those were the last words he said.

Chorus:
Oh, deep in the forest of Wayland,
Too dark for the rays of the sun,
In the homesteads and hamlets of Breckland,
Folk say that a foul deed was done.

Young Thomas, a lad of eleven,
Was walking alone through the glade.
No thought in the mind of the youngster
That murder was crouched in the shade.

Did greed guide the hand of the killer?
Had uncle provided the fee?
The lad's body fell in the twilight
At the foot of a mighty oak tree.

At sunset the robins flew sadly;
One last solemn token they gave
By covering the little lad's body
With leaves they had picked for his grave.

Uncle Robert laid claim to the fortune,
Then tried for the young widow's dower.
She fought the case at the Assizes
And Robert was shorn of his power.

The country folk all turned against him,
They burnt down his barns and his grain.
He was heavily fined and imprisoned.
His sons were both lost on the main.

Whether the folk tradition or the historical fragments from the local history of Griston come closer to the truth, it is now almost impossible to decide with any certainty. The shadowy finger of suspicion may point to young Thomas's stepmother instead of his uncle Robert. One possible and very sinister scenario suggests that, having disposed of her husband, Thomas de Grey senior, she planned to get rid of young Thomas, her stepson, lay the blame on his unpopular Catholic uncle Robert, and ultimately claim the de Grey estates for herself. In the sixteenth century, it was difficult, if not impossible, to distinguish between death from poisoning and death from natural causes such as enteritis or severe salmonella poisoning. Was Lady Heydon of Baconsthorpe a loving and caring stepmother, or yet another Roman Livia, ruthlessly poisoning her way to power?

10

WAS TEENAGED MOTHER MARY MORGAN FRAMED FOR INFANTICIDE?

ary Morgan, from the village of Glasbury near Maesllwch Castle in Wales, may well have been the innocent victim of one of the cruellest, most evil and hypocritical frame-ups in judicial history. When she was scarcely fifteen years old, she went to work as an assistant cook in the kitchens of imposing Maesllwch Castle, home of the rich and influential Wilkins family. Walter Wilkins senior was at that time the local member of Parliament.

The official story, which led to her tragic death at the gallows at the age of seventeen, was that she had become pregnant by one of the other servants, had subsequently murdered her newborn baby daughter, and concealed the infant's tiny body in a mattress in her room in the servants' quarters.

The cook enthusiastically gave evidence at Mary's trial to the effect that Mary had admitted to killing the child, and that a penknife — presumably the murder weapon — had been found under the pillows of the bed where the body was concealed. The first major point worth noting is that the supposed "confession" of which the cook testified with such eagerness was preceded by the strongest possible denials from Mary. When the cook, therefore, testified to having heard Mary's alleged confession, how much pressure had been put on the girl to confess? And had that pressure included threats and intimidation — or something like treacherous plea-bargaining ("If you confess, they'll let you off")?

In the early nineteenth century, infanticide was sickeningly frequent, and only rarely were the hapless young servant-girl mothers punished for it. Can we imagine a scenario in which the cook — sounding suspiciously like the agent, or mouthpiece, of someone with far more power and authority — had told Mary that if she confessed promptly, and implicated no one else, she would be dealt with as leniently as other girls in her situation were normally treated?

In September 1804, Mary had been working in the kitchens as usual when she complained of feeling unwell and was given permission to go up to her room. The child's body, with its head almost severed, was found there later that day — along with the knife Mary had allegedly used to inflict the fatal wound.

The coroner at the time was also the landlord of the Radnorshire Arms in Presteigne. The inquest verdict was that Mary Morgan was responsible for the baby's death. She was imprisoned for seven long months in the diabolical conditions of an early-nineteenth-century jail. As a friendless, unprotected servant girl, she would have had no chance to ward off the sexual advances of any of the prison staff who wanted to abuse her. By the time she arrived in court at Presteigne in April of 1805, she would have been battered, half-starved and so seriously ill that she was in no state to defend herself. Her travesty of a trial before the sanctimonious Judge Hardinge ended on April 11. He condemned her to death, and added that her body was to be given to the anatomists after she had been executed. His whole attitude towards her seems to have been vindictive — as though he was anxious to dispose of her as quickly as possible.

The sentence was carried out on Saturday, April 13. Huge crowds had gathered in Gallows Lane because public executions always attracted a large audience. Mary was a pathetic sight, dressed in a shroud, with her long hair hanging down in tresses over her thin shoulders. She was lifted, barely conscious, from the execution cart and duly hanged at noon. In spite of the judge's reference to sending her body to the anatomists, she

Judge Hardinge who sentenced seventeen-year-old Mary Morgan to death.

was buried in what was then unconsecrated ground, not far from what is St. Andrew's Churchyard in Presteigne today.

So much for the official version: but what might really have happened?

Judge Hardinge himself is not above suspicion. He was a close friend of the Wilkins family at Maesllwch Castle. It is likely that he had stayed there on several occasions before Mary gave birth. It has even been suggested that he was the father of the baby girl who was murdered!

To delve into that suspicion, it is necessary to explore the murkier depths of the human psyche and the terrifying obsessions and perversions it can nurture. The worst thoughts and cruellest atrocities can sometimes lurk behind a cloak of sanctimonious, religious respectability. Victor Hugo was not only a great storyteller, but he understood human nature as well as Chaucer, Shakespeare or Milton. In *The Hunchback of Notre Dame* he gets inside the labyrinthine mind of Archdeacon Claude Frollo — and it is a solemn, mysterious, morose, perverted and austere place. Frollo is tall, dark, menacing and fanatically academic. Second in ecclesiastical power only to the Bishop of Paris, Frollo's priestly celibacy and grim piety exclude him from the wholesome warmth of physical love that his passionate nature secretly longs for. At the lowest depth of his being he craves Esmeralda, the beautiful gypsy dancer. It is her tragedy that he destroys what he cannot possess.

The same sickly sweet, toxic odours of pious respectability and sanctimonious hypocrisy cling tenaciously to Judge Hardinge, a man cast in Frollo's sinister mould.

Another strange link between the judge and Mary's tragedy is that he frequently visited her grave, and even wrote several poems about her. Eleven years after her execution, Hardinge was at her graveside when he collapsed. He died of pleurisy shortly afterwards.

The Earl of Ailesbury, a close friend of the judge, arranged for a stone to be erected over Mary's grave, probably to try to counter the anger and disgust felt at the girl's cruel and unjust treatment. There is a replica on the spot today. The original stone is currently on display in the judge's lodgings — now the Presteigne Town Museum. Part of the inscription reads:

> To the memory of Mary Morgan, who young and beautiful, endowed with a good understanding and disposition, but unenlightened by the sacred truths of Christianity became the victim of sin and shame and was condemned to an ignominious death on the 11th April 1805, for the Murder of her bastard Child.
>
> Rous'd to a first sense of guilt and remorse by the eloquent and humane exertions of her benevolent Judge, Mr. Justice Hardinge, she underwent the Sentence of the Law …

Another stone nearby transmits a very different message:

> In Memory of MARY MORGAN
> Who Suffer'd April 13th, 1805. Aged 17 years.
> He that is without sin among you
> Let him first cast a stone at her.
> The 8th Chapr. Of John, part of ye 7th vr.

Was this raised by her parents, her friends and neighbours, or her defence counsel, Richard Beavan? There is a tradition that Beavan, or another man who was present at her trial and was incensed by the injustice of the sentence, rode to London to obtain a reprieve for her, but his horse went lame and he failed to reach Presteigne in time to save her. It may well be the case, but as far as is known, there is no documentary evidence to support this part of the story.

The waters of suspicion are further clouded by the presence of young Walter Wilkins, son of the MP, as foreman of the jury that condemned Mary. He was also a friend of Judge Hardinge. Some accounts of the tragedy actually suggest that the Wilkins family were related to Hardinge. Walter junior was said to have been engaged to the daughter of a socially prominent family in Hereford. Were he the father of Mary's child, his prospects of social advancement — something vitally important to the nouveau riche Wilkins family — would have been ruined.

Suppose that either Walter junior or Judge Hardinge had made Mary pregnant. Bribery or pressure is put on a footman, or groom, to admit responsibility. Hardinge, or Wilkins, makes the man "an offer he can't refuse." Their sinister influence also ensures that the cook's evidence against the hapless girl is lethal. Mary, weak and in pain after giving birth, staggers from her room for a few minutes, probably to what was then known euphemistically as "the privy." The murderous father slips in unseen, kills the tiny infant and leaves the incriminating penknife hidden under Mary's pillow — ready for the cook to find. Was the real father — Hardinge or Wilkins — afraid that if the baby survived and grew up, it would bear a family likeness that could not be denied? The savage slash that almost severed the tiny girl's head was a very powerful blow: could a girl in Mary's weakened condition have been strong enough to inflict such a decisive wound at such a time? The hand of a desperate criminal father seems more probable.

Mary's supposed confessions are easy enough to explain. She had endured hard labour all through her pregnancy. She had also had the problems of trying to conceal her condition. She had gone through the pain and stress of giving birth entirely alone. Imagine the scene — and the impact on the girl's mind — when she staggers back to her room and finds her baby's body. Panicked, she hides it. Until the cook arrives and searches the room, Mary herself has no idea that the knife that killed the child is hidden under the pillow. (At least one other researcher into Mary's tragedy has suggested that because it was an expensive penknife, it was most unlikely that it would have been Mary's property.) Mentally, she is in no state to defend herself. Browbeaten and threatened, she says anything her tormentors want her to say. The months in prison before the trial weaken her still further. The cruellest trick of all is the deceitful, pseudo-plea-bargain: "Just confess, and they'll let you off."

The weight of evidence seems to suggest that Mary Morgan was innocent, and was the victim of one of the cruellest legal murders in history.

11

MARIA MARTEN IN THE RED BARN

By the standards of the early nineteenth century, farmer John Corder of Polstead, near Stoke-by-Nayland, Suffolk, England, was a happy and prosperous man. With a good wife, three hundred acres of fertile East Anglian soil, and three sturdy sons — John, Thomas and James — to follow him and help on the farm, Corder's life seemed safe and secure. The fly in the ointment was his fourth son, William. Unlike his brothers in every possible respect, William wanted to follow a literary career, as a writer, or perhaps as a teacher. This was the great bone of contention between him and the rest of the Corder family. Learning in general, and such pretentious skills as writing for a living, were regarded with dark suspicion by sturdy, rural East Anglians in the early nineteenth century. Farmer John despised and ridiculed his small, pale, short-sighted youngest son, and made it very clear to him on several occasions that he would not share his brothers' inheritance when the time came, but would have to work for them as a menial hired hand. Although his mother treated him better than his father and brothers did, not surprisingly, young William brooded on escape and revenge.

Corder, the murderer of Maria Marten, once lived here.

His school days at a Hadleigh boarding school were as miserable and unfulfilled as his life at home. At school, the other children called him "Foxy" Corder, laughed at his literary aspirations, and generally made his life close to intolerable. Rejected and bitter, William felt driven to take his small, mean revenge as best he could. He was an inveterate thief and liar who indulged in minor confidence tricks that included selling some of his father's pigs on the sly, and borrowing money in his father's name. Curiously enough, some of the character witnesses who spoke in his defence at the trial maintained that he was kind, humane and good-tempered.

At every possible opportunity, William would sneak away to London with money he had stolen or borrowed. During these clandestine visits to the capital, he met Thomas Griffiths Wainewright, the artist, forger and poisoner who merits a subsequent chapter to himself and was undoubtedly a profound negative influence on the inadequate and impressionable Foxy Corder. Like Corder, Wainewright was constantly in debt, and again like Corder — but on a much grander scale — Wainewright had no scruples about obtaining money. He also shared Corder's literary aspirations — but, unlike the unhappy farm boy from

85

Polstead, Wainewright was the grandson of the famous Ralph Griffiths, founder and editor of *The Monthly Review*, London's first literary magazine.

How close were Corder and his sophisticated London friend? Did the far more able Wainewright pass on his arcane knowledge of poisons to his protégé?

The Maria Marten "Murder in the Red Barn" case became so notorious that various melodramas and musicals were written about it, and these are largely responsible for the misrepresentation of the historic Foxy Corder. In the dramas, he is portrayed as a bold, dashing, romantic, sophisticated seducer of beautiful, innocent country maidens. In fact, he was physically weak, timid, undersized and mentally self-deluded to an almost clinical extent. He was a petty criminal, prone to extravagant Napoleonic gestures, and ridiculed by all who knew him.

Maria Marten, in the Georgian plays about her murder, was a dewy-eyed, teenaged, village virgin, as innocent, delicate and beautiful as a snowflake on gossamer. The real Maria, however, was a very different proposition. She was, in fact, two years older than William, and was generally known to be readily available to any gentleman with a few shillings to spare. She had three illegitimate children, one by William's elder brother Thomas, before her fatal association with Foxy. She was already said to be wanted by police on charges of immorality, although Corder may have made that up to frighten her into agreeing to run away with him. When she vanished from Polstead village, it was widely assumed by the scurrilous local gossips that she had gone to London to work as a professional, full-time city prostitute.

As far as Maria was concerned, the four Corder brothers — and their father — were all wealthy enough to be good potential customers, and, if she was really lucky, one of the boys might even consider marrying her.

Fate intervened: Thomas, the father of one of Maria's children, died in a very strange accident in the frozen village pond. Had Foxy booby-trapped it for him by surreptitiously weakening a section of the ice over which Thomas took a shortcut? James and John both died young from typhus and tuberculosis. Not long after these deaths, John Corder senior joined his sons in the churchyard. Was Foxy in any way responsible?

Even a medieval man at arms knew that catapulting a decaying corpse over a castle wall was likely to bring sickness to the defenders. How much had Foxy learned in London about the ways in which diseases might be spread? Or was Wainewright's knowledge of toxicology involved? Had

Corder, the murderer of Maria Marten, once lived here.

young Corder learned how to administer poisons very slowly and carefully in such a way that the victim appeared to have succumbed to natural causes? This was certainly the case with Wainewright's own killings.

The poor, sickly baby boy born to William and Maria also died promptly, and his parents gave him a swift, informal, irregular burial. Given Maria's lifestyle and her promiscuous, unprotected sexual activities, the cause of death might have been congenital syphilis. Nevertheless, the question also arises as to whether William's knowledge of Wainewright's poisons might yet again have had something to do with the baby's demise.

The deaths of his father and brothers left William as Maria's only hope of getting her hands on the Corder farm. His mother, Mrs. Corder, was still alive and well, but once married to William and ensconced in the farmhouse, the dominant Maria would have been very much the lady in charge of the establishment.

Theatrical versions of the Red Barn melodrama invariably portray Mrs. Ann Marten as Maria's loving and deeply concerned mother. Maria's real mother, however, was Grace Marten, who had died after giving Thomas several other children as well as Maria. Ann Marten was, in fact, mole catcher Marten's second wife — Maria's stepmother — and presumably much younger than her husband — perhaps not very much older than Maria herself. What if she, too, was ambitious to get the Marten family's hands on to the Corder farm?

Imagine a sinister conspiracy: Maria and her stepmother accept that, although the three older Corder boys and their father are all well and good as regular paying customers of Maria's, it would be much better if they were out of the way so that the inadequate and impressionable Foxy could be driven into marrying Maria. Once that was all legally established, perhaps there were plans for him and his mother to join the rest of the Corders in the great beyond.

Detailed analysis of the fatal quarrel in the Red Barn that led to Maria's death raises a number of very interesting questions. Maria was a big, powerful, country girl — stronger, perhaps, and potentially more violent than the slightly built Foxy Corder. Was she threatening him in some way that, unless he agreed to marry her very soon, she would tell the authorities what she knew about his possible involvement in the very convenient family deaths? Or was she warning William that unless he married her, he was likely to go the same way? Knowing her to be ruthless, dangerous and unscrupulous from the death and burial of their infant son — and other events — was Corder afraid that she would one day dispose of him? Was the fatal pistol shot in the Red Barn Corder's version of a pre-emptive strike against a woman he knew to be deadly dangerous?

Suppose that young Mrs. Ann Marten, tired of her much older, low-paid, mole catcher husband, rather fancied Foxy and his farm herself. What if Maria discovered that her stepmother was actually her rival for the control of weak and manipulable William Corder? Was that why she and Corder quarrelled so bitterly in the Red Barn, instead of eloping as they had perhaps originally planned before their final, fatal meeting? What if, at some crucial moment in that deadly interaction between Maria and William, Mrs. Marten had turned up? Infuriated by her stepmother's intervention, Maria attacks William. He draws his gun and shoots her in self-defence. As she helps Corder tuck Maria's body away below the floor of the Red Barn, does Ann now realize that she has the ultimate hold over him? In return for her silence, she makes Corder swear to marry her, as soon as she can get free of old Thomas Marten, the mole catcher. Is his death part of their plan?

It is highly significant that Ann Marten's obsessive "dreams" about Maria being murdered by Corder and buried beneath the floor of the Red

The field where Corder's Red Barn once stood: Maria Marten's body lay below that barn.

Barn began only when he married Kathleen (also referred to as Mary) Moore, a young schoolmistress in London. Corder had met and married Mary (or Kathleen) after she replied to his early-nineteenth-century equivalent of a lonely hearts advertisement, which he had placed in the *Morning Herald* of November 12 and the *Sunday Times* of the 25th:

> MATRIMONY. A private gentleman, aged 24, entirely independent, whose disposition is not to be exceeded, has lately lost the chief of his family by the hand of Providence, which has occasioned discord among the remainder, under circumstances most disagreeable to relate. To any female of respectability who would study for domestic comfort, and willing to confide her future happiness in one every way qualified to render the marriage state desirable; as the advertiser is in affluence, the lady must have the power of some property, which may remain in her own possession. Many very happy marriages have taken place through means similar to this now resorted to, and it is hoped no one will answer this through impertinent curiosity; but should this meet the

Corder's brother drowned in this pond in Polstead, Suffolk, England. Was it murder?

eye of any agreeable lady, who feels desirous of meeting
with a sociable, tender, kind and sympathising companion, she will find this advertisement worthy of notice.
Honour and secrecy may be relied on. As some security
against idle applications, it is requested that letters may
be addressed to A-Z, care of Mr. Foster, stationer, No 68
Leadenhall Street, which will meet with the most respect-
ful attention.

Corder received about a hundred replies: Mary's was the successful one.
They opened a school together in London, and Corder apparently took
to the role of headmaster with great relish. Ironically, their house was
found for them by the infamous Thomas Griffiths Wainewright! Corder's
academic fantasies of becoming a teacher were at last fulfilled. Doom,
however, in the form of Ann Marten's "paranormal dreams," was not far
from the blissfully happy young couple.

There can be no doubt at all from her letters to Corder that Mary loved
him deeply and with boundless loyalty. Mary Corder had taken lodgings

in Bury St. Edmunds, where William was imprisoned, and was allowed to visit her husband. After she had been to see him on the morning of May 3, he wrote to her about his belief in an afterlife. He asked her not to read the papers because so many of them spoke very harshly of him. Mary wrote back the same day:

> My dear husband,
>
> I know that there are a number of idle reports published; but when we consider that it is by such reports those who write them get their living, it is a little excusable. Although no one would like to have all their faults and every error painted in their blackest colours to the world — pray be of good cheer, as we are not to be judged by sinners like ourselves, but by one who will pardon us if we repent. Look at the rich man and Lazarus. Let me beg you to continue fervent in prayer, and end them thus, "Thy will, O Lord, and not mine be done." Write me a few lines every day, if ever so few — I am fearful you do not eat — I have left all to follow you — let me know what you want, and while I stay here; it shall only be to attend to your comforts.
>
> God bless you, Adieu,
> M. Corder

Back to Polstead: how could Ann Marten bring the crime home to Corder without implicating herself? She could scarcely go to the local authorities and say that she had known about it for a whole year without condemning herself as an accessory after the fact. The early nineteenth century was a time of great superstition. People believed in dreams, portents, the writings of Nostradamus, the prophecies of Mother Shipton and the predictions of Coinneach Odhar, the Brahan Seer. Suppose that a dream led to Maria's decaying corpse? According to Ann Marten, she dreamed repeatedly that Corder had killed Maria and buried her under the floor of the Red Barn. She persisted with this account of her gruesome dream until her husband and the Corder Farm bailiff dug up the barn floor and discovered Maria's decomposing body.

Corder's brother drowned in this pond in Polstead, Suffolk, England. Was it murder?

Before discarding the possibility that a totally innocent and caring Ann Marten might really have had a series of frightening, persistent, and inexplicable paranormal dreams, it is worth looking briefly at another, much later, murder case in which a dream was central to the police investigation.

Writing in *The Book of Great Mysteries* in 1986, the brilliant Colin Wilson and his meticulously accurate co-author, Dr. Christopher Evans, provide impressive evidence in connection with the Bertha Huse murder case in Enfield, Vermont, in October of 1898. Following Bertha's disappearance, a widespread and thorough search revealed nothing. There was, however, a witness who reported seeing a woman answering Bertha's description on the Old Shaker Covered Bridge that crosses a narrow part of the nearby Muscova Lake. When divers failed to find Bertha's body, a certain Mrs. Titus, who lived four miles away, had a very strange and unnerving dream in which she saw exactly where Bertha's body rested, head down in the deep mud of the lake floor. At her insistence, a local businessman who had already paid for part of the search sent the diver down again. This time, by descending exactly where Mrs. Titus directed, he found Bertha's corpse, head down in the mud, just as Mrs. Titus had seen it in her paranormal dreams. William James, an eminent contemporary psychologist and a scrupulously accurate scientist, investigated the case thoroughly. He took signed statements from those involved. There seems to be little or no doubt that Mrs. Titus had had an inexplicable psychic revelation in her dreams.

Could the same thing have happened to Ann Marten, after Maria's murder? That possibility cannot be entirely dismissed.

Because Foxy Corder was such a compulsive liar, little or no stock can be placed in his so-called confession, but shortly before he was hanged at Bury St. Edmunds on August 11, 1828, he made the following statement:

Bury [Jail], August 10th, 1828, Condemned Cell, Sunday Evening, half-past eleven.

I acknowledge being guilty of the death of poor Maria Marten by shooting her with a pistol. The particulars are as follows: When we left her father's house, we began quarrelling about the burial of the child: she apprehended the place wherein it was deposited would be found out. The quarrel continued about three-quarters of an hour upon this ... and other subjects. A scuffle ensued, and during the scuffle, and at the time I think that she had hold of me, I took the pistol from the side pocket of my velveteen jacket and fired. She fell and died in an instant. I never saw her even struggle. I was overwhelmed with agitation and dismay: the body fell near the front doors on the floor of the barn. A vast quantity of blood issued from the wound, and ran on to the floor and through the crevices. Having determined to bury the body in the barn, about two hours after she was dead, I went and borrowed a spade of Mrs. Stow, but before I went there I dragged the body from the barn into the chaff house and locked the barn. I returned again to the barn and began to dig a hole, but the spade being a bad one, and the earth firm and hard, I was obliged to go home for a pickaxe and a better spade, with which I dug the hole and then buried the body. I think I dragged the body by the handkerchief that was tied round her neck. It was dark when I finished covering up the body. I went the next day, and washed the blood from off the barn

floor. I declare to Almighty God I had no sharp instrument about me, and no other wound but the one made
by the pistol was inflicted by me. I have been guilty of
great idleness, and at times led a dissolute life, but I hope
through the mercy of God to be forgiven.

William Corder.

This confession was witnessed by John Orridge and checked by W.
Stocking, the prison chaplain, and Timothy R. Holmes, the under-sheriff.
   The central mysteries remain: Did Corder kill Maria? Was it self-defence?
What part did Ann Marten really play in the grim tragedy of Polstead?

12

THOMAS GRIFFITHS WAINEWRIGHT (1794-1847)

Thomas Griffiths Wainewright is a psychological enigma rather than the central figure in a pure murder mystery. Two great questions hover over this brilliantly talented artist, painter, man of letters — and insidious poisoner. The first riddle concerns the real man — Wainewright's true character — and whatever mysterious ambitions, impulses and urges motivated him.

The highly acclaimed Farmington Trust, consisting of outstanding academics in the fields of theology, psychology and philosophy, contributed significant research data to the study of morals and ethics. Their work on psychopaths was important, and was particularly relevant to men like Thomas Griffiths Wainewright. As noted in Chapter One, the Farmington researchers concluded that psychopaths could distinguish right from wrong, what was morally good from what was ethically bad, but only in a non-emotional, non-involved way, in the same way that normal people recognize the difference between up and down, near and far, red and green. Wainewright was a psychopath in the Farmington sense.

Wainewright was a contemporary of Byron and Coleridge. They and other Romantic writers of that era were closely concerned with an examination of "the self" (as was Wainewright). They delved into the balance between good and evil in whatever it was that constituted a human personality. They investigated extremes of emotion and of behaviour. They looked at the relative proportions of love and hatred, gentleness, tenderness and vicious cruelty. They were interested — Coleridge, in particular — in the nexus between crime and creativity.

Born in Chiswick, London, in 1794, Wainewright was orphaned while still very young, and brought up by his grandfather, the famous Ralph Griffiths, founder of *The Monthly Review*, London's pioneering literary magazine. Wainewright was educated at Charles Burney's Academy, and then worked as an assistant to the painter Thomas Phillips. A commission in the Guards was bought for him, but he left the army soon after on the grounds of what were described as "pronounced hypochondria and neurotic symptoms." Contemporary accounts describe him as having "thick, sensual lips." His voice was an affected whisper, and his pale, aristocratic, artistic hands were encrusted with expensive, jewelled rings.

London in the early nineteenth century was a world of artists, writers, poets, painters, dandies and dilettantes — and Wainewright was in his element. His problem — although it ought not to have been — was money. He had exhibited at the Royal Academy several times. He had an inherited income of nearly £5,000 a year. He wrote regularly for various magazines and journals. But his problem was extravagance: he spent as if there was no tomorrow; luxuries became necessities. Debts began to pile up. By the time he married Frances Eliza Ward in 1821, money had become the major problem in his life.

His psychopathic disregard of any ethical standards enabled Wainewright to forge signatures on documents that would release the money held in trust for him. Predictably, because of his unbridled extravagance, those funds melted away like sunlit snow.

Luxurious housing for his wife, his son and himself added to Wainewright's chronic financial difficulties. They moved into beautiful Linden House, Turnham Green, where his wealthy bachelor uncle, George Edward Griffiths, lived. Uncle George died mysteriously soon afterwards, and Wainewright took over the magnificent house — and the substantial estate that went with it. As though inspired by his success in removing George, Wainewright now seems to have turned his attentions to his grandfather, who died soon afterwards — leaving everything he had to young Thomas.

Wainewright next invited his mother-in-law, Mrs. Abercromby (rendered as Abercrombie in some reference sources), and her other daughters, Helen and Madeleine — his wife's half-sisters — to stay with them at Linden House. Wainewright's next move was to set up an elaborate insurance fraud involving his wife and Helen Abercromby. Helen's mother — very astutely, in view of what had recently happened to Wainewright's uncle and grandfather — raised strident objections to the scheme. Predictably, Mrs. Abercromby died soon afterwards, with agonizing stomach pains as the principal symptom.

Just how Wainewright and his wife managed to persuade Helen to go along with the insurance fraud scheme after her mother's very suspicious death is another mystery in its own right. Helen may not have been very perceptive, or she may have been told of some strange, entirely hypothetical, plan whereby she could be made to "disappear," be presumed dead, and then rejoin the other conspirators abroad using a false identity — once the insurance companies had paid out. The insurance policies on Helen's life were now approaching £20,000 in value.

It seems as if Wainewright was beginning to think that if any more people died mysteriously at Linden House, the authorities might grow suspicious. Accordingly, he took the family to the theatre in London and booked overnight accommodation for them at 12 Conduit Street. Helen, up until then a perfectly normal, healthy, twenty-year-old woman, was taken ill there. She died eight days later, screaming in agony and describing her pains as being like "knives in the stomach." Helen's medical attendants and the domestic servants at Linden House commented thoughtfully that her mother had displayed quite similar symptoms.

Wainewright went to claim the insurance, but the companies refused to pay out and more or less hinted that they strongly suspected him of poisoning Helen. Wainewright, never lacking in impudent bravado, took the Imperial Insurance Company to court. Before matters were decided there, however, Thomas fled to France, where his persuasive charm worked wonders on an attractive young French girl living in Boulogne. Her father very foolishly allowed them to insure his life for about £3,000. The ink was scarcely dry on the policy before he, too, keeled over with fatal stomach pains, and the Pelican Insurance Company handed Wainewright the money. With this as his new stake, Thomas moved to Paris and stayed there until 1837.

By this time he had lost in absentia his claims against the English insurers who had refused to pay out on Helen's life policy. Probably thinking that everything in England had now safely blown over, Wainewright finally left Paris in pursuit of a woman he lusted after obsessively, but who had nevertheless had the good sense not to be taken in by his suave flattery and charm. He followed her back to Britain, and while staying at a hotel in Covent Garden, Wainewright was recognized by an alert and observant Bow Street Runner, who arrested him on the spot on an eleven-year-old forgery warrant. Thomas was all too eager to plead guilty and get himself deported for life — a sentence that in his view was vastly preferable to being hanged as a poisoner.

As a convict in Tasmania, he worked on a chain gang at first, was transferred to hospital work, and was finally allowed to exercise his considerable artistic talents once more. Specializing in the portraits of eminent citizens in Hobart, the artwork he produced there during his later years was arguably the best he had ever done.

He died of apoplexy in 1847 — still in Tasmania — at the age of fifty-three.

If he was not, after all, one of history's most callous poisoners, he was a man whose presence at so many deeply suspicious deaths stretched coincidence far beyond the limits of its rational elasticity.

13

THE MOZART MURDER MYSTERY

On his baptismal certificate, Wolfgang Amadeus Mozart's name was entered as Joannes Chrysostomus Wolfgang Theophilus. Amadeus was the Latin form of Theophilus, which translated to German as Gottlieb. (The Joannes was also translated as Johann, a name that is significant later in the story.) The brilliant composer was born in Salzburg, Austria, on January 27, 1756, and died on December 5, 1791.

The great mystery surrounding Mozart's death is whether he was poisoned by Antonio Salieri, who was allegedly insanely jealous of Mozart's genius. Although Salieri has always been the chief suspect — assuming, of course, that Mozart died of something other than natural causes — there was, in fact, another suspect. That man was Franz Hofdemel. The murder theory in Hofdemel's case was that his beautiful and passionate young wife, Magdalena, had had a prolonged affair with Mozart (always a notorious ladies' man) while she had been one of his music students. He had frequently taught her at home — which was not his usual practice with students. Beethoven certainly suspected that there was an intimate relationship between Mozart and Magdalena, and was so incensed about it that he refused to play if Magdalena was around.

One account of the tragedy records that, on the day after Mozart's funeral, there was a terrific row between Magdalena and her husband, Franz. She was five months pregnant at the time — and Mozart was suspected of being the unborn baby's father. A visitor failed to gain admission to the Hofdemels' home, and, fearing the worst, came back with two witnesses and broke in. They found Magdalena terribly injured by razor cuts to her face, arms and neck, and bleeding profusely. Nearby lay Franz, who had seemingly committed suicide by cutting his throat: the lethal razor still tightly gripped in his dead hand. Miraculously, despite her pregnancy, the prodigious loss of blood, and the shock resulting from her razor wounds, Magdalena and her baby lived. She named her son Johann (after Mozart) and Franz (after her late husband). This may have been because not even she was certain of who had fathered the boy — her husband, or her lover.

The details of the Hofdemel tragedy were never satisfactorily clarified, but an alternative theory of what happened suggests that the melodramatic Franz accused Magdalena of infidelity, confessed that he had poisoned Mozart, and then attempted to cut his throat in front of her as a suicidal gesture of the wrongs he felt he had suffered. Magdalena tried to stop him, and sustained her injuries more or less accidentally in the desperate struggle that ensued for possession of the razor — Franz never intended to harm her or the unborn child, only himself.

The possibility that Mozart died of natural causes cannot be entirely ruled out. Reports suggest that his medical history was long and complicated. He suffered at various times from rheumatic fever, arthritis, tonsillitis and even smallpox — from which he was lucky to recover. There is a theory that he finally died of uremia rather than the typhoid that was suspected as the cause. Mozart himself believed that he had been poisoned. During his terminal illness he said, "I have the taste of death on my tongue." That foul taste could equally well have indicated uremia, in which some of the body's waste products accumulate in the patient's mouth. But Mozart had none of the other symptoms: protracted coma, convulsions, fits and chronic skin irritation.

Any later attempt at a forensic examination of his exhumed corpse was thwarted because his wife, Constanze, collapsed and was unable to cope. By the time she had recovered sufficiently to take any effective action, she was unable to positively locate his grave. This, in part, gave rise to the frustrating mystery regarding the identification of what may, or may not, be Mozart's skull.

It is alleged that when Mozart was finally laid to rest, Joseph Rothmeyer wound an identifying wire around his neck: in itself, a very curious action. Although the church and Empress Marie Therese officially disapproved of Freemasonry, Mozart had been an enthusiastic member, as had Franz Hofdemel, and it is possible that Rothmeyer was complying with a mystical Masonic tradition in which the circle of wire — with no beginning and no end — symbolized eternity and immortality. Rothmeyer is said to have claimed that he retrieved Mozart's skull in 1801, using this wire neck loop as a definite identifier. The purported Mozart skull ended up in a rather morbid collection of skulls of the talented, which included those of Schubert and Beethoven. Joseph Hyrtl, who had interesting theories about the correlation between skull shapes and the talents of their owners, examined the Rothmeyer skull carefully and labelled it as Mozart's. It finally came to rest in the Mozarteum Foundation in Salzburg, where more advanced and up-to-date medical knowledge than Hyrtl's put forward the theory that the skull displayed signs of premature synopsis of the metopic suture (PSMS) — a condition which, in effect, cauases the forehead to develop in two halves. This abnormal bone development results in an unusually broad face, a straight, vertical forehead, prominent cheekbones and ridges over the eyes — all of which are revealed in early portraits of Mozart. So perhaps the skull is genuine and Rothmeyer was telling the simple truth.

In order to produce a clear picture of the composer's death and the possible motives behind his murder — if in fact it was murder — it is important to summarize Mozart's life and background.

His father, Leopold Mozart, was a composer and violinist in the service of the Archbishop of Salzburg. Johann had an older sister, christened Maria, but nicknamed "Nannerl." Nicknames were something of a family tradition in the Mozart ménage — Wolfgang was known as "Wolferl." From his early childhood, Mozart's life and music were inextricably intertwined. For example, he was playing the harpsichord at three years old, and actually composing when only five. He was playing before the Austrian empress and the elector of Bavaria a year later. In Vienna, Emperor Francis I referred to Mozart as "my little magician."

Like many other poverty-stricken parents of child prodigies, Leopold looked for ways to make money off his exceptionally gifted young son.

The family set out on various tours, and Wolfgang's performances astounded the crowned heads of France and England, among other distinguished patrons. It was during April of 1764, at the age of eight, that he visited England. He was very well received: there is even a statue of him as a boy between Victoria and Chelsea in London.

While still very young, in December of 1769, Mozart went to Italy to further his musical education. Arriving in Rome on the Wednesday of Holy Week, he went to the Sistine Chapel to hear Allegri's famous "Miserere," and caused an uproar by being able to write it down from memory. This work was securely guarded — singers were forbidden to transcribe it under the threat of excommunication.

While touring Italy, Mozart wrote at least two operas, as well as a serenata that was performed in Milan. In 1773, while still in his teens, Mozart wrote a set of string quartets and a group of symphonies, including Number 25 in G minor, and Number 29 in A. From 1774 until 1777 he worked in Salzburg as konzertmeister for 500 florins a year under the patronage of Archbishop Hieronymus — an arrogant, pompous, self-opinionated prelate who must have been a strong contender for the title of Salzburg's worst employer.

It needs to be emphasized at this juncture that musicians were such vicious rivals in those days because there were very few posts available; even if a man landed a job, the pay was relatively low. This made it very much a buyer's market, an employer's market, and even the most talented composers and performers — such as Mozart — had to put up with extremely unpleasant employers. Archbishop Hieronymus wanted the prestige of having Mozart on his payroll, but he treated the great composer abominably.

So vast was Mozart's talent that Haydn once described him as "the greatest composer known to me." It was because Mozart's musical talent was so prodigious that many other musicians — including Salieri — were insanely jealous of him, and very much afraid of his powers as their rival. In Salieri's case, did that jealousy culminate in murder?

How much is known about Antonio Salieri? He was a competent Italian composer who was born at Legnano on August 18, 1750, and died in Vienna on May 7, 1825. He had gone to Vienna, and met Emperor Joseph, in 1766. In 1774 he became kapellmeister, and in 1788 hofkapellmeister. He remained in that post for fifty years, visiting Italy and Paris on several occasions. He wrote a lot of acceptable music, which was performed in several European theatres. Salieri was also a great teacher of music: his talented students included Beethoven, Schubert and Liszt.

In a time before television, radio, compact discs, the Internet and the like, good composers like Salieri must have been outstandingly important to the embryonic entertainment industry. The Viennese public preferred his work to Mozart's *Don Giovanni*. Salieri's last opera was *Die Neger*, which was produced in 1804. After that, he devoted himself to church music. Salieri was held in such high esteem that he retired on full salary in 1824. Sadly, he had a nervous breakdown before his death, and sometimes, in moments of deep emotional stress, he actually accused himself of killing Mozart. Did he really mean that he had been the one who had told Franz Hofdemel that Mozart was having an affair with the lovely Magdalena, and, in so doing, prompted Franz to poison Mozart?

Mozart's power and passion flowed through his music as wildly as it did through his tempestuous romantic relationships. This shows clearly in his *Don Giovanni*, in which he perceptively examines the interplay of social and sexual stresses and pressures.

Mozart's mother died on July 3, 1778; four years later, in 1782, he married Constanze Weber. She was the younger sister of Aloysia Weber, with whom he had previously been in love. Although he spent the rest of his days based in Vienna, Mozart made several visits to Salzburg, Prague and Berlin. Ironically, his last, unfinished, work was a requiem.

Towards the end of Mozart's life a very odd incident occurred that makes it seem as if Mozart had almost convinced himself he was going to die. Psychiatrists do refer occasionally to thanatomania (derived from the Greek term thanatos, meaning "death") and it seems possible that Mozart was suffering from this strange kind of self-induced death wish. While Mozart was working on *Die Zauberflote*, a mysterious stranger called and asked him to compose a requiem. He offered to pay in advance — an important inducement for Mozart — but the stranger's conduct was so bizarre that Mozart, who was far from well, began to regard the man as some sort of eldritch and arcane messenger of death.

Die Zauberflote, which was filled with Masonic symbolism, was duly produced and ran very successfully. In Mozart's youth, a musical performance that ran for as long as twenty nights was considered to have achieved exceptional success.

The all-important requiem, however, was still unfinished: the stranger came again and paid a further advance. Mozart, now thoroughly con-

The young Mozart: was he poisoned?

vinced that he was writing his own requiem, put his very best music into it. Before the sinister stranger's third visit, Mozart was dead, but his terrified widow, Constanze, had persuaded their friend Sussmayr, one of Mozart's most promising students, to finish the score in an imitation of Mozart's handwriting.

The mysterious patron actually turned out to be a messenger representing Count Walsegg, who wished to have Mozart's requiem performed for his own funeral service.

Some time after Wolfgang's demise, Constanze married Georg Nissen, who set about writing a biography of his illustrious predecessor. To help him with this work, Sophie Haibel, who was Constanze's younger sister, wrote Georg a letter containing a detailed account of Mozart's death. One section of her evidence detailing Mozart's last hours is particularly poignant and moving. Sophie wrote:

> Alas, how frightened I was when my sister, who was almost despairing and yet trying to keep calm, came out saying: "Thank God that you have come, dear Sophie.

Last night he was so ill that I thought he would not be
alive this morning. Do stay with me today, for if he has
another bad turn, he will pass away tonight. Go in to him
for a little while and see how he is." I tried to control
myself and went to his bedside. He immediately called
me to him and said: "Ah, dear Sophie, how glad I am that
you have come. You must stay here tonight and see me
die."

Mozart's son, Karl, who was only seven years old when his father died,
described the gruesome tragedy this way:

Particularly remarkable is, in my opinion, the fact that a
few days before he died, his whole body became so
swollen that the patient was unable to make the smallest
movement, moreover, there was a stench, which reflected
an internal disintegration which, after death, increased to
the extent that an autopsy was rendered impossible.

Constanze, herself an eyewitness of her husband's death, recalled that
Mozart "vomited a great arc of brown fluid" just as he died. Medically, this
could have indicated any one of several horrendous, fatal, visceral conditions.
So, who really killed Mozart? Or did he die of natural causes after all?
For years, Mozart seemed to have been oblivious to the bitter criticisms
of Salieri and many of his other jealous contemporaries. Did that make
Mozart vulnerable? Salieri undoubtedly hated him and showed his dislike
openly. On more than one occasion he seems to have prevented Mozart
from securing lucrative appointments. Persistent rumours certainly accused
Salieri of poisoning Mozart, and this formed the basis of Rimsky-
Korsakov's opera, *Mozart and Salieri*. Beethoven and Schubert, however,
were particularly fond of Salieri, and did not think him responsible for
harming Mozart. Another interesting piece of evidence comes from Salieri's
own death-bed statement in 1825: "I did not poison Mozart." He said this
during several moments of clarity to contradict other statements — in
which he implicated himself — made during his tragic nervous breakdown.
Careful examination of Salieri's exact words still leaves room for doubt: he
did not say that Mozart had not been poisoned — only that he, Salieri, had
not done it! There seems to have been quite a lot of public sympathy for

Salieri at the end — he was given a magnificent state funeral. Hardly the sort of send-off accorded to a treacherous poisoner!

Mozart believed that he had been poisoned. If he did not blame Salieri, then did Mozart suspect Franz Hofdemel, the wronged husband of his beautiful and passionate young student, Magdalena?

Weighing all the evidence, the authors' views of the statistical probabilities would seem to be about 0.7 (70 percent) that Mozart was poisoned and only 0.3 (30 percent) that he died of natural causes. Of the 0.7 probability of poisoning, 0.4 points go to Franz Hofdemel and 0.3 to Salieri.

14

THE BLOODY STEPS AT RUGELEY

On the south side of Rugeley Parish Church stands the memorial stone of Christina Collins, victim of the Bloody Steps Murder, which took place on June 17, 1839. Her inscription reads:

> To the memory of Christina Collins, wife of Robert Collins, London, who having been most barbarously treated was found dead in the canal in this Parish on June 17th, 1839, aged 37 years. This stone is erected by some individuals of the Parish of Rugeley in commiseration of the end of this unhappy woman.

Two men were hanged for Christina's murder, a third was transported to Australia, and significant social reforms affecting the lives of canal boatmen and their families were triggered by her tragic death. But were the men convicted of her murder really guilty? There are significant unanswered questions still attached to Christina's case.

Christina was actually christened Christiana. She was born in New Radford, Nottingham, England, on July 17, 1801, and her life soon became a very mixed and unusual one. Her father, Robert Brown, was an inventor, and initially had great success. In Christina's early youth, the family were well provided for. Robert was granted Patent Number 2766 for "a machine which made lace from animal, vegetable or mineral fibres." He also took out Patent Number 2571 for a network machine. Sadly, his ability as an engineer was not matched by his ability to manage money. Unable to cope with the financial problems that threatened to overwhelm him, he became mentally ill and suicidal. By the time he died in 1818, he was receiving parish relief. Christina had a brother named Alfred, who tried his hardest to follow in his father's footsteps as an inventor, but never succeeded, largely because he lacked the essential investment capital to exploit his good ideas.

Having enjoyed a good education, and with high hopes of a good marriage to a wealthy husband, Christina found poverty uncongenial. Mrs. Brown coped bravely by working as a nurse, and battled on to bring in what money she could until well into her sixties. Christina's first attempt to escape from poverty and the boredom that accompanied it was her marriage to Thomas Ingleby. He was a Scot, originally from Dundee, who earned a reasonable living — a lot more than Christina could aspire to since her father's death — by entertaining as a conjurer. He was, nevertheless, not a high-earning, top-of-the-bill illusionist. Although he sometimes appeared in the more lucrative London theatres, he spent most of his working life touring the provinces. He had also written a book on conjuring in 1815 entitled *Ingleby's Whole Art of Legerdemain*. His tricks included beheading a chicken and apparently restoring it to life, smashing and rebuilding a watch, and — providing he was given notice in advance — eating six knives and forks.

Christina recited, sang, joined in the conjuring tricks and danced to augment their act. Ingleby was much older than Christina, and he died in Ireland in 1832, leaving her a young, childless widow of only thirty-one. If her show business career had been exciting and entertaining, it seems to have lacked the deep and romantic love that she enjoyed in her second marriage, and which led indirectly to her death. Her second husband, whom she married in 1838, was Robert Collins, a hostler. Times were hard, and Robert could not find work no matter how hard he tried. Christina was lucky enough to get sewing work at the home of a Mrs. Grice, who lived at 3 Crosshall Street in Liverpool. Finally, Robert managed to get a job in London, where he lodged at 10 Edgware Road. As soon as he could afford it, he sent Christina a guinea (twenty-one shillings in the money of their day, or £1.05 in modern decimal currency). This would have represented nearly two weeks' wages to him, and be worth approximately £50 at today's prices. (Source: http://eh.net/hmit/ppowerbp/.) It is clear that he missed his beloved Christina desperately, and wanted to be with her as soon as possible. She was equally anxious to be reunited with him, and probably felt that her own chances of employment in London would be better than they were in Liverpool. Accordingly, on the morning of June 15, 1839, Christina packed all her worldly goods into two small travelling trunks and set out for London by canal — which was much cheaper than travelling by rail.

Christina was an attractive girl — not very big, but trim and smartly dressed. Her canal route was scheduled to go from Liverpool via Stoke-on-Trent, Rugeley, Fradley Junction, Coventry and Oxford to London. It was an extremely hazardous journey for a young woman to tackle on her own. She was the only passenger on that particular barge on the section of the canal that passed through Rugeley. The typical boatmen of the early nineteenth-century canals tended to be violent, illiterate and heavy drinkers. It says a great deal about her love for Robert Collins that she was prepared to take such an enormous risk to be reunited with him in London.

The skipper of the barge was thirty-nine-year-old James Owen. He was married and came from Brinklow, not far from Coventry. His crew consisted of twenty-seven-year-old George Thomas from Wombourne in Staffordshire, who had the alias of Dobell, which might, or might not have indicated a past that he was trying to escape from; twenty-eight-year-old William Ellis, also from Brinklow, and another man with an alias (Lambert); and William Musson, who was still in his teens and who hailed from Chilvers Coton in Warwickshire. Christina set out with them at 7:30 p.m. on Saturday, June 15. At 5 a.m. on Monday, June 17, her body was dragged out of the canal at Brindley Bank, close to the notorious Bloody Steps, not far from Rugeley aqueduct.

A coroner's inquest was held promptly at the Talbot Inn in Rugeley. Owen, Thomas and Ellis were charged with Christina's murder and remanded in custody. When their case came before the Staffordshire Summer Assizes in July of 1839, they were also charged with raping her, and with aiding and abetting one another in the rape. Only teenaged Musson was omitted from the indictment. Mr. Justice Williams was in charge of this first trial, and he directed the jury to find them not guilty of the rape charges because of a lack of evidence. Sergeant Ludlow, who was prosecuting, applied to postpone the trial until the next Assizes because he maintained that a vitally important witness would not be available until then.

Ludlow's vitally important witness was Joe Orgill, who was currently imprisoned for bigamy. If and when he was granted a pardon, it would be possible for him to appear and give evidence. Ludlow's argument was that Owen, the skipper of the fateful barge when the murder was committed, had been imprisoned near Orgill during the time that he was remanded in custody. Orgill maintained that Owen had made certain disclosures to him that would provide vital evidence for the murder trial. It was, of course, highly probable that the cunning bigamist had seen a golden opportunity to obtain a pardon by offering to give evidence during this important murder trial. Owen's defence counsel stridently opposed the postponement, but the judge listened carefully to Sergeant Ludlow's arguments and agreed to the postponement.

When the next Assizes got under way, the new judge was Baron Gurney, a very different proposition from Judge Williams. There had been a powerful surge of public outrage over what had happened to Christina, and the case had also attracted the professional attention of several judges, barristers and solicitors. The actual charge was that Owen, Thomas and Ellis had "cast, pushed and thrown the said Christina Collins into the canal, by which means she was choked, suffocated and drowned."

One of Pickford's porters, a sensible and reliable witness named William Brookes, gave evidence that when the barge arrived at Stoke on June 16 the sole passenger was a woman. She actually complained about the conduct of the crew and, according to Brookes, she looked stressed and far from well. He also expressed the opinion that the crew looked as if they were the worse for drink. It was Christina's ill fortune that the cargo consisted partly of alcohol, and there were several bargemen of the period who had worked out various ingenious techniques for extracting a free drink or two without leaving any indication that the cargo had been tampered with! There is a link here with the unknown fate of Captain Benjamin Spooner Briggs, his wife and child, and the crew of the *Mary Celeste*. That mysterious vessel had also been carrying alcohol — but it wasn't the drinkable kind. There were over 1,700 barrels of industrial alcohol aboard the *Mary Celeste* when the captain, passengers and crew simply vanished not far from the Azores in November 1872.

Brookes's evidence made it clear that Christina was so frightened by this time that she enquired about the possibility of getting a coach ticket

The Rugeley canal, where brave little Christina Collins was raped and murdered.

instead. Her tragedy was that there were no convenient or affordable coaches to London — and she was as anxious to rejoin her beloved Robert as he was to be with her again.

Another vital witness, Hugh Cordwell, worked as a checking clerk at Stoke. He not only confirmed that the barge had duly arrived there at approximately 8 p.m., he described his conversation with Christina. She was now very frightened indeed, and Cordwell added that Owen in particular seemed dangerously drunk. Cordwell told the court that he had advised Christina to report the crew's conduct to the proper authorities when the boat finally reached its destination. Perhaps Cordwell was not very big, and not very strong. Maybe he was not the type of man to risk getting involved in a fight with Owen and his crew, but under the circumstances it seems very strange that he didn't insist on taking Christina off the barge for her own protection. He was, after all, a responsible servant of the Trent and Mersey Canal Company, with the rank of checking clerk, and he was by no means uneducated.

The next piece of evidence came from another clerical officer, John Tansley. He had been on duty at Aston Lock, nearly two miles on from Stoke, where Cordwell had talked to Christina. Tansley told the court that he had seen her walking along the towpath. She had decided to get off the boat altogether and rejoin it later if the men showed any signs of sobering up and behaving decently. Tansley also told the court that Christina had sharpened her small penknife on the step of the lock keeper's cottage. At this stage of the story, it's important to recall that Christina was the daughter of an ingenious inventor. Her brother had inherited their father's creativity, and Christina was a girl with plenty of spirit and initiative. Her years in show business as a conjurer's wife and stage assistant had not been easy ones. She was resourceful and defiant. Whoever killed her did not have an easy task. At least one of the barge crew had a cut face. Was that the work of Christina's newly sharpened little knife?

Her nightmare journey continued throughout what was to be her last night on Earth. Sometimes she must have fought the men off while still on the boat. Sometimes she got off and walked along the towpath to escape from their unwelcome attentions.

Witness Tommy Blore, another Pickford's captain, told the court that he had passed Owen's barge near Sandon. It was then around 9 p.m. Owen had exchanged words with Blore about the woman passenger on board. He had also threatened, according to Blore's evidence, to treat her as Burke and Hare, the notorious "resurrection men" — murderers and body snatchers — had treated their victims. Blore also confirmed Tansley's evidence that Owen was wildly drunk when their vessels passed.

James Mills, another vitally important witness, was the lock keeper at Hoo Mill. He testified that he and his wife had seen Christina on top of the cabin, and the three accused standing by the boat. Christina was screaming defiance at them. Anne Mills, the lock keeper's wife, asked who the girl was. The boatmen said that she was a passenger, and that everything was all right because her husband was on board with her. This seemed to satisfy John and Anne, but the evidence again shows great reluctance to intervene to help the desperately frightened girl. The disturbing question is raised yet again: why didn't Mills and his wife insist on taking Christina off the boat and into the safety of their cottage? Why were all those who encountered them so frightened of the three boatmen?

William Hatton proved to be yet another key witness. In the early hours of the morning, he had passed the spot where Christina's body was eventually found. Hatton told the court that he had seen Owen and Thomas standing together on the canal bank. As he came within hailing distance they asked whether he had seen a woman. When he replied that he had-

The notorious Bloody Steps at Rugeley beside the canal where brave little Christina Collins was raped and murdered.

n't, they repeated the question. According to Hatton's evidence, they both seemed very agitated.

Christina's body — still warm — was pulled up out of the water near Brindley Bank and Rugely Aqueduct at 5 a.m. At 5:30, Owen reported to lock keeper John Lee at Woodend that a woman passenger, whom he described as "off her head" and "deranged," had committed suicide by drowning herself in the canal.

The matter was at last reported to the police and the boatmen were arrested by Constable William Harrison. His evidence indicated that they were not only drunk, but abusive, and he testified that one of them had muttered, "Damn and blast the woman!"

Hannah Phillips was called in to remove the dead woman's clothing so that the body could be properly prepared for burial later. Hannah testified that Christina's clothes were torn. It looked as though she had been involved in a desperate struggle — almost certainly while resisting a rapist. One of her arms was badly bruised, as if an assailant had taken her penknife away. The examining surgeon, Samuel Barratt, told the court that in his opinion Christina had died from a combination of suffocation and drowning.

Owen and Thomas were duly hanged — still protesting their innocence. Ellis was transported to Australia.

If there is any mileage in the popular folk belief that ghosts are more likely to be observed in places associated with murders than almost anywhere else, the evidence from Mrs. Southwell and her daughter of Arch Street in Rugely may be highly significant. A century to the day after Christina had been murdered, Mrs. Southwell and her daughter were walking near the infamous Bloody Steps, close to the spot where Christina's body had been pulled from the canal. The two women saw a strange, ghostly male figure that was gliding rather than walking. It came right through the railings as if they were not there, then disappeared. They described the spectre as having a very sad expression on its face. The figure made no sound.

Although the circumstantial evidence pointed damningly to the three accused boatmen, and although there can be little or no doubt that they subjected Christina to an abominable and terrifying ordeal, there is serious room for doubt about whether they actually murdered her. The poor, desperate girl had left the barge more than once during that long terrible night. Was someone waiting for her on that lonely towpath? The early nineteenth century was a grim and terrible place for the poor and the dispossessed. Homeless vagrants used towpaths as frequently as they wandered the highways and byways. Imagine the scene as game little Christina fights off the drunken bargemen with a strength borne of desperation. She cuts one with her penknife. He catches her arm, bruising it as he tears the knife away from her. Her clothes are torn and dishevelled in the struggle. She jumps from the barge to the bank. The barge moves on along the canal. The opportunistic rapist and murderer lurks in the shadows of the towpath. She has no knife to defend herself now — and although courageous and determined she is very small. The end of her last fight is inevitable. Stunned and shocked, fighting for breath, she is flung into the muddy depths of the canal.

Whose sad ghost did the Southwells see in 1939? One of the bargemen, hanged for a murder he did not commit? The unknown lurker on the towpath? Or even the heartbroken Robert Collins, wishing even after death that he had gone to Liverpool to escort the wife he loved so much safely back to London?

15

THE MYSTERY OF
SPRING HEELED JACK

C o-author Lionel's father, Robert, was born in 1880. A fascinating character, he ran colourful businesses of the more adventurous kind — ranging from a pub with a boxing booth and lodging house attached to it to a scrap-metal yard and a coal delivery round. He also told Lionel stories from his boyhood in Victorian England, several of which featured his personal reminiscences and his reflections on the two terrifying "Jacks" of the nineteenth century — Spring Heeled Jack and Jack the Whitechapel Ripper.

The very earliest reports of a jumping daredevil making a vicious nuisance of himself in London pre-dated Victoria by several years. Whispers of someone — or something — very like the powerful, jumping creature described in the later, fuller reports of Spring Heeled Jack circulated as early as 1817, but it was another twenty years before Spring Heeled Jack was truly established as part of London's urban folklore. These first reports came from London's Barnes Common area.

In 1837, Barnes Common was not the safest place to walk alone in the dark. There were known to be pickpockets and more violent thieves in the area, but because time was pressing and the Common offered a good shortcut, a businessman who had been working late one September night took the risk. He was shocked and horrified when Jack bounded over a cemetery wall and confronted him. The startled businessman ran for his life. Jack's description included pointed ears; an abnormally long, pointed nose; reddish-orange eyes that bulged and glared horribly; what seemed to be a tight-fitting white oilskin costume; hands that felt more like iron claws or talons; and the ability to breathe some weird type of electric-blue fire in the faces of his victims. Jack frequently arrived very suddenly with his characteristic leaps and bounds — and he often left in the same way. By leaping over high walls, hedges and fences, Jack baffled his pursuers time after time.

Polly Adams, a pretty teenager, was making her lighthearted way home from Blackheath Fair, where she had been having a good time with her friends, when Spring Heeled Jack attacked her. She said afterwards that the hands that had torn her clothes away felt more like iron hooks than ordinary fingers. She also said that her attacker was very thin and tall — but far stronger than such a slightly built man would have been expected to be. Three other victims confirmed Polly's description, adding that the glaring, bulging eyes of whatever had attacked them had been particularly prominent and horrible.

Another of Jack's well-documented and authenticated attacks took place in Cut Throat Lane near Clapham Common. Mary Stevens was a pretty little teenaged housemaid who worked in Lavender Hill. Her employers had given her permission to visit her parents' home in Battersea, and she was walking back via Clapham when Spring Heeled Jack attacked her. He locked her helplessly in what Mary later described as a grip like a steel vice and began to fondle her. When she screamed for help, he laughed insanely, let go of the terrified girl, and sprang away into the surrounding darkness. Unlike the screams of poor little Christina Collins on the Rugeley Canal, Mary's cries were heard, and elicited an instant response from a group of burly, well-meaning Clapham citizens. They raced purposefully after Jack, and would have caught him had it not been for his superhuman leaping powers.

Very soon after the attack on Mary Stevens, Jack struck again quite close by. He leapt into the road immediately in front of a horse-drawn carriage. The terrified horses bolted, causing a devastating crash that seriously injured the coachman. Once again, public-spirited bystanders tried to detain him, but Jack bounded effortlessly over a wall nearly ten feet high and escaped into the night once more.

His next attack was on another lady in Clapham, not far from the churchyard. On this occasion he left a very important clue behind — one that could have helped not only to identify whatever, or whoever, Jack really was, but could also have shed light on his mysterious, superhuman jumping ability. The clue in question consisted of two unusually deep footprints that penetrated seven or eight centimetres down into the earth. Whatever had created those strange markings had either been abnormally heavy, or had descended from a prodigious height. Some accounts maintain that when the prints were examined it looked as though an odd mechanism in the shoes or boots had made them. Unfortunately, none of the investigators at the time had the wisdom to take plaster casts of the mysterious prints for long-term analysis. The mechanism-in-the-boots theory was later said to have been tested by a group of young soldiers, the majority of whom suffered broken ankles when the springs in their boots turned out to be a catastrophic failure.

The next two girls who encountered Spring Heeled Jack did so in 1838. They were two young sisters, Lucy and Margaret Scales, who had been visiting their brother in the Limehouse area of London and were making their way home again between 8 and 9 p.m. Lucy was in front, and was growing rather impatient with Margaret, who seemed to her to be dawdling unnecessarily. Spring Heeled Jack suddenly confronted Lucy and breathed what she described as blue fire into her face. She screamed and collapsed. Margaret ran to help her, and Jack bounded lightly over the two terrified girls. According to the report they gave, he then leapt on to a house roof and vanished away into the darkness at the rear of Green Dragon Alley.

Shortly after this episode with the Scales sisters, Jack attacked eighteen-year-old Jane Alsop. She lived with her father and two sisters in Bow, and had been sitting quietly reading when the doorbell rang. When she answered it, she saw a caped figure who she thought at first was a policeman. He told her that he was indeed a policeman, and that he needed a light. He went on to explain that they had just caught Spring Heeled Jack in the lane. Jane was very excited by the news. She ran quickly back into the house and returned with a candle — but as she held it out to the supposed policeman, Jane had a terrible shock. The light from the candle fell on the weird, shiny, oilskin-like face of Spring Heeled Jack himself! He blew fire into her face, half-blinding the girl, and then began ripping enthusiastically at her clothes with hands that felt more like metallic claws. Jane screamed and punched hard at his prominent, pointed nose. This made him recoil a little, and she tried to get back indoors. He seized her long hair and dragged her back towards him. Her desperate screams, however, had alerted her sisters to the danger. They bravely rushed out to rescue her, and somehow the three girls succeeded in getting inside the house and slamming the door in Jack's hideous face.

From the safety of an upstairs window, the Alsop girls shouted for the police — the relatively new force established by Sir Robert Peel's Metropolitan Police Act, which had been passed only nine years before.

Once again, Jack was able to escape by bounding away with enormous leaps across the fields at the rear of Bearhind Lane. He dropped his cloak, but before this could be retrieved by the police and used as a vital clue, someone else picked it up. Did this mean that Jack had an accomplice? Was there, perhaps, a Spring Heeled Jill?

When Jane and her sisters described Jack to the police in Lambeth they said that he seemed to be wearing a helmet of some kind; he had a cloak — the one that was subsequently dropped — like a policeman's; and he wore a costume that fit him very closely. They described it as resembling oilskin. His claw-like hands, Jane noted, were very cold. She also emphasized the terrifying effect that his glowing, orange-red eyes had had on her: "They were like balls of fire," she said.

By this time, the lord mayor, Sir John Cowan, publicized a letter about Spring Heeled Jack that had been sent to him in his official capacity. Once this became public knowledge, other victims who had been too afraid, or embarrassed, to speak began to come forward and tell their own stories of encounters with Spring Heeled Jack. As a result of all this extra publicity, the fearless Duke of Wellington — the veteran victor of the Battle of Waterloo in 1812 — decided to ride out again in pursuit of the weird creature that was unnerving half the teenaged girls in London. Armed with a pair of trusty pistols, Wellington — as bold and fearless at seventy as he had been thirty years earlier — mounted his war steed and rode through the areas where Spring Heeled Jack had been seen up to his tricks. The Iron Duke never caught him, but if he had, Jack's mysteriously charmed and apparently invulnerable life might well have been terminated by an ounce or so of well-directed pistol ball!

A week after his vicious attack on Jane Alsop, Jack called at a house in Turner Street, off Commercial Road, and asked the young servant boy who opened the door whether his master was in. The lad was on the verge of summoning his employer when the lamplight illuminated Jack's weird, inhuman face. The boy saw the hideous red-orange eyes and stood for a moment, paralyzed with fear. But as he stood there, the lad also noticed some significant details about Jack. The claw-like hands were easy to recognize, and under the cloak there was a delicately embroidered design that made the lad think immediately of a coat of arms. He also saw the letter W embroidered in gold thread.

As the young servant screamed out a warning, Jack shook his fist in the lad's face, before hurtling over the roofs of Commercial Road and away into the darkness once more.

The coat of arms and the golden W might have been vital clues — or they might have signified nothing. Henry de la Poer Beresford was the Marquis of Waterford. Some accounts suggest that he was a notorious practical joker and that the wilder aspects of what he regarded as humour were irresponsible, cruel and sadistic. Further accounts of his life describe him as an expert oarsman and boxer while at Eton and Oxford. He must therefore have had the kind of physique that would have enabled him to perform some of the minor feats attributed to Spring Heeled Jack. There is also the strong possibility that his boxing career had left him with slight brain damage — perhaps enough to account for at least some of his eccentric behaviour. He is said to have been in the habit of galloping through busy streets in his coach, from which he and his equally wild friends threw eggs at passers-by. It is recorded that he once tried to negotiate with a railway company, offering to pay for all necessary replacements and repairs, to make two trains collide head-on so that he could witness the spectacle. His idea of "painting a town red" was also a simple, direct and literal one — and it included painting a hapless night watchman along with the town he was trying to guard! In view of all the marquis's reported eccentricities, the W below the coat of arms on Jack's costume might have stood for "Waterford," but heraldic experts tend to disagree with this theory.

Whoever (or whatever) Spring Heeled Jack really was, by far the worst of his attacks on young women was the murder of poor little Maria Davis. She was one of the desperate teenaged prostitutes who plied their trade in the impoverished slums of Jacob's Island in Bermondsey, just south of the Thames. Jack breathed fire in the girl's face and then threw her down into a deep open sewerage ditch where she drowned. The leaping figure escaped, laughing insanely, before any of the angry Bermondsey witnesses could stop him.

If some of Spring Heeled Jack's exploits could be laid at the feet of the Marquis of Waterford, others were far beyond the strength and ability of even the most powerful and athletic human being. On one occasion, Jack — seemingly invulnerable to musket shot — leapt lightly over an Aldershot sentry and his box. Some reports suggested that the sentry's gun was loaded with a blank charge, but on another occasion, Jack angered some agricultural workers and farmers, who blazed away at him with shotguns. They reported that they could hear the pellets rattling harmlessly off his strange costume and one of them described the sound as "like shot hitting a metal bucket."

A carter encountered Jack in Shropshire in 1879. He struck at the hideous-looking creature that had leapt onto his horse's back, but it clung on with superhuman strength, and the terrified horse bolted. When the burly carter — with nerves of steel — finally got things under control again, the weird figure leapt off the horse and disappeared among the trees by the side of the road, cackling with insane laughter.

Another episode in 1904 reported Jack leaping prodigiously near a reservoir in Liverpool, after which he appeared on the steeple of St. Francis Xavier's Church in Salisbury Street, Everton!

According to Thomas Slemen's research in 1998's *The Giant Book of Strange but True*, Jack appeared again, wearing his characteristic white costume, as late as 1920. This episode took place in Horsemarket Street in Warrington. He was seen jumping from pavements to rooftops and back again, and finally leapt right over the buildings of the Warrington Central Railway Station — after which his pursuers lost sight of him. Slemen also refers to an appearance reported in Monmouth, where Jack (or someone very like him) was seen jumping over a stream in the aptly named Watery Lane.

So the mystery of sad little Maria Davis's murder in Bermondsey remains unsolved. Her killer was undeniably Spring Heeled Jack — but was he human? Was he an extraterrestrial? Could he have been a weird visitor from another dimension? Or was he just a leaping animal — such as a wallaby, or a kangaroo — dressed in a curious costume by a dangerous lunatic of a keeper? Was he the product of a laboratory, like Frankenstein's monster in Mary Shelley's famous novel?

In the twenty-first century, bioengineering has outstripped the science fiction of yesteryear. Cloning, the application of stem-cell healing techniques, nanotechnology and micro-miniaturization beckon us towards a future where the most wonderful and most ambitious human dreams can be fulfilled. This is a future where the only limits are those of human courage and imagination. Is it possible that a real-life Frankenstein stumbled upon a way to produce strange, dangerous hybrids in his Victorian laboratory? Did one or two of these weird creatures terrorize Victorian England — and especially the servant girls of nineteenth-century London? There are cryptozoologists who think that the dreaded chupacabras of Puerto Rico and Central and South America were produced in a top-secret military lab as a living weapon. Splicing the genes of alligators and those of kangaroos would notionally have created a nightmarish killing machine with huge reptilian jaws and the ability to jump high. Add the genes for gibbon-like arms and razor-edged feline claws, and the product begins to resemble a conglomerate of the varying descriptions of Spring Heeled Jack. Was Jack a product rather than a person?

16

THE QUEST FOR
JACK THE RIPPER

Every pragmatic and realistic hunt for Jack the Ripper begins with a survey of his environment in London's East End in 1888, and in particular with a study of the prostitution that was prevalent there in those days. Additionally, a major social fact that is sometimes overlooked, misunderstood or ignored is the tension between the East and West Enders in London at that time; an awareness of that very real tension may provide the Ripper investigator with a few additional clues.

The poverty and deprivation that darkened the lives of the 900,000 people who lived in the East End during the closing decades of the nineteenth century is literally unimaginable by today's standards. The East End had become a demographic symbol of poverty and hardship. For example, during the Ripper's era, Whitechapel had a population of roughly 80,000, of whom 32,000 were subsisting well below the poverty line. Many jobs — when the necessitous and underprivileged could get jobs at all — were irregular, unreliable and poorly paid. Wages were abysmal and hours were long — up to eighteen hours a day for some sweatshop victims — and workshops were dangerously overcrowded, insanitary and unhealthy. Only the hell of unemployment, homelessness and starvation kept the brutally exploited poor grinding away at their boot-making, tailoring and cabinet-making.

There were also deep-seated prejudices against certain social groups in London during the 1880s. The large influx of immigrants from continental Europe and Russia added to the social strains and pressures. With jobs so scarce, newcomers weren't welcomed.

Taken together, racism and corrosive poverty created a dangerously volatile social mix in the East End, and when the West End's fear of a revolution similar to the one that had rocked France only a century before was stirred into the Whitechapel cauldron, the situation became even more inflammable.

Working conditions in the sweatshops were bad enough, but living conditions were, if possible, worse. Every social reformer of the time reported grimly on the chronic overcrowding, incest, drunkenness, dirt, squalor, illegitimacy, prostitution, poverty and rags that were prevalent throughout the East End. Water supplies were hopelessly inadequate, and a shortage of mortuaries often meant corpses were kept in the living room until the day of the funeral.

Attempts to improve things often made them much worse. For example, the 1875 Artisans and Labourers Dwelling Act created a few newer, cleaner, better homes as unsanitary slums were demolished and better buildings erected. The trouble was that the poorest people, with the greatest need, were unable to afford the rents of these new, improved dwellings. Consequently, slum properties in the area immediately surrounding the new buildings became even more hopelessly overcrowded.

Common lodging houses offered the very poor their only alternative to sleeping in the filthy streets. Such institutions gave the police extra control over the poor who were forced to sleep there. The residents could be observed, and the owners were only too keen to "assist the police with information" from time to time. Reformers reporting on the Whitechapel of the 1880s were convinced that the existence of these common lodging houses made a big contribution to prostitution in the East End. In 1888, for example, Whitechapel alone was said to contain over sixty brothels, close on fifteen hundred prostitutes, and two and a half thousand common lodging houses with accommodation for approximately ten thousand impoverished residents. A girl who slaved away as a seamstress or lace-maker all day would often have to take two or three clients for sex every night in order to raise enough cash to pay her rent.

Two more well-intentioned attempts at social legislation did as much damage to these desperately poor part-time prostitutes as the 1875 Artisans and Labourers Dwelling Act had done to those impoverished families in need of an affordable home. During the 1860s, the Contagious Diseases Act was passed. The idea here was that members of the armed forces — traditionally likely to patronize prostitutes while stationed away from home — would be less prone to catch sexually transmitted diseases if the women were medically inspected and incarcerated if infected. To some reformers, the Contagious Diseases Act seemed to condone and regulate prostitution, and they objected stridently to what they saw as its supervision — and, therefore, implied acceptance — by the state. These middle-class reformers, with their puritanical moral and ethical obsessions, opposed the Contagious Diseases Act and worked instead to suppress prostitution altogether. They regarded themselves as a sort of social purity movement, and a singularly intolerant one. They failed utterly to recognize that by striving to prevent impoverished and exploited working girls from augmenting their impossibly low wages with a little harmless, government-regulated, medically inspected, part-time prostitution, they were condemning them to poverty and starvation. Furthermore, they were forcing the girls to take unacceptable risks with potentially dangerous and dubious customers because they could no longer ply their trade openly. It was in this environment that Jack the Ripper could flourish.

How many of the murdered women in and around Whitechapel in 1887–88 were genuine Ripper victims? It is almost as difficult to identify them as it is to identify Jack himself. The first question surrounds the death of a prostitute named Emma Elizabeth Smith. In her mid forties, Emma was either a widow, as she sometimes claimed, or was permanently separated from her former husband. She had been drinking, and was staggering towards the house where she lodged, 18 George Street, Spitalfields. She had made her way down Osborn Street as far as the corner of Brick Lane when she was attacked by a gang who beat her up, robbed her, raped her, and inflicted appalling internal injuries on her with a stick. She was admitted to the hospital in Whitechapel Road, described her attackers, lapsed into a coma and died. It is remotely possible that the Ripper was a member of that brutal street gang, and later went solo.

In March 1888, a seamstress and part-time prostitute named Ada Wilson narrowly escaped death when a man aged around thirty —

possibly a client, although Ada said he was an intruder to her home at 19 Maidman Street — produced a knife and demanded money from her. She described him as being around five feet six in height, and wearing a broad-brimmed hat. His coat was dark, his trousers lighter in colour. From what she could remember, his face was sunburnt and his moustache fair rather than dark. This description was reasonably close to later ones of men seen near Ripper victims, and it seems just possible that Ada had a very narrow escape. The man slashed at her throat twice, and although very seriously injured, Ada survived.

Monday, August 6, 1888, was a Bank Holiday. Buxom, big-built Martha Tabram and her friend Pearly Connolly, another prostitute of similar size, went looking for customers. They met a pair of soldiers, had some drinks with them, and went off to have sex. Pearly took her client into what is now Angel Alley and Martha took hers into what is now Gunthorpe Street, off Whitechapel High Street. Pearly came to no harm, but Martha's body was found later with nearly forty deep stab wounds.

Had one of those two soldiers been the Ripper? Among the many theories about Jack's identity, hypotheses involving soldiers are strangely rare — which seems odd at a time when many of the Whitechapel prostitutes' clients were men in uniform. Despite all the efforts made by the police and army authorities, Pearly failed — probably quite deliberately — to identify the two soldiers who had been their clients on that fateful August Monday. It is possible that Martha was a genuine Ripper victim — but there can be no certainty about it.

The first victim about whom Ripperologists express broad agreement is Mary Ann (also known as Polly) Nichols. Her marriage to William Nichols had been neither happy nor successful. They had five children. Polly was not only alcoholic, she was an aggressive one who would start a fight at the drop of a hat, even though she was only five feet two and had already lost several front teeth because of her frequent brawls.

On the night of August 30–31, Polly had been told to leave the common lodging house in Thrawl Street because she hadn't paid her four pence for the night's lodgings. She laughed with brash drunken humour, asked the man in charge to save her bed for her, and staggered out in search of a client. "I'll soon get my doss money!" she shouted. "See what a jolly bonnet I've got now!" Polly met her friend Jane Oram — also known as Emily, or Nell, Holland — who shared a room with her at 18 Thrawl Street. It was then somewhere between two and three in the morning. Nell had been out watching a fire on the docks. It was the last time she was to see her roommate alive.

An hour after Nell had tried unsuccessfully to persuade Polly to come home, Charlie Cross, who worked for Pickford's, was walking to work to make an early start. In Bucks Row, opposite the Essex Wharf and close to Barber's Yard, where the men in the abattoir normally worked all night, Cross saw what he thought was an old tarpaulin. He went to examine it and found the body of Mary Ann Nichols. When Dr. Llewellyn was called to examine the corpse, he said that the wound to her throat was so deep that it had cut right into the spinal column, and her head was all but severed. While the body was being washed and laid out in the mortuary attached to Montague Street Workhouse, the attendants discovered a huge gash in Polly's abdomen. In view of the injuries, Dr. Llewellyn suspected that the murderer was left-handed. They were arguably consistent with a right-handed killer working from behind his victim, or a left-handed killer attacking her from the front.

Naturally, Bucks Row became notorious during the period of the Ripper murders, and the residents petitioned for a change of name: it is now called Durward Street.

The next victim was Elizabeth Stride — known as "Long Liz" because, at around five feet five inches, she was significantly taller than the average height of the poor women eking out a wretched subsistence in the Whitechapel slums. Various witnesses saw her chatting with a few clients and prospective clients in Henriques Street around midnight on Saturday, September 29. An hour or so later, the steward of the International Workers' Educational Club, a man named Louis Diemschutz, found her body very close to the club itself in Berner Street.

She was not the only Ripper victim to die that night. Those who knew Catherine Conway would have described her as perky and amazingly cheerful for a girl whose life was a mixture of alcohol, prostitution and malnutrition. She was also known as Catherine Eddowes, and she had been taken to Bishopsgate Police Station for her own safety when she was found helplessly drunk on the pavement in Aldgate High Street. George Hutt was the constable in charge of supervising the cells, and at about one in the morning he decided that Catherine had probably recovered sufficiently to be allowed home. No charges were brought against her for being drunk and disorderly, and she bade Hutt a cheery "good night" as she left the station. She was last seen alive walking rather uncertainly towards

Aldgate. Hutt would have expected her to head the other way, towards Church Street, Spitalfields, as she was known to have lodgings there. A witness named Lawende saw Catherine chatting to a prospective client near Mitre Square at about 1:30 a.m. Less than a quarter-hour later, Police Constable James Harvey — one of several extra officers patrolling the Whitechapel district because of the great public concern over the Ripper — inspected Mitre Square, which was part of his beat, and found all that was left of Catherine.

Kearley and Tonge's had a warehouse adjacent. Its door was open, and George Morris, the night watchman, was a sturdy and reliable retired police officer. He and Watkins went together to properly inspect the body of Catherine Eddowes where it lay in an ominous pool of blood. Jack had somehow travelled half a mile from the spot where he had butchered Long Liz, avoiding all the extra constables and the vigilant neighbours whose one thought was the vital importance of catching him and putting a stop to the savage slaughter. Dr. Frederick G. Brown reported his findings. Catherine lay on her back, with her head turned towards her left. Her arms lay naturally at her sides as though she had simply fallen there. Her throat was cut and her lower body slashed open. Her face was horribly mutilated and her intestines were draped over her right shoulder. Her right ear was also severely cut.

Ghastly as Catherine's injuries and mutilations were, they paled into insignificance alongside what the Ripper did to his last victim: twenty-five-year-old Marie Jeanette Kelly, or Mary Jane Kelly. On November 9, 1888, she was disembowelled, her face mutilated almost beyond recognition, and severed parts of her once-beautiful young body arranged around the room like bizarre "decorations." All this happened in her rented room in Miller's Court, and it was the rent collector who discovered her when he came to press for the arrears.

There were several stories about her past that are difficult to corroborate. She seems to have come from Ireland; in 1879, when she was sixteen, she married a young Welsh miner in Carmarthenshire. It is probable that they had at least one child before her husband, whose name was Davies, was killed in a tragic mining accident. With scant compensation, Mary went to Cardiff, where she supported herself and her child, or children, by joining the prostitutes in Cardiff's world famous Tiger Bay. There are records of a girl named Agnes Kelly, who was married in Cardiff in 1908, and it is just possible that this was Mary's daughter.

These are the victims about whom most Ripperologists are in broad agreement.

What of the theories about the Ripper's identity?

First, there is the very reasonable possibility that the Ripper was really James Maybrick, and that the challenging and disturbing document known as the Ripper Diary was a genuine, factual record of his gruesome work. It is a theory that cannot be lightly discarded. Maybrick was a Liverpool cotton merchant. He died — poisoned — at the age of forty-nine on May 11, 1889. Much about Maybrick was highly suspicious; he might well have been the Ripper.

Another interesting suspect was Sir William Gull, a fanatically loyal doctor who attended the royal family and was also a high-ranking Freemason. Author and researcher Stephen Knight said that he got his Ripper information from Joseph Sickert, the son of Walter Sickert. In outline, Knight's theory was that Prince Eddy, the Duke of Clarence, had met and secretly married a Catholic girl named Alice Mary Crook, also known as Cook. According to this involved but ingenious theory, Alice had met Eddy via her friendship with Walter Sickert, an artist, for whom she posed as a model, and Walter was also a friend of the prince. As the son of Edward VII, Eddy was in line for the throne, and at that time the thought of the future king of England marrying a Catholic would have caused apoplexy amongst the establishment! Alice, it was said, had been a friend of Marie Jeanette Kelly, the last Ripper victim, who had, in some versions of the story, been employed as the children's nanny to look after Alice and Eddy's child.

The establishment was said to have found out about the secret wedding and consequently sent in its ruthless undercover agents to abduct Eddy and Alice. Kelly somehow escaped that abduction raid and went off to the East End to work as a prostitute. Here she met the other future Ripper victims and told them about Eddy and Alice. Together, they hatched a blackmail plot. Dr. Gull was commissioned to silence them. According to some versions of the story he had already performed a brain-wrecking operation on Alice and had her confined to an asylum. From there, practically mindless, the poor girl was passed through a series of workhouses and similar institutions until she died thirty-two years later.

Gull, meanwhile, invented the character of Jack the Ripper, and made it look as if his careful and deliberate silencing of the prostitute blackmailers was the random work of a psychotic serial killer.

Knight did immense amounts of diligent, painstaking research, and his highly complex but well-integrated theory cannot be lightly discarded — except for the fact that Joseph Sickert (his main informant) inexplicably changed his statement a year or two later and claimed that the story was all a hoax, and entirely his own invention. A strange and perplexing question mark still hangs over Sickert's alleged denial — and the serious researcher is tempted to echo Pilate's famous question "What is truth?" Did someone ruthless, with a vast amount of power and influence, pressurize Sickert?

Prince Eddy himself was another sensational suspect, but the records show that he was in either Scotland or Norfolk when the Ripper murders took place.

Prime Minister William Ewart Gladstone was also on the suspect list because of the scandal attached to his interest in "rescuing fallen women" from the East End brothels. Gladstone's diary was so full, his movements so public and easily accounted for, that it is very unlikely indeed that he could have been the Ripper. Nevertheless, in all fairness, he has to be included on the suspect list because at least one Ripperologist, Graham Norton, writing in the September 1970 issue of *Queen* magazine, put his name forward as a serious possibility.

Leonard Matters wrote *The Mystery of Jack the Ripper* in 1929 and theorized that the Ripper was an eminent Harley Street surgeon whose son had died of syphilis contracted from an East End prostitute. According to Matters, once the deadly doctor had taken his grotesque vengeance on Marie Kelly in Miller's Court, he vanished to South America. Syphilis takes many years to kill; the mysterious doctor's son would probably still have outlived his father in spite of the disease — and there was no medical evidence that Marie was infected with it herself. But mad doctors, like mad scientists in science fiction and horror films, are very popular stereotypes.

Dr. Thomas Neill Cream, whom Ripperologist Donald Bell proposed, comes into the same category. There was a traditional story around at the time that just before the hangman despatched Cream — also known as the Lambeth Poisoner — in November of 1892, Cream shouted: "I am Jack the —" The rope did its job before he could finish the statement! It seems to have been a wild, idle boast — literally gallows humour — and Cream had about as much respect for the truth as he did for human life. Records show that he was in jail in the United States between 1881 and 1891, so the probability of his being Jack was extremely slim — unless, as some researchers believe, the sinister Dr. Cream had a double. If he had, who served time in the American prison: Cream, or the doppelganger?

Another suspect was the redoubtable Severin Antoniovich Klosowski. He had some medical knowledge — particularly the surgical and anatomical type that the Ripper was thought by some researchers to have possessed. Klosowski had served at one time as an army surgeon's assistant in Russia. Inspector Abberline, who was one of the most competent Ripper investigators while the murders were taking place, favoured Klosowski as a prime suspect. Calling himself George Chapman while in the United Kingdom, Klosowski came fairly close to matching the description of a man seen talking to some of the victims before their mutilated bodies were found. Klosowski came to London in 1888 and worked as a barber in Whitechapel. He was also a bigamist who married Lucy Baderski even though his original wife was still alive. Klosowski next lived with Mary Spink, Bessie Tailor and Maud Marsh, all of whom he systematically poisoned. It was Maud's mother who suspected him — although her suspicions came too late to save her daughter. When the dead girls were exhumed, their bodies were so well preserved that it was clear (even to those working with the limited forensic science of the time) that they had been poisoned with arsenic. Chapman, or Klosowski, was hanged in 1903. He might have been the Ripper but, like the odious Dr. Cream, he was a poisoner rather than a knife man — despite his tenure in the Russian army.

The next candidate also had Russian connections. This was the strongly suspected — and heavily sensationalized — Dr. Alexander Pedachenko. The most melodramatic version of this dimension of the story is that Pedachenko — alias Vasilly Konovalov, and known to be a dangerous, homicidal maniac — had been deliberately allowed to reach the U.K. to perpetrate a series of sensational murders in the East End. With its high numbers of political refugees from Russia and Eastern Europe, ran the Pedachenko argument, Whitechapel harboured a number of communists and anarchists whom the Tsarist secret police wanted to discredit. If the mass murderer was caught and identified as an Eastern European, then it was thought that the British authorities would be less sympathetic and tolerant towards such potentially dangerous refugees. It was also argued by supporters of the Pedachenko-Konovalov Ripper hypothesis that the Tsarist police might be trying to discredit Scotland Yard as well because they were unhappy about the Yard's lack of action against the cells of anarchists and communists — whom the Tsarists regarded as highly dangerous — operating in the East End of London.

This particular version of the Pedachenko story came to prominence via the writings of William le Queux in 1923. Le Queux claimed that papers found among Rasputin's effects revealed that Pedachenko had come to London with the blessing of the Tsarist police. Rasputin was still highly newsworthy in the twenties, and le Queux probably thought that bringing him in would help to sell his Pedachenko story. Le Queux also maintained that he had heard from a Russian newspaperman named Nideroest that Zverieff — one of the anarchists — had given him the details about how Pedachenko and two accomplices carried out the Ripper murders in order to spread alarm and despondency in London. Pedachenko's callous assistants were a thug named Levitski, who acted as their lookout man, and a cold-hearted tailoress called Winberg. Her job was to chat with the unsuspecting victims; while their attention was distracted, Pedachenko would creep up behind them and begin his murderous assault. Pedachenko was also described as fitting the Ripper descriptions — such as they were — and, according to le Queux, the mad doctor had died in an asylum in 1891.

Another medical suspect was Dr. Roslyn d'Onston Stevenson, who clearly suffered from Munchausen syndrome — chronic compulsive lying, or factitious illness — to a pronounced degree. Stevenson was living in Whitechapel in 1888, which put him in the right place at the right time to be a strong Ripper suspect. Melvin Harris's 1987 book *Jack the Ripper: The Bloody Truth* gives all the gory and complex details about Stevenson. His fantasies — if they were only fantasies — were fuelled by his alcoholism and drug dependency. He claimed to have married a former prostitute named Ada, who had committed suicide when he left her and went back to the family that had ostracized him for marrying her. Stevenson was heavily interested in magic and the supernatural, and claimed that Ada's ghost had kept her pact with him on Westminster Bridge after her suicide. His other strange Munchausenesque tales included world travel, gold prospecting in the United States, African slave trading, and fighting for Garibaldi in Italy. The great majority of his stories were high adventures, in which Stevenson cast himself as an outstanding hero.

After losing Ada, Stevenson took up with a new partner called Mabel Collins, who claimed that among his possessions was a tin box containing bloodstained ties. Confronted with her discovery, Stevenson boasted to her that he was, in fact, the Ripper, but that he had committed the murders only in order to increase his magical strength. He told Mabel he had kept pieces of his victims hidden under these ties, and eaten them raw as part of various magical spells aimed at enhancing his power. Stevenson's alleged Ripper claims are further shadowed by doubt because the black magician Aleister Crowley — never regarded as an inviolable sanctuary of the truth — later maintained that he had acquired Stevenson's sinister tin box.

One pointer to Stevenson's possible guilt is that he laid the Ripper murders at the feet of a certain Dr. Morgan Davies — even though this is wildly contradictory to what he had privately bragged to Mabel Collins! Blaming Davies enabled Stevenson to reveal his own special, detailed knowledge of the circumstances of the victims' deaths, while deflecting suspicion in another direction. Edgar Allan Poe might have done something equally sinister in his story "The Mystery of Marie Roget." His fictional detective hero, Dupin, on the verge of naming the girl's murderer, is prevented from doing so by a curious editorial comment:

> For reasons which we shall not specify, but which to many readers will appear obvious, we have taken the liberty of here omitting, from the MSS placed in our hands, such portion as details the following up of the apparently slight clew obtained by Dupin. We feel it advisable only to state, in brief, that the result desired was brought to pass; and that the Prefect fulfilled punctually, although with reluctance, the terms of his compact with the Chevalier.

What did this unbelievably weak "editorial excuse" for not disclosing the murderer of Marie Roget — alias Mary Rogers — really signify? Was Poe himself the killer of the beautiful New York cigar girl Mary Rogers, whose decomposing body was lifted from the Hudson River (then called the North River) on July 28, 1841? Was the story his means of releasing facts known only to the killer without incriminating himself? And is that what Stevenson was doing when he put the blame for the Ripper murders on Dr. Morgan Davies?

According to some theorists, Pedachenko had a female accomplice, and that leads to another interesting theory that makes the prime suspect a woman — Jill the Ripper, rather than Jack. These hypotheses make her a nurse, a midwife — or an East End abortionist. One variation makes her the disappointed wife of a returning sailor who began his shore leave with a drunken tour of the East End pubs and brothels, where he became the client of one of the prostitutes. When his wife realized what had happened, she felt that she could never have sex with him. If she was in fact a nurse, she would have been well aware of the dangers of sexually transmitted infections. In frustrated fury, she decided to wreak a terrible revenge on the women who had ruined her love life. Those Ripperologists who look for special medical knowledge as part of the killer's characteristics would nod approvingly at the idea that the Ripper was a woman with nursing experience. In favour of this hypothesis, it may be added that a nurse, or midwife, carrying a bag of surgical instruments through the East End and wearing bloodstained clothing would not arouse any suspicion.

One of the favourite suspects is Montague John Druitt. Known to be mentally ill, Druitt committed suicide shortly after the spectacular murder and mutilation of Marie Kelly in Miller's Court. His body was found in the Thames on December 31, 1888. Montague was born on August 15, 1857, into a family who were preeminent in medicine. His father was a distinguished surgeon in Wimborne, Dorset, as his grandfather had been. Young Montague started well enough and went on from Winchester College to New College, Oxford, in 1876, when he was nineteen. He later enrolled in the Inner Temple to train as a barrister, but after he qualified he failed to attract any clients, and worked instead in a small private school — such establishments were referred to as "crammers." He was sacked in 1888.

Meanwhile, his father had died and his mother, Anne, had become mentally ill. After visiting her at a private asylum in Chiswick, Druitt is said to have become very depressed and mentally unstable. He often expressed the fear that he had inherited her predisposition to insanity. In fact, he left a note that read, "Since Friday I felt I was going to be like mother and the best thing for me was to die." Druitt was definitely mentally unstable; and he was also in the right places at the right times to have committed the Ripper murders. Furthermore, they stopped when he died — but that is the only evidence against him.

Just as Dr. Neill Cream had claimed to be the Ripper, even though he was recorded as having been in prison when the Whitechapel murders were committed, so the next suspect, Frederick Bailey Deeming, made a similar seemingly impossible claim — as he too had been in prison during

1888. Deeming was certainly mentally unstable, although the doctors who examined him after his arrest refused to go along with his claim that he was legally insane. Like Dr. Roslyn d'Onston Stevenson, Deeming suffered from factitious illness, or Munchausen syndrome. He persistently told wild, adventurous, self-aggrandizing stories of his largely imaginary exploits. There was something about him, however, that made him fatally attractive to the women he met.

At Dinham Villa, Rainhill, near Liverpool, he murdered his wife and four children and put them in cement under the kitchen floor. He then remarried and took his new wife to Australia. Within a month of landing there, she, too, was under the floorboards. The discovery of her body led to Deeming's arrest, the subsequent recovery of the remains at Dinham Villa, and Deeming's execution. While in prison awaiting the hangman, Deeming made his claim to be the Ripper, and, in consequence, his death mask was sent to the famous Black Museum at Scotland Yard, where it was actually labelled for a time as the Ripper's.

In connection with the death of Mary Ann (Polly) Nichols it was noted that there was an all-night abattoir in Barber's Yard, very close to Essex Wharf, adjoining the spot where her body was found. The next suspect was, therefore, a slaughterman, perhaps even a Jewish shochet — a highly trained and experienced ritual butcher who knew how to prepare animals for the table with great skill and in strict accordance with the ancient Jewish traditions. After cutting the throat, a shochet had to examine the heart, lungs and viscera to be certain that the animal was free from disease. If it passed all his tests, it was kosher, meaning fit to eat. If it failed any of the tests it was trefah, meaning forbidden. There can be no doubt that any experienced, professional butcher would have had all the necessary skills and anatomical knowledge — and a shochet would have been even more knowledgeable. This is borne out by the evidence of a butcher named Hull, living in Bow in 1888, who wrote to the police to say that not only would an experienced butcher and slaughterman know how to extract the organs that had been cut from the Ripper's victims, he would also know how to do it while minimizing the risk of getting blood on himself.

Another suspect, John Pizer, was also referred to as "Leather Apron," and he came close enough in some respects to fitting the Ripper's profile. The long knives he used in his work as a boot finisher would have been more than adequate for the grisly mutilations the Ripper carried out, but

Pizer's alibi stood up to all police investigations, and he was erased from the suspect list by most Ripperologists.

Armed with that list of suspects — and others — the Ripperologists doggedly continue their unresolved debate. The appalling mutilations seem to suggest some medical or anatomical knowledge, or at least some experience in an abattoir, but this is only a suggestion — the indications of such knowledge are not conclusive. Was it a mad doctor, or a crazy slaughterman? The horrific brutality of the murders indicates either a wildly deranged psychotic personality — or someone coldly sane, with an entirely different set of cunning and complex motives, setting out to impersonate a psychopath for some reason of his own. Why did Sickert initialize such an intricate, integrated and plausible story about Prince Eddy and Dr. Gull — and then deny it all, falling back weakly on the excuse that it was merely a hoax? Is it possible that secret forces and powerful organizations such as those Stephen Knight described still exist — and made Sickert an offer he dare not refuse?

There also remains the possibility of the Ripper being a Jill rather than Jack — it covers the point about the killer being able to pass unhindered and unsuspected through a panic-stricken and vigilant East End.

Finally, there is as much sound evidence in favour of the Maybrick Diary being genuine as there is against it. James Maybrick of Liverpool has to stay close to the top of the suspect list.

Of all the tantalizing murder mysteries, the Whitechapel Enigma of 1888 is still the greatest and most complicated riddle.

17

WHO KILLED MARY ROGERS?

As noted in Chapter Sixteen, at the centre of the mystery of who killed Mary Rogers, the beautiful young New York cigar girl, stands the tragic, enigmatic figure of Edgar Allan Poe. Was he her killer? Her decomposing body was lifted from the Hudson River (then called the North River) on July 28, 1841. Poe's detective story "The Mystery of Marie Roget" was published only sixteen months after Mary Rogers was killed. Was it his vehicle through which to communicate details that only the killer could have known, without incriminating himself?

Poe's life was a strange, difficult, sad and mentally disturbed one. He was born on January 19, 1809. His mother, Elizabeth Arnold Poe (maiden name Hopkins) was an actress; she died on December 8, 1811. His father, David, was also dead before Edgar's third birthday. Young Edgar was taken in by the Allan family, and his adoptive father, John Allan, had him baptized Edgar Allan Poe.

Nothing seemed to go right for the boy. He quarrelled with John Allan over gambling debts — a dispute that ended young Edgar's university career. Allan was also instrumental in breaking up Edgar's plans to marry Sarah Elmira Royster.

Because he had no other source of income, Poe enlisted in the U.S. Army under the name of Perry. He achieved the rank of sergeant major before leaving the army, and later tried to train at the U.S. Military Academy at West Point: that effort failed, too, because Allan would not provide adequate financial support. The whole of Poe's literary career was a series of brilliant short stories and poems, editorial appointments that were wrong for his type of genius, and financial disasters made worse by his heavy drinking.

On May 16, 1836, Poe married Virginia, the teenaged daughter of his widowed aunt, Mrs. Clemm, with whom he had gone to live in Baltimore. Virginia contracted tuberculosis and died on January 30, 1847. The desperate poverty the Poes and Mrs. Clemm suffered contributed significantly to Virginia's death. Poe's own death on October 7, 1849, was as mysterious as it was tragic. The *Baltimore Clipper* allocated him a brief obituary and reported that he had died of "congestion of the brain."

The terrible chronic stress of poverty, the terminal illness of the beautiful young wife he adored, his failure to keep an editorial job for any length of time, and his continual disappointment when his brilliant work failed to find a publisher all took their savage toll on Poe's physical and mental health. There is no denying that he also had psychiatric problems, and was probably schizophrenic. But was his macabre mind sufficiently deranged to make him murder Mary Rogers in that fateful autumn of 1841? At that time, his beloved Virginia was still alive, although in poor health. Had Poe — in other respects a faithful and attentive husband to Virginia — impulsively succumbed to the vivacious young cigar girl's nubile charms? Had he then immediately regretted it, and murdered Mary to make absolutely certain that she could never tell anyone about their relationship?

There is conflicting evidence about Mary's character. Some of her friends and neighbours described her as demure and modest, with no sexual experience. Other evidence suggests that when she went to work as a cigar girl for John Anderson, she also moved in with him as his mistress. Some reports make out that Mary was so attractive and outgoing that male customers came to Anderson's just for the pleasure of flirting with her — and perhaps for something more.

In October 1838, she was away from the cigar store for two weeks. Her own explanation for that absence was that she had felt tired and had gone to stay with her aunt in Brooklyn for some days to rest. When questions were asked after the murder, it seems that she had not been in Brooklyn with her aunt, but in some unspecified love nest in or near Hoboken with her then boyfriend, who was supposedly an officer in the U.S. Navy — but that was almost certainly a pose on his part.

She was also seen during that fortnight with a well-dressed man with what was then described as a dark complexion. Could this second man have been Edgar Allan Poe? Despite his chronic poverty, Poe always did his best to dress smartly, and contemporaries described him as walking with an upright, soldierly bearing. He was also said to have had an attractive, olive-skinned, or lightly tanned, complexion.

After this strange, uncharacteristic episode, Mary ceased to work at Anderson's and went home to live with her mother, ostensibly to help her with the work of the boarding house. One of their lodgers was Daniel Payne, and he and Mary got engaged. Her mother, Phoebe, disliked Payne, who had a problem with drink. A rival suitor, whom Mary's mother much preferred, was also on the scene. This man was Alfred Cromelin (or Crommelin). One version of events records that Mary was hesitating between the two men, and tried to contact Cromelin with a view to getting back together with him. Having been rejected once, however, Alfred wanted nothing more to do with Mary. Was there some deeper reason for his refusal to take her back? Did he know, or suspect, what might really be going on? She was apparently in some kind of serious financial trouble, and having failed to get the money from Cromelin, she borrowed it from Anderson, her former employer — and the man who was almost certainly her former lover as well.

On the morning of her disappearance, Mary told Payne that she was going to stay with her aunt, Mrs. Downing. This seems to have been her stock alibi for her mysterious absences. Again, she never went there. When she had not returned by Monday morning, enquiries were made. It was established that Mary had not stayed with her aunt, and the police were called. When her body was dragged from the North River on the following Wednesday, the medical opinion was that she had been savagely beaten, repeatedly raped, and then strangled.

According to some reports, a Mrs. Frederika Loss ran an abortion clinic in the Hoboken and Weehawken district of New Jersey. It was also alleged that Frederika worked with Madame Restell, who operated a Manhattan home for unmarried mothers. Here, she arranged discreet

Edgar Allan Poe. Did he kill Mary Rogers, the Cigar Girl?

abortions for the wealthy and privileged. Girls with modest financial resources went to less salubrious establishments — like Frederika's — but were still under Madame Restell's overall jurisdiction.

Why had Mary Rogers been so desperate to borrow money? Was it possible that she needed it to pay for an abortion at Frederika's place? Or was it possible that she had become ensnared in a vice ring operated — at least in part — by Anderson, the cigar store owner? If so, who were his underworld associates in the organization? Had Anderson, in fact, sold Mary on to the mysterious man who took her away for a couple of weeks? Had she, on her return, left Anderson's and gone home to her mother in a vain attempt to escape from the vice ring? If that was what was really happening, her escape plan didn't work.

When she went to Anderson for the abortion money as a last resort, did he contact the rest of the gang — not with a view to having her killed, but beaten and gang-raped as a grim warning to her to get back to work? There were notorious, but colourful, gangs of criminals in the area, any of whom could have been hired to do the job — including the Plug Uglies, the Forty Thieves, the Chichesters and the Kerryonians.

According to Frederika, she had neither seen nor heard of Mary Rogers — but she did say that she had heard repeated screams and the sounds of a struggle from the undergrowth near the Hoboken-area farmhouse that formed part of what was alleged to be her cut-rate abortion clinic. When this patch of undergrowth was investigated, some of Mary's bloodstained clothing was found. Evidence was also given that Mary had been seen in that vicinity in the company of a man with an olive-tan complexion answering — at least in part — Poe's description.

Several biographers and literary critics who have made detailed examinations of Poe's work — especially stories like "The Pit and the Pendulum," published in 1842 — have commented on his interest in sadomasochism. Is it possible that he watched from a place of concealment in the thicket while Mary's attackers handed out the "warning" that Anderson and the other vice ringleaders had ordered for her? Imagine the scenario: the gang leaves her, badly bruised and shaken, to make her way back to Anderson — or the new pimp to whom he had sold her. Mary is determined now to do as she's told in future, and be what the gang describes as a "good girl" rather than risk another punishment as devastating as the one she's just endured. Her murderer — Poe, or someone else — emerges from concealment, strangles Mary and drags her body to the river, using the cloth around her neck as a convenient handle. After what the gang has just done to her, she is in no condition to put up much resistance.

Her killer is never apprehended.

Anderson, who is very wealthy, retires to Paris. Did he amass all his wealth by selling tobacco? It hardly seems likely. Wasn't there a more secretive — and lucrative — living to be made by other means? In retirement, John claimed to have seen Mary's ghost more than once. He is alleged to have begged it to forgive him before he died in 1881. Was he asking forgiveness for being an innocent girl's original corrupter? Was he asking her to forgive the punishment beating and gang rape he had ordered for her, to bring her back into line after she had tried to leave?

Daniel Payne's behaviour also aroused suspicion. He committed suicide in the exact spot where Mary's bloodstained clothing had been found. He left a note suggesting that he was in some way involved in Mary's brutal death. Was it Payne, perhaps, rather than Poe who was the concealed watcher?

Frederika Loss, the abortionist, died not long afterwards — apparently shot "accidentally." She lingered for several days, moaning that a ghostly figure was haunting her last hours — did she think it was Mary's ghost? Her sons, one of whom was responsible for firing the "accidental" shot that killed her, were said to have been very worried in case her delirious ramblings revealed some sinister secret. What could Frederika possibly have known that could have caused so much trouble if it got out? Were her sons involved in the supposed vice ring controlling Mary and the other girls?

There is far more to Poe's "Mystery of Marie Roget" than meets the eye, and it is incontrovertibly tied to the tragic mystery of Mary Rogers.

18

THE BORDEN AXE MURDER CASE

The bare outline of the Borden axe murders is a very simple one: seventy-year-old Andrew Jackson Borden of 92 Second Street, Fall River, Massachusetts, Lizzie's father, was a prominent and very wealthy citizen of the town. Beginning as an undertaker, he had made his way up steadily by hard work, frugality and good business sense. He was a prosperous property developer and textile mill owner when he died on August 4, 1892. He was killed by repeated axe blows — several of which landed in his skull. His sixty-four-year-old wife, Abby Durfee Gray Borden, Lizzie's stepmother, already lay dead in an upstairs bedroom when Andrew was killed as he lay downstairs on the couch. Abby was so over-weight — in excess of two hundred pounds — that she rarely went out because she found walking difficult and strenuous.

Lizzie, who was subsequently tried for their murders, had been born in 1860. She was a thirty-two-year-old spinster when her father and step-mother were killed.

Other crucial members of the Borden household included Emma Borden, Lizzie's elder sister, who had more or less been a substitute mother for Lizzie — there was an age gap of eleven years between the two girls. Lizzie's maternal uncle was visiting at the time the murders took place. His full name was John Vinnicum Morse. Born in 1833, Uncle John did not die until 1912. The Bordens' live-in maid was Bridget Sullivan, usually referred to as Maggie. Born in 1866, Maggie survived until 1948.

Doctors Dolan and Wood were the medical examiners in the case, and the city marshal was Rufus Hilliard. His deputy, John Fleet, also played a prominent part in the investigations. Four judges were involved in the legal proceedings following the murders: Josiah Blaisdell, Albert Mason, Caleb Blodgett and Justin Dewey. Alice Russell, a long-standing friend of the Borden sisters, was a key witness.

It was just after 11 a.m. on Thursday, August 4, when Maggie Sullivan heard Lizzie shouting: "Maggie, come down! Come down quick! Father's dead! Somebody's come in and killed him!" Maggie hurried down from her attic bedroom where she had been resting. It was a singularly hot, sultry day in Fall River — over 100 degrees Fahrenheit — and Maggie had earlier been hard at work cleaning the windows on Mrs. Borden's instructions. Lizzie told her not to go into the room, but to hurry to fetch Dr. Bowen, the Bordens' family doctor. Maggie hurried over to Dr. Bowen's house, only to find that he was out on his rounds. She told Mrs. Bowen that Andrew Borden was dead. When she got back to number 92, Lizzie asked her to go to find Alice Russell.

The next development came when their next-door neighbour, Mrs. Adelaide Churchill, who had clearly seen and heard that something was very seriously wrong, called out to Lizzie to ask if they needed help. Lizzie begged Adelaide to come over because Andrew had been killed. Mrs. Churchill's first question was, "Where's your mother?"

(When one considers the details of the Borden case, it is particularly significant to note that Lizzie did not refer to her stepmother as "mother," but always as "Mrs. Borden." Even allowing for small-town, late-nineteenth-century formality, this was decidedly cold and distant.)

Anxious discussions turned next to Mrs. Borden's probable whereabouts. Maggie offered to go and look for Mrs. Whitehead (Mrs. Borden's sister). Lizzie then recalled that someone had brought a note asking Mrs. Borden to go to visit a neighbour who wasn't very well. Lizzie also remembered that she was almost certain she had heard her stepmother coming back into the house after this visit. Suppose, for the sake of argument, that Lizzie was telling the simple truth at this point. Suppose that she had heard a noise that suggested Abby had returned — but what if that sound had been made by the homicidal intruder coming in?

Maggie was asked to go upstairs to see if her mistress was there; understandably, Maggie refused to go alone. Confident and robust, Mrs. Churchill volunteered to go with her. They found Abby Borden lying face-down on the floor of the guest bedroom — and very clearly dead. Detailed medical examination showed a total of nineteen axe blows, all of them delivered from behind.

When one searches for motives — and tries to identify the murderer — one strange detail forces its way ruthlessly through the much greater tragedies of the Borden axe murders. Lizzie loved birds and animals, especially her pet pigeons and squirrels. There had been two break-ins to the outbuildings where she kept her pigeons. After the second burglary, Andrew Borden had decided that it was the pigeons that were attracting the thieves — who were possibly impoverished, hungry men who wanted the birds as food. Andrew's brutal and heartless remedy for the burglary problem was to behead Lizzie's pigeons. Consider the lengths to which some extremist animal rights campaigners will go today to shut down vivisection laboratories and intimidate the staff who work there; is it possible that Lizzie was so emotionally distressed by what Andrew had done to her pets that she paid him back in his own coin — an axe to his head in return for his axe to her pigeons' heads?

The wholesale damage to both the dead Bordens was more in keeping with an outburst of uncontrollable emotion than with the simple, callous, pragmatic blow of a professional, murderous thief. The sane — but highly dangerous — armed robber kills swiftly, with maximum economy of effort and time. It is the emotionally crazed, psychotic murderer who strikes his victim's corpse repeatedly after the last hint of life has left it.

The medical evidence threw up other strange and puzzling questions: Abby had died at least two hours before Andrew. How had her body remained undiscovered? And, if it was an opportunistic thief who had somehow broken in and killed the Bordens, how had he (or she) avoided detection during the two hours between the murders? The house wasn't that big; wouldn't someone have heard the crash as the heavy body of Abby hit the bedroom floor?

Then there was the vexing question of the Bordens' blood. When you end a human life with an axe — especially if a strong man is wielding a heavy axe — blood tends to fly in all directions. Medical evidence described the blood as still oozing from Andrew's body when Dr. Bowen examined it. The axe man, or woman, had administered at least eleven blows to Andrew's face. One eye was sliced through and protruding. The nose was severed. Blood had splashed onto the wall above the couch where his body lay, and onto a picture. There was also a considerable amount of blood on the floor. It appeared that, as Borden slept, the attacker had struck downwards at his defenceless, upturned face. Unlike the blood still oozing from her husband's injuries when Dr. Bowen got there, Abby's blood had already congealed because of the time that had elapsed between her death and the discovery of her body.

The highly effective city marshal, Rufus Hilliard, was there within half an hour, along with seven or eight of his officers and the Fall River medical examiner. The investigation that Marshal Hilliard led can be studied in four stages, matching the legal processes that followed the murders: first came the inquest, then the preliminary hearing, the grand jury, and at last the trial itself.

One of the first things to be investigated was the poisoning allegation made by Abby on August 3 — the day before she died. She called on Dr. Bowen very early in the morning and reported that she and Andrew had both been repeatedly sick during the night. Maggie had also complained of feeling ill. Bowen reassured her that it was nothing serious — and he seems to have been right, because no poison was found in the Bordens' systems during the autopsy.

Although the postmortem examination revealed no trace of toxins, there is evidence that Lizzie had attempted to buy prussic acid from a local pharmacy. The assistant there was a certain Eli Bence. Lizzie had explained to Eli that she needed the poison to destroy insect pests that were infesting her sealskin cape. Bence said that he regretted that he was unable to sell prussic acid without a prescription, and Lizzie left the pharmacy empty-handed. Two witnesses supported Bence's story, but Lizzie denied that she had been in the pharmacy, which was known as Smith's Drug Store, even though she said at first that she had gone out that morning. Curiously, she subsequently changed her testimony altogether and said that she had not gone out at all.

In jurisprudence, there are two diametrically opposed theories concerning the accuracy and honesty of evidence. The first argument is that if a witness is telling the truth, and repeats his or her story without deviation during subsequent retellings, then that story is probably true and accurate.

Lizzie Borden. Was she innocent of the axe murders?

However, there are psychological reasons to support the belief that in the normal course of events, the human brain tends to recall not the events themselves but rather the first retelling of the events. Human fallibility and imperfection being what they are, there is a case to be made for an honest witness coming up with variations of an account simply because that witness is a human being, not a recording machine. This argument would suggest that when a witness repeats a story word for word, precisely and accurately, the story may well have been a dishonest invention, memorized and parroted by rote to make it sound reliable and convincing.

The investigation also revealed that Lizzie's uncle, John Morse, had arrived at 92 Second Street on the afternoon of August 3. His declared intention was to stay overnight with Andrew and Abby, although he had brought no luggage with him. The great significance of his evidence was that, although he and Lizzie were both in the house, they did not see each other until after Abby and Andrew were dead — the point being that 92 Second Street was the sort of building which made it possible, and even likely, that a member of the family in one part of the premises might not be aware of what was going on in an adjacent room. Lizzie could have been genuinely and innocently unaware of what had happened to her father and stepmother even though she was in the vicinity.

It was also found that Lizzie had visited Alice Russell on the evening of August 3. Alice testified that Lizzie did not seem herself, but was worried and anxious about her father. She had returned to Second Street around 9 p.m. and had overheard John Morse, Andrew and Abby talking. She had gone up to her room without speaking to any of them.

Life started early in the Borden household on the fatal fourth. Maggie was up just after 6 a.m. John also rose early. Abby was next to stir, and Andrew was close on her heels. Lizzie appeared shortly after John went out. It was then close to 9 a.m. Mrs. Adelaide Churchill, their neighbour, seemed to know more about the Bordens' comings and goings than they themselves knew! She said that Andrew had left number 92 at about 9 a.m. Subsequent enquiries revealed that he had made the rounds of the banks where he was a major shareholder, then inspected the progress of renovations at one of the shops he owned. The workmen said that he had left them between 10:30 and 11 a.m. They presumed that he was then heading home.

While Andrew was attending to his various commercial interests, Abby was instructing Maggie to wash the windows — strenuous work on a hot day, especially when Maggie was far from well. Abby went into the guest room herself to clean and tidy it while John was out. Medical evidence showed that she had been butchered there at approximately 9:30 a.m. So much for the story of a note from a sick friend asking for a visit! Despite a meticulous search, that note was never found. Lizzie, apparently uncertain of so many things, said that perhaps she had burned it!

Maggie's evidence at this point was also very odd. When Mr. Borden came home, Maggie had to let him in because the door was secured firmly from the inside. She said that she recalled hearing Lizzie laughing upstairs as she let Andrew into the house. Lizzie's own testimony — again, very uncertain — was that she was in the kitchen when her father came home. The sequence of events, as far as they can be reconstructed from evidence that is frequently missing or contradictory, seems to have been that Andrew went upstairs, but saw no sign of Abby's corpse in the guest bedroom. Lizzie did some ironing. Maggie continued washing the windows. As soon as she'd finished, she went up to her room to rest — this appears to have been just a few minutes before 11 a.m. Mr. Borden came down again and decided to take a nap on the living room couch. Lizzie maintained that she had gone out to the yard, then the barn, then the loft above the barn — her testimony being particularly vague and confusing at that point. She was out of the house for some considerable time, and when she came in again at approximately ten past eleven, she found Andrew, still bleeding from the fatal axe attack, lying dead on the couch.

There were numerous axes in the house and the outbuildings, any one of which might theoretically have inflicted the fatal injuries. One was, indeed, covered with blood and hair — which turned out to be bovine rather than human.

While the police investigations continued, John strolled in nonchalantly, picking and eating fruit from the pear tree in the Bordens' garden as he walked towards the house. He said that Andrew had asked him to share the midday meal with the family. He could not be certain whether or not the cellar door — which provided access to the house — had been secured when he left earlier that morning. Clearly, if there were numerous axes lying around, and the cellar door was unfastened, any psychotic prowler could have entered unseen, committed the murders and left before Lizzie came back from the barn. If he had had any motive, John himself could also have done them, and pretended to arrive later.

Lizzie's vague evidence about visiting the barn loft grew even more curious. She said that she had gone up there to try to find some small pieces of discarded metal to use as weights when she went fishing. It can be said in her favour that she was known to be a keen angler, but the loft above the barn was not likely to be a fruitful source of the type of metal she was allegedly looking for while the murder was committed. The investigating officers also thought that the thick layer of undisturbed dust up there did not support Lizzie's story that she had been rummaging around looking for scraps of metal! Nevertheless, a witness named Lubinsky testified at the trial that he had seen Lizzie go into the barn.

Many unanswered and unanswerable questions hang over the Borden axe murders.

It is perfectly possible that Lizzie was responsible — although she was found not guilty. It is equally possible that someone with a grudge against the Bordens paid an opportunistic, murderous visit to number 92. Maggie might have done it, but there doesn't appear to have been any motive. Andrew Borden does not seem to have been the kind of philanderer who would have tried to take unfair advantage of his maid.

Lizzie's supposed "friend" Alice Russell saw Lizzie burning a dress on the Sunday after the murders, and commented that it would not be a good idea to let anyone see her doing it! Lizzie explained that the dress was in no way sinister — it was simply stained with paint and was therefore of no more use. Lizzie was frequently eccentric and occasionally irrational, but for a suspect to burn a dress in her circumstances was practically suicidal! It was Alice's comments on this dress-burning incident that were largely responsible for Lizzie's being charged with murder. (With friends like Alice, who needs enemies?)

At the trial in June of 1893, Thomas Kiernan was brought in as an expert witness to conduct "visibility experiments" involving lines of sight in the Borden house. When questioned by the defence, he accepted that it was perfectly possible for someone to walk around in number 92 without seeing the bodies. He also had to admit that if a murderous intruder had got in early, killed Abby and then lurked to wait for Andrew's return, there were several places where such an intruder could have hidden undetected. All this favoured Lizzie's acquittal.

Another vitally important issue at the trial was the question of whether Lizzie's dress was bloodstained. All the witnesses who saw her within a few minutes of the death of her father were quite clear that they had seen no evidence of blood either on Lizzie or on her dress.

A rather salacious and melodramatic theory suggested that Lizzie had committed the murders naked, and washed off the blood before getting dressed again. It's not impossible, and she was capable of odd behaviour at times!

Another theory posited the idea that Andrew Borden had an illegitimate son, William, who was mentally ill. This young man was said to have displayed a morbid interest in axes, and was thought to have been seen in the vicinity of number 92 on the day of the Bordens' double murder. He may even have been implicated in the later axe murder in Fall River of a Mrs. Bertha Manchester. However, a Portuguese immigrant named Jose Corriera was later charged with that one. Corriera certainly could not have killed the Bordens as he was not even in the United States in August of 1892.

A further ingredient that thickens the plot without solving anything is that Maggie (otherwise known as Bridget) was given money to return to Ireland. There are versions of the story that say she was given enough to buy a farm when she got there! If this is correct, it makes the suspicious investigator wonder exactly why Lizzie and Emma thought it necessary to give Maggie quite such a generous bonus — unless hush money was involved. Whether or not she purchased that farm in Ireland, Maggie/Bridget returned to the States and died in Montana in 1948 at the age of eighty-two.

There are whispers of a supposed "confession" from Maggie, made when she was seriously ill and thought she was dying. As it happened, she recovered and the alleged "confession" was either retracted completely, or modified and placed quietly on the back burner.

All things considered, our analysis of the evidence leads us to agree with the "not guilty" verdict on Lizzie, and to suggest that a sinister, unknown, psychopathic intruder was the most likely perpetrator of the Borden axe murders on the morning of August 4, 1892.

19

WAS NAPOLEON POISONED?

Born in Ajaccio on Corsica on August 15, 1769, Napoleon was the second son of a lawyer named Carlo Bonaparte, who took an interest in local politics and came out in favour of remaining with France rather than campaign for Corsican independence. His pro-French attitude enabled his son, Napoleon, to live and study in France. This was the fuse that ignited the future emperor's rocket to fame and his unique place in world history. By 1799 he was to all intents and purposes the real ruler of France. He was officially recognized as emperor in 1804.

The fortunes of war between Napoleon and his various enemies — including Britain, Austria, Prussia, Russia, Spain and Portugal — fluctuated until Napoleon's defeat and subsequent exile to the Isle of Elba in 1814. He made his way back to France in 1815 and, incredibly, succeeded in raising another army with which he met Wellington at Waterloo. After the British victory there, Napoleon was exiled again, this time to the remote and rocky island of St. Helena in the South Atlantic. It was there that he — or one of his doubles — died at 5:49 p.m. on May 5, 1821, at Longwood House.

Whomever the so-called Napoleonic remains really belonged to, they were exhumed in 1840 and reburied in Paris in the Palais des Invalides, where they still rest.

Was Napoleon murdered? If so, how was it done? And who did it?

Some of the best evidence, valid even after almost two centuries, concerns his valet, Louis Marchand. History reveals that Napoleon thought the world of Marchand, treating him more as family than as a servant, and Louis repaid the emperor with unfailing loyalty and devoted service. Today's professional management consultants would readily agree that any modern Napoleon of industry or commerce needs the unconditional support of a colleague like Louis Marchand.

The faithful Louis kept a diary of the days on St. Helena that was not published until 1955. So detailed was Marchand's account that it provides vital evidence for any contemporary pathologist or diagnostician. But even more important than Louis's meticulously detailed case notes were the hairs shaved from Napoleon's head the day after he died. Marchand put some in an envelope and labelled it. Those hairs later revealed telltale traces of arsenic.

Pathologists have almost forty ways of describing the symptoms of arsenic poisoning. Marchand's diary, and other contemporary eyewitness accounts, show that Napoleon — or the double who was dying in his place at Longwood House — demonstrated some 80 percent of those symptoms. In addition to Marchand's fundamental work, eyewitnesses to Napoleon's decline included the Marquis Las Cases, Baron Gourgaud and Marshall Bertrand.

All kinds of medical theories have been set out to account for Napoleon's death. Some have suggested a sexually transmitted disease, like syphilis; others have hypothesized hepatitis. History officially records that it was stomach cancer, but Napoleon showed no signs of the gaunt loss of weight that so often accompanies cancer.

The brilliant Swedish scientist Sten Forshuvfvud reported that the arsenic in Napoleon's hair clearly revealed that he had been given massive doses of arsenic on some days, and little or none on other days. Tests at the Harwell Nuclear Laboratories did not contradict Forshuvfvud's findings.

Modern toxicological light is thrown on the difficulties of diagnosing arsenic poisoning by Dr. Ben Weider, another brilliant scientist and a colleague of Forshuvfvud's. Weider studied and reported on a Canadian case that occurred in 1967. Mrs. Esther Castellani had died in Vancouver after being ill for nearly a year. Some while later, the court was approached by a woman claiming that she knew Mrs. Castellani had been murdered. In return for immunity from prosecution, she would provide evidence against the murderer. When this protection was granted, she explained that Mrs. Castellani's husband had poisoned his wife with arsenic so that he could claim the insurance and then marry the witness. After getting his hands on his dead wife's insurance money, however, it was reported that he had changed his mind about the promised marriage! Hence her call to the court.

The body was exhumed. Tests similar to those used on Napoleon's hair were carried out on Mrs. Castellani's hair — with parallel results! Like Napoleon's doctors, Dr. Moscovitch of Vancouver General Hospital had not suspected arsenic poisoning. Although the attentive, expert care given to Mrs. Castellani had included more than a hundred sophisticated tests, none of them pointed to chronic arsenic poisoning.

The medical experts were strongly in agreement that arsenic poisoning can produce many different symptoms, which make diagnosis extremely difficult. Dr. O'Meara, for example, who had attended Napoleon, had thought that the emperor was suffering from one or more of a range of unpleasant illnesses including gout, scurvy and dysentery. Dr. Antommarchi, the emperor's personal physician, referred to Napoleon's bouts of nausea, vomiting, coughing and a terrible, persistent thirst.

Expert toxicologists and forensic scientists divide arsenic poisoning into two phases: cosmetic and lethal. The purpose of the cosmetic phase is to make it appear that the victim's health is merely deteriorating naturally. In Napoleon's case, it is believed by some highly reputable and knowledgeable researchers that the cosmetic phase may well have begun in 1816 or, even earlier, around the time of Waterloo!

Politically, those plotting the emperor's death had to be extremely careful to make it seem accidental, or completely natural. He was still a powerful icon in France, where he had many fanatically loyal followers, including most of the army. His health had to be shown to be deteriorating over years rather than months. Medical experts who have studied the case closely are of the opinion that the lethal phase was launched in February or March of 1821.

The postmortem, after his death on May 5, clearly revealed that something horrendously toxic had partially destroyed the lining of his stomach — yet the verdict stubbornly remained either cancer, or a pre-cancerous condition.

If, as now seems almost certain from the evidence, Napoleon was poisoned, who is the prime suspect? Only two people had constant and unfettered access to the emperor. One was his loyal valet, Louis Marchand, who would have died defending him. The other was the devious Comte de Montholon, who almost certainly nursed a grudge against Napoleon after being dismissed from his post at Wurzburg for marrying Albine — a woman of whom the emperor had then strongly disapproved, but who was now, ironically, almost certainly sharing his bed at Longwood House on St. Helena! Montholon was linked with Louis XVIII and with the Duke d'Artois, who became Charles X.

If, as seems probable, Montholon was the poisoner, how did he get the fatal doses into his victim? Napoleon was, in a sense, the architect of his own destruction. He enjoyed one particular wine, imported specially for him from Cape Town. This was a vintage called vin de Constance, and he alone drank it. For a poisoner with the cunning and subtlety of Montholon, opening a bottle of wine, adding tasteless, odourless arsenic, and refastening the bottle to make it look as though it had come straight from Cape Town was simple enough. He had all the time in the world to carry out the wine bottle deception with slow, careful, diabolical craftsmanship.

What if the St. Helena plot is deeper and subtler yet? Is it absolutely proven beyond the faintest shadow of doubt that the man who looked like Napoleon and died in Longwood House on May 5, 1821, was really Bonaparte the emperor?

Mabel Brookes, an expert on Napoleon with ancestral family ties to St. Helena, identified no fewer than four doubles who had served the emperor at one time or another. The most interesting of them is a man named François Eugène Robeaud. According to an eminent Russian researcher, Dr. Alexander Gorbovski, Robeaud was the man who went to St. Helena in 1818 to stand in for the exiled emperor. The real Napoleon was then spirited away by a daring American captain who smuggled him safely to Verona, where he took the name of Revard and pretended to be a diamond trader. He went into partnership with a local businessman named Petrucci. Signor Revard was a fluent Italian speaker who bore an uncommon resemblance to Napoleon Bonaparte! Ironically, his neighbours in Verona nicknamed him "Napoleon" — a friendly, local joke to which Revard seemed to have no objection. On August 23, 1823, he received a message that caused him great anxiety.

He raced off and was never seen in Verona — or anywhere else — again.

Before leaving, however, he gave a sealed letter to his partner, Petrucci, to be delivered only if Revard failed to return within ninety days. When that time had elapsed, Petrucci, a man of honour, delivered the letter — to the king of France! He was given a vast amount of money as a reward, and not until 1853 did he tell his story: Petrucci then testified that his mysterious partner, Revard, was really Napoleon.

The great escape from St. Helena, however, seems to have come to an ignominious and inglorious end. The urgent message that took Revard away from Verona concerned the serious illness of Napoleon's twelve-year-old son known as l'Aiglon (meaning "the young eagle") whose mother was Marie-Louise. The boy's full name was François Charles Joseph, and she and the lad were then accommodated in the castle of Schönbrunn in Vienna. On September 4, 1823, an intruder to Schönbrunn was challenged and shot by a sentry while attempting to climb the castle wall. As soon as the body was seen in clear light, there was a great commotion and the French Embassy in Vienna was notified. Marie-Louise, however, swiftly asserted such authority as she still possessed and arranged for the body of the mysterious intruder to be buried in an unmarked grave at Schönbrunn.

Complication piles upon complication as the mystery of Napoleon's death is analyzed more deeply. There are detailed accounts of Napoleon's burial on St. Helena in 1821. At that time his Legion of Honour medal was placed on top of his coat, his hat covered his feet, and he wore his boots — complete with silver spurs. His viscera were contained in silver jars located in the corners of the coffin. His face and skull were clean-shaven. The body was not embalmed, and the face, according to some reports, was already so badly decomposed as to be practically unrecognizable, but the mouth was closed. When the body was exhumed in 1840 on its way to rest in a place of honour in the Palais des Invalides, there were a number of disturbing discrepancies: there was hair on the skull and face; the Legion of Honour decoration was under the coat; the hat was above his knees; the silver visceral jars were between his legs. The face was well preserved, but the mouth was open. The body seemed to have been embalmed and the embalming had proved very effective. One sure clue to arsenic poisoning is that the body is very effectively preserved for much longer than a normal corpse which has been allowed to putrefy naturally. The inference is that the body that was taken away from Napoleon's grave in Saint Helena in 1840 was not the body which had been placed there in 1821. But if the exhumed corpse of 1840 was neither Napoleon, nor François Eugène Robeaud, whose was it?

The most likely candidate would seem to have been another of Napoleon's loyal men, Franchesi Cipriani, who was as faithful to his beloved emperor as Marchand was. Like his master, Cipriani was a Corsican and was of similar stature and general appearance. Previously in excellent health, he had complained of agonizing stomach pains shortly before he died, and his body had been removed from its original grave and hidden somewhere before exhumation and an autopsy could reveal the undeniable presence of arsenic. Whoever poisoned Napoleon almost certainly poisoned his loyal follower, Cipriani, as well. Perhaps Cipriani was beginning to suspect Montholon. There was no time for the poisoner to carry out the same elaborate cosmetic phase as he had done on Napoleon. If Cipriani was getting close to the truth, the murderer would have to go straight to the dangerously incriminating lethal phase.

Why not try to remove Franchesi by some other means, if speed was of the essence? A sword? A dagger? A pistol or musket shot? If the tough little Corsican was a hardened soldier, and anything but a soft target, the foppish playboy Montholon would not have wanted to risk a direct attack that might well fail and then turn into hand-to-hand combat. In those circumstances, the odds would heavily favour Cipriani.

So the man who resembled Napoleon and who died on May 5, 1821, was very probably Robeaud. The man interred in honour in the Palais des Invalides is probably Cipriani, whose loyalty to Napoleon deserves that place of honour anyway. The mysterious Signor Revard, shot by a vigilant sentry on the wall of Schönbrunn Castle on September 4, 1823, was almost certainly Emperor Napoleon Bonaparte.

20

WHO MURDERED PRINCE RUDOLPH AND COUNTESS MARIA VETSERA?

During the night that separated Tuesday, January 29 from Wednesday, January 30, 1889, Prince Rudolph of Habsburg and his beautiful, passionate, romantic, teenaged mistress, Countess Maria Vetsera, died violently. During the century and more that has passed since, the rumours and legends about the lovers' tragic deaths in the hunting lodge at Mayerling have become confused and distorted almost beyond recognition. One thing is grimly certain: they did not commit suicide.

To investigate the mystery of their double murder, it is essential to look at the background of Austrian and Hungarian politics. The old Habsburg Empire had brought the two countries together in an uncomfortable and uncertain bonding of very different aspirations and characteristics. Another problem that threatened the empire's stability and continuation was the tension between the progressive liberalism of the young Habsburgs — especially Rudolph and his cousin, close friend, and confidant Johann Salvator — and the reactionary ultraconservatism of Emperor Franz Josef.

*Prince Rudolph of Habsburg,
murdered with Maria Vetsera in
Mayerling.*

*Countess Maria Vetsera,
murdered with Prince Rudolph in
Mayerling.*

Twisting and writhing his way through the hazardous political and social jungle that was the Austro-Hungarian government was the dangerously enigmatic and underestimated Count Eduard Taaffe (spellings vary slightly). Born in Vienna on February 24, 1833, Taaffe was twice prime minister, and he remained in power longer than any other politician during Franz Josef's reign. Of Irish descent, Taaffe was a boyhood friend of the emperor. His supporters — an agglomeration known as Taaffe's Iron Ring — consisted mainly of Polish and Czech landowners and reactionary senior clergymen. Taaffe went to great lengths to disguise his grim ruthlessness by pretending to be lighthearted and laid-back. Under this cloak of supercilious humour, however, lurked a deadly and determined politician who, among his other instruments of power, seems to have controlled an Austro-Hungarian secret police force that was, in its day, as effective and as feared as the KGB or the Gestapo.

Rudolph, Johann and their liberal entourage were a constant thorn in Franz Josef's side. The younger Habsburgs were impatient for reforms; they wanted to introduce rights and freedoms for the citizens of the old Habsburg Empire that were diametrically opposed to the fundamental, authoritarian principles which meant so much to Franz Josef and his right-hand man, the sinister Eduard Taaffe.

With or without the emperor's knowledge and connivance, it is highly likely that Taaffe decided to remove Rudolph. Crafty politician and ruthless secret police commander that he was, Taaffe knew full well that the assassination must be carefully stage-managed. Nothing can be calculated to deceive the public more effectively than the controlled leak, or the double bluff. Taaffe was looking for an opportunity to put forward one fragile smokescreen, or ineffectual cover-up, and then blow it away with a second one which would seem to be an unwelcome intrusion into what the government had hoped to keep strictly under wraps.

His opportunity came when the colourful Countess Larisch introduced the philandering Prince Rudolph to the passionately eager and melodramatic young Maria Vetsera. Perhaps Larisch was a genuine friend to both lovers, but she might have been working undercover for Taaffe. The question as to whether she was actually in Taaffe's employ, or whether her role as a go-between for the clandestine lovers was played honestly and with their interests at heart, cannot now be answered definitively — but the suspicion lingers that there was more than chance behind their introduction.

Rudolph had inadvertently placed a trump card in Taaffe's hands by talking of love and death with the characteristic fervour of the extravagant nineteenth-century poets. It was a stark and challenging idea that also appealed to the wild emotions of excitable young Maria. Rudolph was gloomy and Byronic at times. She was reckless and immature. Provided Taaffe could ensure that those who knew about the affair also knew of the lovers' romantic notions concerning love and death, his second smokescreen was likely to be widely accepted.

Rudolph and Maria were duly found compromisingly naked, and conveniently dead, in the prince's bedroom in the hunting lodge. The first official account — the camouflage that was intended to fail — reported that Rudolph had died in a hunting accident. No mention was made of Maria's presence, or her death, in this first version. The method by which the second layer of camouflage — the one that was intended to hold — was released to the general public, seems to have been that a servant at Mayerling allegedly walked past the well-lighted room, with its curtains open, and saw the telltale bodies on the bed! That scandalous news travelled like wildfire throughout the empire. Various feeble official denials were made: traditional religious leaders frowned piously on suicide, and on suspected suicide. Rudolph was eventually buried honourably and with due respect paid. Poor little Maria's body was deposited in a shed for a couple of days, and her family were pressurized into signing an official statement to the effect that she had killed herself. She was eventually buried in an unmarked grave.

There is evidence that the future King Edward VII, who was then Prince of Wales, wrote a letter to his mother, Queen Victoria, saying that Salisbury (the prime minister of Britain at that time) had expressed the view that "poor Rudolph and that unfortunate young lady were murdered ..." An autopsy report, which did not surface until many years after the Mayerling tragedy, came to similar conclusions. It noted that the track of the bullet through Rudolph's head was an odd one for a suicide, and that the gunshot that killed Maria had hit the top of her head. It was also noted that the revolver found near the prince did not belong to him, and that all six shots had been fired. The bodies of both lovers showed other injuries besides the fatal ones. The probability that Taaffe's secret police agents attacked them, injured them badly and then killed them remains a strong one.

The mysterious Countess Larisch comes into the Mayerling equation again via her memoirs. She maintains that Rudolph was very much afraid of someone — Taaffe, or Franz Josef — during the closing weeks of his life. Larisch says that Rudolph gave her a strongbox for safe-keeping until someone gave her the secret code RIUO. After Rudolph's death, his cousin and trusted friend, Archduke Johann Salvator, duly turned up and gave Larisch the necessary code. She handed the box over to him with a great sense of relief. After what had happened to Rudolph and Maria in the hunting lodge, no one wanted to risk a similar visit from Taafe's homicidal thugs.

Salvator's next course of action added still further to the mystery of Rudolph's box and its unknown contents. He renounced his title, changed his name to plain John Ort — taken from Castle Ort, not far from Gmunden in Austria — qualified as a master mariner, and was officially recorded as lost at sea when his ship, *Saint Margaret*, failed to return.

After Rudolph's death, Johann's life was in the boiling centre of an emotional and political maelstrom. He was a good, loyal and honourable man, and when he fell in love with the beautiful actress, Milli Stubel, he was determined to marry her at whatever cost.

Castle Ort enshrines the myth of a giant named Erla who fell in love with a water nymph and asked a friendly enchantress to reduce him in size so that they could marry. Metaphorically, Archduke Johann — a social giant by virtue of his title and his membership of the Habsburg Dynasty — reduced himself to the size of an ordinary citizen in order to marry his beloved Milli. They sailed away together on the *Saint Margaret* and were never seen or heard from again. The cover story was that their ship had gone down with all hands trying to round Cape Horn.

Modern witness protection programs and sophisticated government intelligence and espionage organizations have the capability of making it seem as if the person being protected has died — and then giving him or her a new, secure identity and a home in an undisclosed, faraway location. Is that what John Ort and Milli Stubel managed to do? Did they still have Rudolph's box with them? Most intriguingly of all, what deadly secrets might that box once have contained?

21

THE MURDERS AT RENNES-LE-CHÂTEAU

The mystery of Father Bérenger Saunière and the secret of his sudden, vast, unexplained wealth remains one of the greatest unsolved mysteries of all time. The Rennes treasure is often referred to as an accursed one, and there is more than enough violence and tragedy associated with it to justify that sinister adjective. Saunière himself may well have been poisoned. The discovery of three unidentified corpses — all shot, and all males in the prime of life — under Saunière's lawn, and the brutal axe murder of old Father Antoine Gélis of Coustaussa, near Rennes, in 1893, may well have a link with the Mayerling tragedy and the riddle of Rudolph's mysterious strongbox.

In outline, Bérenger was an impoverished parish priest, barely subsisting on the charity of his Rennes parishioners and an official stipend so small that it was practically nonexistent. Then, in 1885, everything changed for him: he became one of the richest men in the South of France and went on spending money as if there was no tomorrow until 1917, when he died in debt to a furniture company.

One of the many theories that we and other experienced Rennes researchers have examined for more than a quarter-century is the possible

*View of Coustaussa,
where Father Gélis was
murdered.*

*The grave of Father
Antoine Gélis, murdered
in Coustaussa.*

Marie Dénarnaud, Saunière's loyal companion and housekeeper.

BERENGER SAUNIÈRE

Father Bérenger Saunière, mysterious Priest of Rennes-le-Château, France. Was he a murderer?

connection between this unusual French parish priest and the House of Habsburg. There are clues that suggest that Saunière may have found something of enormous historic and religious value hidden at Rennes. There are also clues that his lineage may have been older and nobler than that of the Habsburgs. It has even been hinted that he was descended from the ancient and arcane Merovingians.

As a practising Catholic priest, Saunière could hardly try to sell back whatever priceless religious relic he had discovered to the church he supposedly served — but the Habsburgs were a different matter altogether. They had been Holy Roman emperors at one time. As it wasn't possible to sell his unique discovery to the Vatican, Bérenger might well have considered offering it to a descendant of the last Holy Roman emperor: Franz Josef of Austria-Hungary.

Franz Josef was sanctimonious — a formal, rigid traditionalist to whom respectability was the ultimate virtue. He was also obsessed by the desire for power, authority and control. If something was in the offing that would increase his power, Franz Josef was extremely interested — but if that coveted object had the faintest whiff of scandal or suspicion attached to its acquisition, Franz would use an expendable intermediary rather than become directly involved.

Upon analyzing the character of the authoritarian Austrian emperor, it is possible to hypothesize that if Saunière hinted that he had an ancient artefact — a symbol of social, religious or political power — that Franz Josef would dearly love to possess (something like the Grail, the Lance of Destiny or the Crown of St. Stephen), then Franz would send out a junior Habsburg to reconnoitre the situation.

Whatever else Saunière had uncovered at Rennes-le-Château, it certainly wasn't the grail, the lance or St. Stephen's crown — but it might well have been something in their league.

As part of this scenario, Franz Josef sends his expendable son, Crown Prince Rudolph, and the even more expendable cousin, Johann Salvator, to negotiate with this mysterious French priest. The hypothesis goes on to suggest that the young Habsburgs agreed to buy the mysterious artefact from Saunière, and that its value was so enormous — literally beyond price — that he would have to be paid in instalments over many years. This could well explain why his money dried up before his death in 1917. As a patriotic Frenchman, Bérenger could hardly be seen visiting Vienna and drawing money from the Royal Bank of Austria while World War I raged across Europe.

So who were the three dead men beneath Saunière's lawn? One explanation is that they were three of Austro-Hungarian Count Taaffe's hit men, agents of his lethal secret police — and perhaps even the same men who had murdered Rudolph and Maria. Now they were being sent to silence the French priest who knew too much, the man who had all the politically inflammable information about how the Habsburgs had acquired the mysterious artefact. Rudolph and Maria Vetsera had been soft targets; the hard-drinking prince was neither robust nor in good health, while Maria was a small, teenaged girl. Her physical strength and fighting ability could not match her courage or her devotion to her prince: sadly, devotion and courage are not enough to hinder brutal assassins.

In thinking of Bérenger as merely some innocuous, ineffectual little village priest, Taaffe's agents fatally underestimated him. Saunière enjoyed shooting and was an expert marksman. He was tall, athletic and powerfully built. In a brawl, he would have been more than a match for any two ordinary men. In addition to his physical advantages, he was ruthless, shrewd, an experienced and sophisticated man of the world — and was not overburdened by scruples.

Most serious Rennes researchers agree that Saunière went through the unavoidable years of misery and deprivation as a theological student simply to obtain the living of Rennes-le-Château once he was ordained. It may seem uncharitable to judge him in this light , but he does not appear to have had any deep sense of religious vocation. He had clearly worked out that there was something priceless hidden in the area, and that there was no greater vantage point for a treasure hunter than to become the parish priest of Rennes.

Taaffe's men went to Rennes expecting to assassinate an ingenuous and more or less defenceless village priest. They ran into a man who was bigger, stronger and more aggressive than any of them, and who had no compunction at all about shooting first.

Saunière had a beautiful teenaged mistress, Marie Denarnaud, who was officially his housekeeper. Marie doted on him. Imagine that it is midnight, or the early hours of the morning. Taaffe's three butchers, brashly overconfident, stroll casually past Saunière's presbytery. One muscular arm slips out gently from under Marie's shoulders. Bérenger draws his heavy-calibre revolver from under the pillow where it always lies loaded and ready for any emergency. The three secret policemen are silhouetted by the moonlight as they advance towards the presbytery door. Like some silent angel of death, Saunière looks down at them from the bedroom window. The southern French night is hot. The window is open. Calmly, resolutely, he takes aim. Three deadly accurate shots crash from Saunière's gun. He dresses quickly. "Marie, my darling, bring the spade if you please." Loyally, unquestioningly, she helps him to bury Taaffe's men under the presbytery lawn — where they are destined not to be found for more than half a century.

There are, of course, many other possible explanations for the presence of those three corpses under the Presbytery lawn at Rennes. They might have been French hostages shot by German soldiers. They could have been German soldiers killed by French Resistance forces. They might have been rashly adventurous treasure hunters who got too close to the strange secrets of Rennes-le-Château.

The murder of Father Antoine Gélis, the parish priest of Coustaussa near Rennes, however, is a very different matter. There are numerous, controversial, versions of how Saunière located whatever it was that had made him so rich. Several of these theories depend upon his discovery of ancient coded manuscripts of one sort or another. Theories abound; proof is scant; facts are scarce. It is possible, however, that Saunière needed more scholarship than he had managed to acquire during his reluctant years at the

The grave of Father Antoine Gélis, murdered in Coustaussa.

Monsieur Rousset, the Doyen of Coustaussa, who led us to Father Gélis's grave.

seminary in order to translate and decipher these arcane documents — always assuming that such documents actually existed. Gélis, the old priest of Coustaussa, is a real scholar, so Saunière goes to him for help. Gélis realizes from the curious coded documents Saunière leaves with him that a great deal of money could be at stake — and Gélis gets greedy. It is possible that he made the same fatal misjudgment of Saunière as Taaffe's men had done. Unless, of course, it was Taaffe's men who killed Gélis before making their unsuccessful attempt on Saunière.

For whatever reason, Gélis was terrified of something, or someone. He would allow no one into his presbytery except his niece, who called daily to attend to his food and laundry needs. Each time she left, he insisted that she wait on the doorstep until she heard him secure the bolts on his heavy presbytery door. Was he merely paranoid, or did he suspect with good reason that someone wanted him dead?

Despite the care that he always took with his security, someone gained admission to the presbytery and attacked him viciously with the heavy fire irons. Gélis, as far as the tragedy can be reconstructed from what was found, seems to have run, badly injured, towards the window — as if to try to summon help from a passer-by. His unknown assailant then finished him off — very bloodily — with an axe. The strangest detail of all is the way the body was arranged: whoever killed Gélis laid him out with dignity and respect — as a priest, or a professional funeral director, would have done — with his arms crossed reverently across his chest. This little gesture makes it look more like the work of Saunière than of Taaffe's minions.

When Saunière himself lay dying in January of 1917, the story told in the village is that a young priest was called to take his final confession and absolve him. This young man apparently heard something from Saunière so traumatic that he fled without granting absolution. Word in the village was that he was too ill to work for months afterwards. Had Saunière confessed to the murder of Antoine Gélis more than twenty years before? Had the young priest been overcome with horror because Saunière had celebrated Mass for two decades with the same hands that had butchered Antoine Gélis — a brother priest — with an axe?

The mystery of Gélis's death is as baffling today as it was in 1893, but either Saunière or Taaffe's men are the most likely culprits.

22

WHAT BECAME OF THE SERIAL KILLER BELA KISS?

Not much is known for sure about the Hungarian mass murderer Bela Kiss. He moved into the little town of Cinkota, where he rented a modest house at 9 Kossuth Street, in the early 1900s. By trade, Kiss was a metal worker who specialized in tin — he had taught himself all the necessary skills of a professional tinsmith and did good work. It seems that he had not had the benefit of any formal education, but somehow he had made himself numerate, literate and much more. It was said of him that he could speak knowledgeably and fluently on most of the humanities, especially literature, history and art.

His personal appearance was described as both striking and attractive. He had fair hair and penetrating blue eyes that were said to be hypnotic in their intensity. He was popular in Cinkota because of his generosity — he often paid for parties at a local hotel — and he was especially popular with the ladies of the area, many of whom regarded him as a particularly good catch.

There are contradictory versions of this background material. One alleges that when Kiss first came to live in Kossuth Street he was, in fact, already married. His wife, Marie, was at least fifteen years younger than Bela, and she soon struck up a relationship with a Cinkota man named Paul Bikari. In December 1912, Bela reported that Marie and Paul had run away together and gone either to Canada or the United States. If that version is correct, then it was as an eligible young man, abandoned by a callous wife, that Bela appealed to the Cinkota girls.

His next move was to engage the services of a more mature lady, a Mrs. Jakubec, to run the house for him, cook his meals and undertake general cleaning and domestic duties. She went back to her own home every night when her daily work in Kossuth Street was completed.

Despite their eagerness to apply for the role of the second Mrs. Kiss, the Cinkota girls were discouraged by Bela's frequent visits to Budapest, apparently in search of a wider range of female company. It was even whispered that he was a well-known and frequent patron at some of the city's brothels.

Rumours of war were growing more sinister with each passing day; those who started to think seriously about its practical implications realized that shortages of food and other essentials would accompany any widespread armed conflict. Fuel would be as scarce as food. It would be prudent to lay in a supply. No one was surprised, then, when Bela began gathering large metal drums — presumably to store oil, petrol and other fuels. The local police asked routine questions about the drums, and Kiss assured them that he was simply amassing a precautionary fuel store against shortages in case war came. The police were satisfied with this explanation.

In 1914, Kiss got his call-up papers. He enlisted and was posted very quickly. The First World War took a desperate toll, and it was no surprise to the townspeople of Cinkota to hear in the spring of 1916 that their popular tinsmith had either been killed in action or taken prisoner.

One version links the discovery of Kiss's victims with soldiers foraging for petrol and oil for their military vehicles; they paid a routine visit to Cinkota.

"Has anyone," they asked, "been known to store fuel?"

"Oh, yes," replied the townsfolk. "Bela Kiss, our tinsmith, has several large drums of it, but the poor fellow was captured or killed in action a few months ago. We'll show you where he used to live." In this version, it was the fuel-foraging soldiers who uncovered Kiss's hideous secret stashed away inside the big oil drums.

Another variation suggests that Bela's landlord, the owner of 9 Kossuth Street, went to inspect his property to assess how much renovation and repair work were needed before it could be re-let now that Bela had reportedly died in action. The landlord found seven big metal drums, and punched a small hole in the top of one to try to find out what was inside. The fetid odour of human decay drifted overpoweringly out of the hole. The pharmacist from the adjoining shop sniffed it cautiously and confirmed the landlord's worst fears: as far as he was concerned that unique stench meant there was a decaying corpse inside the drum.

Whether the landlord and neighbouring pharmacist made the initial discovery, or whether the soldiers did, it was the landlord who seems to have contacted the Budapest police. He was put in touch with Dr. Charles Nagy, head of the detective unit, who came over to Cinkota with a small force of detectives to assist him with the gruesome investigation. Bela Kiss, however, had made just as powerful an impact on the mature Mrs. Jakubec, his housekeeper, as he had on the younger women who were so eager to marry him. She was angrily defensive of her master's property. He had asked her to guard it while he was away doing his duty in the army — and guard it she would. Nagy overcame Mrs. Jakubec's vituperative streams of protest and opened the nearest drum in spite of her.

It contained the naked body of a once-beautiful young woman — only partially preserved by the industrial alcohol in the drum. It also contained the rope with which, presumably, Bela Kiss had strangled her. Each of the six remaining drums also held the body of a naked girl. The industrial alcohol had slowed down the putrefaction process sufficiently for each victim still to be recognizable. Nagy's team extended their search to the house and grounds: more bodies were discovered. The detective immediately informed the military authorities that, if the accounts of Bela's capture or death were inaccurate, he wanted him arrested and sent to him at Budapest.

Locating the suspect was easier said than done. Thousands of Hungarian soldiers had already been taken prisoner or killed, and Bela Kiss was a common name — it was the Hungarian equivalent of Pierre Bonhomme in France, David Jones in Wales, or John Smith in England. There might well have been twenty or thirty brave and honourable Hungarian soldiers bearing the name quite correctly and legally.

Nagy found it impossible to accept that Mrs. Jakubec could have been unaware of Bela's homicidal activities. He interrogated her intensively, and she disclosed the existence of what Bela had referred to as his "secret room," which she was forbidden to enter.

It is at this point that Bela's real-life atrocities take on elements of Charles Perrault's grim 1697 story of Bluebeard. In Perrault's version, the fictional bride escapes with her life by a hair's breadth when her soldier brothers turn up at the last minute and rescue her. She had disobeyed Bluebeard's instructions about never entering the locked, secret room in which all her predecessors' bodies hung. The magical key took on sinister, irremovable bloodstains that indicated that she had disobeyed him and used it.

The Bluebeard folktale may have been a distorted memory of Giles de Rais, a contemporary of Joan of Arc in the fifteenth century. After his early life as a hero of France, Giles went to live in Brittany, where he became involved in black magic, alchemy and serial murder. Unlike Perrault's heterosexual villain, Giles murdered several hundred young boys. When the Duke of Brittany finally investigated all the stories of missing children from the villages near de Rais's estates, his men uncovered the remains of more than fifty bodies. At his trial, Giles confessed to having killed far more than that. He was executed rather spectacularly on October 26, 1440.

The secret, locked room in number 9 Kossuth Street adjoined Bela's bedroom. Mrs. Jakubec did have the key — although she had had strict orders from Kiss never to enter the room and never to allow anyone else to enter it. Half expecting to find yet more drums with sinister contents, Nagy and his men were relieved to find that the interior was more like an archive. It was lined with shelves crammed with books; a convenient desk and chair suggested that Kiss had used it as his private study or office. Of maximum interest to Nagy's team were the records they discovered about the women he had contacted — all too often with lethal results.

Had Kiss got the idea for a secret, forbidden room from reading Perrault's version of Bluebeard? Did Bela even consider himself to be a type of Bluebeard, another Giles de Rais, perhaps? Or did he see himself as another Jack the Ripper? Several of the girls he murdered were thought to have been prostitutes from the Budapest brothels he was said to have patronized. Even the most expert criminal psychiatrists, and those with the longest experience of studying psychotic serial killers like Bela Kiss, recognize the extreme difficulty of getting inside these weird killers' minds and divining their real motivations. Why was Kiss preserving some of his victims in drums filled with industrial alcohol? In his insane imaginings, was there some perverted streak of religious mania? Did he select the most attractive of his victims for the alcohol-filled drums, so that like the Pharaohs, kings, emperors and warlords of the ancient world, he would have his heavenly harem to satisfy his desires for eternity? Were the select seven to be his wives in the hereafter, while those who were consigned to the garden or the chicken-shed were to be his concubines?

As the army was unable to produce Kiss — alive or dead — Nagy directed his resources towards trying to identify some of the victims. His efforts paid off. One of the ladies was Katherine Varga, an attractive young widow who had been the proprietor of a highly successful dressmaking venture. Another was Margaret Toth. Nagy's research in Bela's secret room was beginning to illuminate the serial killer's methods. Bela had placed notices in the lonely hearts columns of newspapers, advertising for a wife — just as Foxy Corder had done in the United Kingdom — and suggesting that the lady should have some financial means.

He would arrange to meet the victim, and turn on all his charismatic charm. His suave conversation would contain seemingly innocent little questions about her relatives and friends as well as her bank balance. Those who had no close relatives, but considerable financial assets, were cajoled into parting with the money and were then invited down to stay with him in Cinkota. A day or two later they would end up in an oil drum, or in the garden. Katherine Varga sold her business and went to Cinkota to marry Bela. Margaret Toth's mother parted with money when Kiss promised to marry her daughter. Margaret visited Bela in Kossuth Street — never to return. Before killing her, Kiss had forced her to write her mother, explaining that she had become angry with him for delaying the promised marriage and had set off for America in the hope of finding a new lover there. As soon as he had the necessary letter, Bela strangled Margaret and sealed her body inside one of the oil drums.

The great mystery is where Bela Kiss went and what happened to him in the end.

Because the name was so widely used in Hungary, various reports reached Chief Detective Nagy, including one that said Kiss had died of typhoid in Serbia in 1915. Another lead said that he was a patient in hospital, recuperating. Nagy and his team hurried over. When they reached the ward, there was a corpse in Bela's bed — but it wasn't his! Other witnesses claimed to have spotted him walking around Budapest a couple of years after World War I ended. In 1920, a French Foreign Legionnaire reported seeing Kiss, who was then calling himself "Hoffman." By the time the police followed up on the legionnaire's evidence, "Hoffman" had deserted and vanished.

Did he cross the Atlantic to find refuge and obscurity in Canada or the United States?

Henry Oswald was a New York detective with an eidetic memory. He was the envy of police colleagues because of his strange ability to "photograph" faces into his memory and then use his own, private "rogues' gallery" to identify suspects. Oswald claimed that he had seen Bela Kiss emerge from the Times Square subway station in 1932. Kiss was also thought to have been seen working as a janitor in a high-rise building in 1936. When police followed up on that alleged sighting, the caretaker had vanished — and Bela Kiss was never seen or heard from again.

23

WHO KILLED
LORD ERROLL AND WHY?

To give Lord Erroll his full title and description, he was the Honourable Captain Josslyn Victor Hay, Twenty-Second Earl of Erroll, Hereditary High Constable of Scotland and Assistant Military Secretary to Kenya. Josslyn was born in London on May 11, 1901, and murdered in Kenya on January 24, 1941.

He was the eldest of his mother's three children and undeniably her favourite. Perhaps it was his excellent relationship with his mother that attracted him to older women when he was an adult. Like many other aristocrats reaching their majority in the Roaring Twenties, Josslyn had a somewhat complicated love life involving a wife, a main mistress and a subsidiary mistress.

Although he was born into a well-connected aristocratic family, they had relatively little money — and finance was a problem that hounded Erroll until his dying day. Their noble Scottish home of Slains had to be sold off and they moved — albeit reluctantly — to the south of England.

Show business was a lure as far as the Errolls were concerned, and Josslyn took a great interest in the technical and artistic side — a far cry from his decision to be a farmer in Kenya, but whether he was on stage, in the wings, or working his land, he was reliable and conscientious. His love of show business was one outlet for his exceptionally brilliant mind: passing his Diplomatic Service Examinations at a very high level was another. Whether in a lady's boudoir, an examination room, his desk in the Diplomatic Office, or a military operations room during World War II, Erroll always gave his all to whatever he was doing.

There were many theories about Erroll's murder. The problem was too many suspects with too many motives — rather than too few. As a consequence, no one was ever convicted, although suspects ranged from an indignant mob of outraged, vengeful husbands to state-sponsored assassins (even a British Special Operations Executive wireless operator).

What evidence is there?

Erroll's corpse was found in a rented car by two men driving a dairy truck. The auto's headlights were on full, dazzling the milk truck drivers' eyes because of the odd angle at which the car was wedged in a drainage ditch. Erroll's corpse was in a kneeling position in the passenger well at the front. His head was turned towards the door, and the .32-calibre bullet that had killed him had gone in behind his left ear. At first glance, it was not apparent that he had been shot; the obvious conclusion to be drawn was that the car had gone off the road accidentally for some reason — perhaps a brake or steering failure — and the driver had died as a result of the impact.

Geoff Timms, a local pathologist, happened to be driving past the scene at about 8 a.m. and stopped to see if medical help was needed. As the body was removed from the car under his direction, some serious trouble was encountered because the left foot was wedged under the accelerator. Once the body was clear of the vehicle, Timms recognized it as Lord Erroll's. At this point, no one had yet realized that Josslyn had been shot. It was not until his body was being washed in the mortuary that the wound and the bullet in his brain were discovered.

There was a vague report of a second set of tire tracks in the vicinity of the car Erroll had been driving, but this evidence was apparently never followed up, and the tracks do not seem to have been investigated properly. As far as can be ascertained, the car was not fingerprinted, and it was washed immediately after it was returned to the garage from which Josslyn had hired it. Curious onlookers with a macabre sense of occasion were actually allowed to sit in the car for effect before the police retrieved it from the garage. After all that, the investigation was doomed — not even Sherlock Holmes, Sexton Blake and Dr. Watson would have been able to help!

The body had been removed from the car without any proper examination being made or any detailed records kept. Vitally important opportunities to take forensic photographs were lost. It seems that only one or two photos were taken — the most important being one of the interior of the car with Erroll's body in its odd kneeling position on the floor. Some investigators commented on a powerful perfume lingering in the vehicle, but Erroll himself was known to use a scent. The Public Works Department was allowed to continue digging in the area, which must have disposed very effectively of several important potential clues. Their continuing excavations also pretty well neutralized the value of the few exterior pictures the police had taken.

The car, a large Buick, was fitted with arm slings, and its owners were certain that they had been securely in their correct places on either side of the Buick's back seat the day before. There was no way that they would have fallen out. Someone must have deliberately unscrewed them — but why? During the investigations, this curious little detail was never regarded as important, but whatever else might have happened to them, those arm slings didn't unfasten themselves. There were also some very distinctive pipe-clay marks on the back of the seat. They, too, might have provided significant evidence — but they were not investigated at all.

Superficially, the prime suspect was Sir Henry Delves Broughton. Also known as Jock Broughton, Sir Henry came to live in Kenya in November of 1940; his arrival was like that of a glowing match thrown into an explosives factory. Broughton's first wife had divorced him in 1939, and he had promptly proposed to the stylish, beautiful and aristocratic young Diana Caldwell. Diana piloted her own plane and ran a successful cocktail bar in Mayfair. Broughton was thirty-five years older than she was, but he overcame her hesitation by promising that if she met and fell in love with someone younger, he would grant her a divorce with no qualms and no rancour — and he would provide her and her new partner an income of £5,000 a year. A very conservative estimate would make that the equivalent of around £250,000 today. (Source: http://eh.net/hmit/ppowerbp/.) With a safety net like that to fall back on, Diana accepted him.

Diana was a talented and intelligent woman with confidence and courage to match her stylishness, but Broughton was definitely bad news.

He was dour, uninspiring and unpopular. The truth was often a stranger to him, and when he needed money, he was prepared not merely to bend the rules but to tie them in a Gordian knot!

The effervescently attractive Diana met and fell in love with the seemingly irresistible Erroll almost as soon as the mismatched Broughtons reached Kenya. She told Sir Henry that she wanted to exercise her marital escape clause — but Broughton at that time was a man of straw. There was no way he could produce the stipend he had promised her.

On the evening of January 23, 1941, Sir Henry decided to throw a farewell party for Diana at Kenya's fashionable Muthaiga Country Club. The other guests were Erroll and a friend named June Carberry. Later events suggested that June had been invited either as some sort of chaperone, or to provide Broughton with an alibi. Bizarre as the whole thing seemed, Broughton actually proposed a toast to Erroll and Diana. Behaving more like a protective father than an abandoned husband, Sir Henry asked Erroll to make sure that Diana was safely home by 3 a.m. The lovers then left the Muthaiga club to go dancing. In this Kafkaesque Kenyan world of the 1940s, Erroll chivalrously complied with Broughton's request and duly brought Diana home at around 2:30 a.m. It was less than an hour later that the two dairymen discovered the Buick with Erroll's corpse in its anomalous position in the well on the passenger side.

As the prime suspect, Broughton was in a similar position to Lizzie Borden — a load of circumstantial evidence indicated that he had been in the vicinity and had had the opportunity to carry out the killing. In Sir Henry's case, two of the most powerful motives known to the human race also highlighted him as Erroll's probable murderer: jealousy and revenge.

The sensational trial began on March 10, 1941, and ended on May 26. Broughton testified that he had tapped on June Carberry's door twice on the night of the murder: once at around 2 a.m. and again at 3:30. As an alibi, this was about as convincing as telephoning the speaking clock! In any case, he could easily have slipped out, murdered Erroll and got home in time for the second contact with June Carberry.

There is some evidence to suggest that June Carberry admitted much later to lying under oath during the trial in order to protect Broughton. She testified that she had heard Broughton walk past her bedroom door during the night at roughly the time when Erroll was killed. She appears to have thought that Sir Henry committed the crime, but explained that she did not want to see him convicted and hanged.

Broughton also reported — predictably — that his pair of .32-calibre revolvers had been stolen a few days before the murder. The prosecution theory was that Broughton had concealed himself in the Buick while Erroll was enjoying a passionate goodnight kiss and warm embrace with the lovely Diana. Sir Henry was thought to have waited until Josslyn slowed down, and then shot him. The missing arm slings came into the plot when Sir Henry was alleged to have held on to them — thus tearing them away from the bodywork — as the car jolted to a halt. Broughton's barrister, Henry Harris Morris, was an acknowledged expert in ballistics, and he soon made it unequivocally clear that the bullet that killed Erroll could not have been discharged from either of Broughton's guns. Their convenient disappearance was said to have been due to yet another timely robbery.

It is significant that Broughton never appeared to be in the least worried about the trial proceedings or their outcome. In fact, he expressed surprise that he should ever have been regarded as a suspect worthy of arrest. It was almost as though someone very highly placed in a clandestine "old boy network" had tipped off Broughton that it would be expedient for him — as a wronged husband — to be the prime suspect, to divert attention from the cold, sinister, political truth. This parallels the Mayerling situation, in which the idea of a melodramatic lovers' suicide pact involving Prince Rudolph and Maria Vetsera was almost certainly seen by Taaffe's homicidal secret agents as a convenient diversion from the political assassination that they had actually carried out on Taaffe's orders.

A simple lack of substantive evidence, or skulduggery between highly placed legal fixers? For whatever cause, Broughton was duly acquitted, although there were highly suspicious findings among the remains of rubbish that he had burned soon after the murder: these finds included part of a bloodstained sock and some charred trainers.

Just as Broughton had celebrated Diana's impending departure with Erroll by throwing a "farewell party" for them, so now he again used the Muthaiga Club as a venue to celebrate his acquittal. His membership was promptly cancelled.

Broughton's life went steadily downhill after Erroll's death. He went to Sri Lanka for a while. Then Diana left him, accusing him of Erroll's murder — whatever the official Kenyan court verdict might have been. Sir Henry returned disconsolately to the U.K. in 1942, and an old fraud charge from 1938 was resurrected and brought against him. He was

Lord Erroll, killed in his car.

alleged to have defrauded an insurance company over two robberies: the so-called "Broughton Pearls" and some paintings. The thefts had netted him a considerable sum at a time when his financial tide was at one of its recurring low ebbs. It was later alleged that one of his friends had carried out the robberies on Broughton's behalf. Once again, lack of evidence — or powerful, hidden protectors in high places — led to a questionable acquittal. Sir Henry then quarrelled with his son over the family estate — which Sir Henry had apparently "milked" so extensively and illegally that there was little or nothing left to pass on. Finally, Broughton took an overdose in the Adelphi Hotel in Liverpool, taking the real facts about Erroll's death to the grave with him.

Could Broughton's hypothetical high-level guardians grown tired of covering an operative who was becoming less and less reliable? He alone could have answered the question as to whether or not he had killed Josslyn Hay, and perhaps the real killers didn't want Sir Henry to talk to the wrong people in the wrong place at the wrong time.

There is some evidence to suggest that Sir Henry told an acquaintance of his, Alan Horne, that he had given Erroll his just deserts for stealing Diana. He might also have made a similar boast to June Carberry's daughter, Juanita, who was only in her teens when Erroll died. According to the Horne version, Broughton claimed that he and another enemy of Erroll's (presumably another angry husband) had paid a hit man £1,000 to do the job for them. Juanita allegedly said that Broughton had told her he had thrown his guns into a deep pool below the Thika Falls, where the police could never hope to retrieve them — thus implying that he, rather than a hired gunman, had shot Erroll.

Both of Sir Henry's so-called confessions have a suspiciously hollow ring to them. They sound more like the clumsy, unsubtle fictions invented by a rejected, depressed and disappointed man trying to convince his listeners and himself that he has the necessary guts to kill the man who has dared to steal his wife. The "confessions" might also have been a pathetic attempt to gain popularity, for Sir Henry had the appearance of a bleak and lonely man at this period.

The philandering Erroll was lower than zero in the popularity stakes in Kenya. To claim that you are the man who got rid of the hornets' nest, the skunk colony, or the rattlesnakes, is to win the approval and friendship of those who were also troubled by those snakes, hornets and skunks.

In the brilliantly plotted western film *Paper Gunman*, an unscrupulous journalist created a legend by attributing every unsolved shooting for miles around to an intellectually challenged drifter. This sad and unfortunate man — desperate to create a powerful, dangerous image of himself and so win respect — finally came to believe the propaganda the journalist had created around him. Consequently, the paper gunman picked a fight with a real gunman who, albeit rather reluctantly, felt forced to kill him in self-defence. Was Broughton another paper gunman, trying to cover his inadequacies by creating an image of himself as a murderously vengeful and jealous husband who commanded respect because he had eliminated the wife-seducer everyone hated?

If this theory is correct, things didn't work out the way that Sir Henry had hoped. He was ostracized in Kenya, and received numerous unpleasant anonymous letters. The typewriter on which they had been created was never traced.

But if Sir Henry Broughton didn't shoot Erroll, who did — and why? Among the many suspicious cover-ups that surrounded Erroll's death was the downright alacrity with which his secretary cleared his filing cabinet and desk of all his personal correspondence before the police had a chance to see it. Again, the burning question is why.

As if to lend credence to the Alan Horne story, that a hit man had been paid to kill Josslyn Hay, Broughton's Somali chauffer vanished immediately after Erroll's murder. No attempt was made to trace him, and he never resurfaced after that fatal January 23, 1941. Perhaps the Horne story was true after all? Maybe Broughton and a fellow conspirator had paid Sir Henry's chauffeur to do something more than drive the limo.

Or was Broughton himself trying very discreetly to drop gentle hints to close and trusted family members that, far from being a murderer, he was acting as a loyal and cooperative servant of the Crown? His letter to his Aunt Evelyn after the trial was satisfactorily completed was dated July 29, 1941. Part of that letter is alleged to read: "I was just a victim of unfortunate circumstances, some clever person, or persons, took advantage of an unrivalled opportunity for getting rid of Erroll and most successfully throwing all suspicion on me."

Could that mysterious "clever person or persons" have been connected with the highest echelons of government? Had someone very high in official circles made the decision that Erroll needed to be silenced — permanently, and in the most effective way known? With jealous husband Broughton as the decoy-suspect to draw attention away from any political motivation, it would have been very easy for a professional killer to dispose of Erroll.

It has already been noted that Broughton was reported as almost enjoying the trial. Clearly, he knew in advance that everything had been squared in his favour. What was very odd indeed, however, was that his supposedly unhappy wife, Lady Diana, who ought to have been in mourning for her dashing new lover Erroll (with whom she had seemingly been on the point of eloping), went cheerfully from Kenya to South Africa and purchased an entire new wardrobe specially for the trial.

Could this possibly mean that Diana and Broughton were really secret agents, working together in the pay of the British government? Had they been sent to Kenya specifically to eliminate Erroll? It would have been the ideal set-up. Josslyn would have been certain to fall for Diana, and that would have provided Broughton with a highly visible, personal motive to murder him — thus taking attention away from any consideration of a political reason for Erroll's death.

Walter Harragin was the Prosecuting Attorney General at Broughton's trial. According to information alleged to have come from Walter Harragin's son, Lee, Broughton teased Harragin after the trial, saying, "You know, that I know, that you know, that I did it."

Could Harragin — and perhaps the judge as well — have been part of the old boy network that destroyed Erroll and let Broughton off the hook? How does all this square with Sir Henry's supposed suicide? Broughton, even though he had chronic money problems and had quarrelled with Diana and his son, seems to have been far too tough a character ever to have contemplated suicide. He would, in extremis, have been far more likely to kill someone else than to take his own life. Which sinister top politician was hiding in the shadows in the early 1940s, ruthlessly deciding that Broughton had to be sent the same way as Erroll, just in case he said too much about Erroll's murder and the real reasons behind it?

Erroll's death, like Caesar's in Shakespeare's Roman tragedy, illustrated the view that:

> The evil that men do lives after them
> The good is oft interred with their bones.

Erroll's reputation certainly went from bad to worse after the assassin's bullet ended his philandering career, but it seems probable that his enemies — personal, political or both — wanted to depict him as a useless womanizer who was incapable of any worthwhile work or any helpful act for someone in difficulties. This was frankly not true. He may not have been the most ethical man on the planet, but many of his contemporaries were worse. Erroll can probably best be described as misguided and irresponsible, but he was also brilliantly intelligent and very conscientious at work. He held a seat representing the constituency of Kiambu on the Legco — the Legislative Council of Kenya — but his death did not receive the public recognition that a Legco member would normally have been accorded.

Isher Dass was a member of this same council. He was originally from the Punjab and had an English wife — which was rare in those days. Isher was a friend of Erroll's, although it did not mean they automatically agreed. In some ways Dass was not unlike Erroll in character: he liked female company, was confident and flamboyant — and did not hesitate to support and speak up for important issues he believed in. The Indians in Kenya considered Dass to be very much on the side of the people. Some of the wealthy European settlers disapproved of him, and found his support of what they thought of as "ordinary" people irritating.

Isher Dass was murdered eighteen months after Erroll's death. He was killed in the same way — a bullet in the head — and his murder, like Erroll's, was never solved.

As a representative, Isher Dass was almost certainly involved to a greater or lesser extent in the investigation of Erroll's murder: perhaps his ability and persistence began to unearth something that the sinister behind-the-scenes powers wanted concealed. It may simply have been that Isher used his official position to put pressure on the police to work harder to bring his friend's killer to justice. The police investigations into the Erroll case seem to have left much to be desired. It is tempting to ask whether they had been secretly instructed to make sure the crime was never solved. Almost unbelievably, no one even bothered to rope off the crime scene. A second set of tire tracks was ignored and rendered useless as evidence because several people walked over them on the wet ground. More crucial evidence was lost when the body was moved.

A motor engineer named J. E. Butcher thought that the car's speed could not have been more than eight miles an hour when it hit the section of ground that brought it to a halt. He went so far as to venture the opinion that it might even have been pushed into that position. The Buick's hand brake was off. Butcher also discovered a cigarette butt with blood on it, and a hairpin in the same condition. Was it possible that a female assassin had fired the fatal shot into Josslyn's brain?

According to one set of records it seems that Erroll's body had not reached the medical laboratory until after 9 a.m. The senior government pathologist, Dr. Vint, then began to examine it. As part of their procedure, his assistant was mopping blood from behind the corpse's left ear when he found the bullet wound. Vint promptly telephoned the police.

Oddly, these medical laboratory details seem to contradict a parallel version of events. It was said that Leslie Condon, manager at the Grange Park Dairy where the two milk truck drivers worked, had noticed the bullet wound and personally told Assistant Inspector Frederick Smith, on duty at the Kilimani police station. Smith, on the other hand, said that he had received a telephone call. No one asked him in court to explain the apparent discrepancy about the gunshot wound report. Dr. Vint testified that death would have been immediate, and, as Erroll had been right-handed, suicide was highly unlikely — if not actually physically impossible.

Errol Trzebinski, in her superbly authoritative and meticulously detailed work *The Life and Death of Lord Erroll*, reports that she was able to obtain information from a very well-concealed informant to the effect that Erroll's death was part of a secret operation called "Highland Clearance." It was alleged that Erroll had been involved with Oswald Mosley's fascists and possessed information that could be extremely embarrassing and damaging to the British government. This highly confidential material which Erroll was alleged to have held was supposed to have concerned a scheme the British government had reportedly considered very early in the war. The gist of this secret plan, had it really existed, was to try to make a deal with certain German generals, depose Hitler and institute a new alignment of states that was to be called the Nordic Alliance. The Nordic Alliance's purpose, were it ever formed, would be to fight the Soviet Union. Economic and political advantages — in addition to the military ones — were foreseen. Had the plan succeeded, it envisaged that the U.K. and the dominions would not fight Germany or other partners of the Rome-Berlin Axis.

It was also hypothesized that this alleged plan was somehow connected with Rudolf Hess's otherwise totally inexplicable landing in the U.K. Significantly, the Duke of Windsor was also mentioned in relation to it.

An integrated rationale can be observed behind these allegations. There were insidious whispers that the Duke of Windsor was supposed to have had some sympathy towards certain Nazi ideas. Erroll was believed to have been a friend, supporter and admirer of Oswald Mosley. Was it possible that the British government had ever considered removing Hitler and doing a deal with the German generals? To what extent might Hess's visit have been connected with all this?

The Duke of Windsor's name crops up persistently during research into the mystery of Lord Erroll's death. While the duke was governor of the Bahamas, two of his eminent friends, Lord Rothermere and Sir Harry Oakes, both died there. Oakes was a multimillionaire who had made a substantial part of his vast fortune through an incredibly lucky gold strike in northern Ontario, in Canada. Rothermere's so-called "breakdown" was suspicious: he died on November 26, 1940.

Oakes's charred and battered remains were discovered on July 8, 1943. (His death is the epicentre of another sinister, unsolved murder mystery covered in depth in another chapter.) Just as Broughton provided an ideal prime suspect in Lord Erroll's case but was acquitted, so Oakes's son-in-law, Fred de Marigny, provided an ideal prime suspect for the Oakes murder — and Fred was also acquitted. Another very odd parallel was that, just as Broughton had been unpopular with those who thought of themselves as the elite in Kenya, so de Marigny was unpopular with those who regarded themselves as the elite in the Bahamas.

Another important factor in the Erroll case was that Josslyn was chronically short of money. Is it possible that he tried to extort hush money from the British government in return for keeping quiet about their supposed consideration of the alleged scheme to form a Nordic Alliance with Germany and Scandinavia? History has taught many a pragmatic government that the most effective way to deal with blackmail is to eliminate the blackmailer, his associates and all traces of evidence.

The complexities of the plots and counterplots were considerable, but in essence it was believed that Oswald Mosley, the British fascist leader in the 1930s and '40s, had put Erroll in touch with a sinister, ultra-right-wing cabal. This included influential establishment figures ranging from Anglican and Roman Catholic church leaders, through top civil servants, high-ranking police officers and Foreign Office officials, to senior people in the armed services. It was alleged that this powerful, clandestine organization had been in direct contact with Germany and with von Ribbentrop, the German ambassador to the U.K. from 1937 until 1939. These furtive, surreptitious negotiations stopped when war broke out in 1939, but it was alleged that the work continued in a modified form via the German ambassador in Stockholm.

Lord Moyne, who was secretary of state to the colonies during 1941–42, was also thought to have been involved. His connection with Broughton was that he had had an affair with Sir Henry's first wife, Vera, and in some circles it had been expected that they would marry in due course. Moyne, however, met a violent death in Cairo in 1944, which was officially blamed on Jewish terrorists — but in view of what happened to Erroll, Dass, Oakes, Rothermere and Broughton, there could well have been different killers involved.

An alternative theory about Erroll's death is also perfectly tenable: far from being a dubious, untrustworthy blackmailer, he could equally well have been involved with secret service work for the British government all along — perhaps as a double agent to keep an eye on Mosley and his group — and it was not the British Special Operations Executive that killed Josslyn Hay but German agents. Erroll had a photographic memory and kept very few files and notes in his office. It is possible that someone very high up was frightened in case Erroll had seen something he shouldn't have, and that that same someone was homicidally nervous in case he remembered it — and talked about it!

The key to Erroll's mysterious unsolved murder may well be fastened to the same key ring as the key to the mysterious deaths of Sir Harry Oakes and Lord Rothermere in the Bahamas while the Duke of Windsor was governor there.

24

THE MYSTERY OF SIR HARRY OAKES

On the morning of July 8, 1943, the burned, battered body of multi-millionaire Sir Harry Oakes was found on the bed in his luxurious home in Nassau in the Bahamas. His wife and four of the Oakes children had already left for their summer home at Bar Harbour, but Harold Christie, whom Oakes had known for years and trusted as a friend, was supposedly sleeping in a nearby room. Christie later gave evidence that he had heard nothing unusual during the night of the murder.

The subsequent police investigation and autopsy results were as curiously ineffective and suspicious as those surrounding the death of Lord Erroll in Kenya. The plane carrying Oakes's body, for example, was recalled because the investigators wanted some additional photographs. The official autopsy report gave the cause of death as a blow — or series of blows — from a blunt instrument. There were also, apparently, four neat, small-calibre bullet holes through the mastoid bone below Oakes's right ear. During the autopsy, the skull was not opened to search for the four bullets that should have been somewhere inside it. That skull is now with the rest of Sir Harry's mortal remains in his crypt in the East Dover Cemetery in Dover-Foxcroft, Maine.

Oakes's son-in-law, Freddie de Marigny, was the prime suspect and — much as Sir Henry Broughton had been in the Erroll case — was tried and acquitted. He reportedly said that a doctor in Nassau had told him of the existence of the four bullet holes that contradicted the blows-to-the-head conclusion drawn at the postmortem. It is interesting to recall that Erroll was also shot with a small calibre weapon, and that the bullet that killed him also came in from behind and below the ear. The same grim professionalism would appear to have been the common denominator.

The Duke of Windsor, who was the governor of Bahamas at the time when Sir Harry was murdered, did not request the help of expert investigators from the FBI or Scotland Yard. Instead, he sent for two Miami detectives he knew personally, as they had been assigned to him as bodyguards when he had visited Florida. They were Captain Edward Melchen of homicide and Captain James Barker, the supervisor of the police crime laboratories there.

Who exactly was Sir Harry Oakes?

He was born in Sangerville, Maine, on December 23, 1874, the third of the five children of William and Edith Pitt Oakes, whose family had been in Maine since at least 1808. The family moved from Sangerville to Foxcroft so that their children could benefit from the schools there. Harry studied at Bowdoin College in Brunswick, then completed two years at Syracuse Medical School in upstate New York.

The iron core that marks most self-made millionaires became apparent in Harry when he was just twenty-three. In 1897, he abandoned his studies and set out for Seattle. His family were supportive of the move: his elder brother was running a lumber business and promised to send young Harry $75 a month to cover the essentials; his mother gave him money from her savings; his sister promised to send all she could afford from her wages as a secretary in New York. Part of Harry's success came from his own unconquerable self-confidence; another vital part came from his family's reinforcing faith in him. The most important element of all was his absolute determination never to give up his quest.

Harry went to Skagway, Alaska, in 1898, where he worked as a medical assistant. The Alaskan gold rush was waning by the time he got there. During the next few years, he prospected in Dawson City, got shipwrecked off the Alaskan coast — but somehow survived — and was even imprisoned by Tsarist Russia. Later travels took him to Alaska once more, then all the way to what was then the Belgian Congo in Africa.

His big break came in January of 1912, when he made friends with the well-named Tough brothers: George, Tom, Bob and Jack. A group of mining claims near Kirkland Lake, Ontario, were up for grabs because the prospector who had originally staked them had not done sufficient work to maintain his right to them as "active" workings. Harry and the Tough brothers battled their way through temperatures of fifty degrees below zero to stake their claims — they were just three hours ahead of their nearest rival. Life was still a battle for Sir Harry, but he was on the first rung of the ladder that was to make him a multi-millionaire.

Within eight years, Sir Harry was the richest man in Canada. His Lake Shore Mine at Kirkland Lake was second only to the fabulously productive Homestead Mine in the Black Hills of Dakota. In the early 1930s, Sir Harry's income was $60,000 a day — it would be necessary to multiply that by more than 100 to get a rough twenty-first-century equivalent.

A round-the-world cruise took him to Australia, where he met and fell in love with beautiful young Eunice McIntyre. They were married in Sydney on June 30, 1923. She was twenty-six years younger than Sir Harry — and noticeably taller than the stocky multi-millionaire. Eunice was one of the few people who could penetrate Harry's rock-hard outer personality to find and release the goodness and generosity that were an integral part of the real Oakes. They came home to live in Canada, on his Kirkland Lake estate.

In 1924, Sir Harry became a Canadian citizen and did vast amounts of good work for the unemployed in the Niagara Falls area during the grim years of the Depression. His kindness and great generosity — undoubtedly encouraged and nurtured by Eunice — are still remembered there with much affection and gratitude. Sir Harry deliberately created jobs when work could make the difference between life and death. And he created them indiscriminately: his foreman, Ed McClement, was told to turn no one away, regardless of age or ability. The going rate was $2 for a half-day's work with a shovel, and one of Sir Harry's idiosyncrasies was to insist that the wages be paid with two-dollar bills. Sometimes Ed McClement had to scour the town to find enough of them!

Sir Harry was also a great advocate of sports and games, and of recreational facilities for public use. In a typical example, he gave sixteen acres

Sir Harry Oakes,
Canadian millionaire.

of land at the corner of Morrison Street and Stanley Avenue to the people of Niagara Falls to be used as an athletic field. The construction of the necessary facilities on that site had the added advantage of providing more work for the unemployed.

Sir Harry and his family then moved to the tax haven of Nassau, where his charitable gifts continued in full flow. He built a waterworks and a golf course, set up a charity to help single mothers, provided a public bus service and an air service to deal with medical emergencies. He also laid on free milk for children.

In addition to all his generosity in Niagara Falls and the Bahamas, Sir Harry gave $400,000 to help St. George's Hospital in London. A grateful King George V recognized that gift — and Harry's many other good works — with the baronetcy that made him Sir Harry Oakes.

On the night of July 8, 1943, everything came to an end. The great man's burnt and battered body left behind it a murder mystery that is as far from being solved today as it was then.

Freddie de Marigny had arrived in the Bahamas with the reputation of being something of a playboy, and with two marriages already history as far as he was concerned. In 1942, he married Sir Harry's eldest daughter, Nancy, who was then barely eighteen. The ceremony was conducted almost in secret in the Bronx County Courthouse. Freddie and Nancy queued up with a line of GIs and their prospective spouses. Meanwhile, Sir Harry and Eunice were relaxing in Bar Harbour, Nassau. When Nancy's parents were informed of the marriage, Sir Harry took the news surprisingly well. He is reputed to have asked Nancy, "How much money do you want?" She replied, "Nothing!" Freddie was a very competent and effective sailor, and a successful businessman in his own right. When Sir Harry offered Freddie a directorship in the Lake Shore Mine, Freddie declined.

Their relationship started unexpectedly well, but it slowly deteriorated. By July 1943, when Sir Harry was killed, it was widely known that the two men disliked each other. Freddie, meanwhile, had incurred the hostility and jealousy of the Bahamian elite, largely because his superior seamanship had beaten them in their beloved yacht races, and because he treated all men as equals regardless of their race, creed or colour.

At the trial, it was brought out that Oakes had quarrelled loudly with Freddie on the night of the murder, but the case against de Marigny was so slender that he was acquitted in less than two hours.

Much more serious evidence seemed to point to Harold Christie, Harry's so-called friend. This evidence included a statement by Edward Sears, a Bahamian police officer who testified that on the night of the murder he had seen a station wagon driving along George Street around midnight. The front-seat passenger had looked remarkably like Harold Christie — supposedly asleep in bed in a room not far from Sir Harry's. There were further allegations that the two night watchmen at the Oakes estate had seen a vehicle arrive at the house just after midnight; two men had allegedly alighted from it; the watchmen heard several shots and then saw flames in Sir Harry's room. The security men were then said to have seen two men running from the house back to the car, and they were further said to have reported that they could see a third man in the car quite clearly — allegedly, they identified that man as Harold Christie.

According to de Marigny, who said he got the information from one of the watchmen years after the killing, Christie had paid the men to leave Nassau and never return. A further element in the allegations against

Christie concerned a report to the effect that the local harbourmaster had been found floating — apparently drowned — in the harbour. This was odd, to say the least, because according to the report he was an experienced swimmer and diver. If the allegations are correct, the dead harbourmaster was the only witness to the furtive, nocturnal arrival of a boat shortly before midnight. Putting all of these reported sightings together creates an interesting but very sinister theoretical scenario. With Christie in the role of Judas, leading the killers to his erstwhile friend Sir Harry, it seems highly probable that hired gangsters — possibly from the Florida underworld — actually carried out the hit on the multi-millionaire.

The question of motive remains, and here again the allegations parallel Lord Erroll's murder in Kenya. According to de Marigny's theories, Christie, Oakes and the Duke of Windsor had all been involved in a colossal conspiracy to smuggle millions of American dollars in directions that defied the strict wartime currency regulations. Christie might have killed Oakes out of sheer greed, or because he thought that Sir Harry might be thinking of tearing the wraps off the scheme. Whistle-blowing, however, doesn't seem to have been Sir Harry's style. It seems much more likely that Oakes had been doing some careful checking up and found that one, or perhaps both, of his associates had been embezzling his share. If Christie discovered that Sir Harry had found something incriminating, that would have been motive enough. If, as was alleged, the Duke of Windsor, as governor, had been protecting Christie, it is small wonder that he was never arrested and tried for Sir Harry's murder. De Marigny also alleged that his own life had been threatened on at least two occasions — even a considerable time after the murder.

Perhaps the most intriguing mystery of all is what happened to Sir Harry's missing millions. Only about $12 million was accounted for when he died — even a cautiously conservative estimate would have put his fortune at $300 million — an astronomical sum in twenty-first-century money!

25

THE MYSTERY OF ALBERT JOHNSON WALKER

Murder is not only the result of misdirected and uncontrolled emotions; in certain strange cases it also generates a wide range of profound, but seemingly contradictory and paradoxical, sentiments. Very rightly, we feel deep, natural sympathy for the victims, their loved ones and friends. There is also considerable bafflement and bewilderment concerning an alleged murderer's real character and motivations. We feel justifiable and implacable anger at the atrocities committed, and absolute determination that society must be protected, permanently and effectively, from such appalling killers and their crimes. Finally, there is consideration for the murderer's own innocent family and friends.

The psychopathic murderer frequently causes deeper and wider grief than most. The Farmington Trust's experts in the 1960s described psychopaths as "moral cripples, able to distinguish right and wrong — but only cognitively, never emotionally." Dr. Robert Hare of the University of British Columbia, today's leading world authority on psychopaths, is just as brilliant and unequivocal. His outstanding book *Without Conscience* defines psychopaths as: "Completely lacking in conscience … they selfishly take what they want and do as they please, violating social norms and expectations without the slightest sense of guilt or regret ..."

Because psychopaths think and behave as they do, it is extraordinarily difficult for police detectives, psychiatrists and criminologists to discover all the facts in cases where psychopaths are involved. This extreme difficulty certainly seems to apply in the convoluted case of Albert Johnson Walker.

Born on August 9, 1945, at Mountain Avenue Hospital in Hamilton, Ontario, Walker was convicted of murder in Exeter in England on July 6, 1998. His father was William G. Walker, and Albert was one of a family of five siblings — the others were all daughters. On Friday, October 25, 1968, Albert, then twenty-three, married Barbara McDonald, who came from a devout Scottish Presbyterian farming family. Their church in Ayr, Ontario, was known officially as Knox United, and Albert's apparent professional charm and ingratiating social skills not only won him membership, but he soon became an elder there as well. He always dressed smartly, and promptly volunteered to help with everything that was going on — although one or two of the more sagacious churchgoers noted that he rarely, if ever, actually turned up to help with the activities on which he had promised to work. He became an especial favourite of his mother-in-law, Hilda, and it was remarked on by some friends and neighbours in Ayr that she made more fuss over Albert Walker than her own son.

In his deeply perceptive children's books on Narnia, C. S. Lewis makes singularly observant comments on two of the villains — the sinister White Witch and Uncle Andrew. Lewis says that witches and magicians are very practical: they only bother with people when they want to use them, or to get something out of them. The same comments were allegedly made about Albert Walker. It was thought that he was interested only in people he believed would be of use to him. Although his religion was apparently only superficial, he liked to create the image of a committed Christian, one who could be trusted completely in business and commercial ventures. That seems to have given him an edge when it came to pulling off one deceptive confidence trick or swindle after another.

Many of Walker's victims had come into his social orbit through his church connections. Throughout all of his highly questionable dealings, Barbara, his wife, seems to have been loyal and protective towards him. In her eyes, Albert was perfection clad in human form: he could do no wrong of any kind. He and Barbara produced three daughters and a son: Jillian,

*Albert Walker, alias
David Davies, alias
Ronald Platt.*

born January, 19, 1972; Sheena, born July 28, 1975; Duncan, born June 25, 1979; and Heather, born June 14, 1982.

They had a bookkeeping business in Ayr, and in 1980 Walker bought Oxford Bookkeeping, in Woodstock, from Al Boggs, who was getting on in years and considering retirement. Al was honest and reliable and had run the business well for over two decades. Walker was keen for Boggs to stay on as a consultant, or in an advisory capacity — entirely for Albert's benefit, so that he could trade on Al's good name and established reputation. It was alleged that Jim Wilhelm, a young finance expert, began to see that Walker had feet of clay, and tried to warn others about him — but, unfortunately, no one at the time took much notice of Jim's warnings.

Confidence tricksters, "stingers" and fraudsters, as Walker was alleged to be, usually tend to operate in a particular style. They go to great lengths to dress smartly and always take pains to be well groomed. They effervesce with what seem like good ideas for making money. They are persistent in their approaches to their victims, and always appear opulent. They flash money about ostentatiously, and at the start of every scam they honour all their cheques and make a point of paying up front. Having demonstrated that their moneymaking ideas clearly work, they offer the victim "an investment opportunity." The trap is sprung and the victim loses heavily — sometimes millions of dollars.

Walker apparently blew his church cover when he was alleged to have had an affair with a minister's wife, but despite that peccadillo he apparently performed a major trick on two of his church acquaintants. At the heart of the situation was a parcel of land that had been in the seller's family since 1812. It seems that Walker was able to initiate a bidding war between two keen rival property developers. As a result, the Staleys sold their land for over $5 million, and so did the Richardsons. Both turned to Walker for "investment advice" and lost everything shortly afterwards. By the time he was tried for murder in Exeter, England, in 1998, records indicated that Walker could have been responsible for embezzling well over $10 million during his career as a confidence man.

From being unquestioningly loyal, and oblivious to any imperfections Walker might have had in the beginning, Barbara had now had enough of his strange lifestyle, and there was an acrimonious divorce. Once again, it appeared that Albert's charming façade had triumphed, because all the children expressed a preference to be with him rather than their mother. The final outcome was that Sheena, their second daughter, born in 1975, left Canada with her father in 1990. Walker seems to have made adequate financial provision for their travels: $20,000 apparently went from his Crédit Suisse account in Toronto to his private account in Switzerland. He also manipulated another $23,000 in Swiss francs. By taking out a second mortgage on his Canadian home, he was thought to have shipped a further $90,000 to Europe. Records indicated that about three-quarters of a million Canadian dollars left the country when Walker did. It is said that his Swiss bank provided the Canadian police with information — but refused to grant access to Albert's Swiss account.

It was reported that when Walker was arrested on October 3, 1996, for the murder of Ronald Platt, the remote farmhouse where Albert and Sheena lived contained gold bars, Scottish £20 bank notes totalling over £10,000, English notes in excess of £10,000, and some investment certificates. Later searches of the premises turned up rubber-stamp signatures in two different names, a credit card in the name of murder victim Ronald Platt, and a diploma in Platt's name — as well as several other very interesting pieces of evidence, including driver's licences and business cards. Walker said his name was David Davis, but when his fingerprints were sent to Interpol it seemed that they matched those of a certain Albert Johnson Walker who was wanted by the police in both Canada and the United States. It emerged in later investigations that there was a real David Davis, and that he had once approached one of Walker's finance companies for a loan. Walker had asked for his birth certificate in connection with the transaction and, as he had also kept Davis's books at one time, was aware of his social security number. The real Davis was English by birth — an ideal situation for Walker if he planned to impersonate Davis and settle in the U.K. Davis was a tall man with brown hair and brown eyes. So was Walker — and so was Platt.

What is known, or hypothesized, about Ronald Joseph Platt, the murder victim?

He was generally thought of as a mild-mannered type, not in the least aggressive; he was rather shy, and did not find it easy to mix, or meet new people. He seems to have spent his younger years in Canada, and had been very keen to go back there. An attempt to settle in the 1980s failed because he had neither a visa nor a work permit. He tried again in 1987, but returned to the U.K. because he wanted to be with his girlfriend, Elaine Boyes. It was through her, ironically, that Platt was introduced to the man who was later convicted of his murder!

Ron's father, Eric Platt, had once worked as a teacher in Saskatchewan, but as soon as he was old enough, Ron had left Canada and gone to England, where he had served for a while in the British Army. His elder brother Brian spoke well of him, adding that Ron was a bit of a loner. Platt had married in 1965, and a son, Malcolm, was born to him in 1967. Sadly, the marriage ended in divorce a few years later, and Platt seems to have lost touch with that part of his family. He left the army in 1973, having learned about electronics and radio and TV engineering. With these relevant, modern skills behind him, Platt worked for DER Ltd. for a while, and then ventured out into contract work on radios, TVs and videos.

Walker encountered Elaine Boyes in 1989 when she was employed by Spencer's, the Harrogate auctioneers. Walker used the name of David Davis when he met her, and claimed to be a financier from the States. His cover story to Elaine was that he had just got in from Geneva and was looking for a suitable house in Harrogate. In Elaine's opinion, he was an exceptionally charming person. Shortly afterwards, he offered her a job as his personal assistant, and when she explained to him that her boyfriend,

Ronald Platt, was hoping to relocate in Canada, Walker convinced her that if she worked for him, she would soon be able to afford it.

Subsequently, she arranged a meeting with Platt at Walker's suggestion, and — superficially, at least — the two men seemed to form positive opinions of each other. Walker again asked Elaine to work for him, offering her a salary of £12,000 a year compared to the £9,000 she was earning with her auctioneering employers. On May 10, 1991, she left Spencer's and went to work for Walker.

Still thinking that Walker was Davis, she and Platt accepted directorships in his company, which he called the Cavendish Corporation. Odd conditions were attached to the company's banking arrangements: Elaine could sign cheques, but Platt could not, and cheques were not to be made out to Davis. He explained that this was because his Canadian wife was taking him to court in connection with alimony and child support payments.

Walker's apparent Munchausen syndrome, or factitious illness, reportedly led to his creation of strange fantasies about meetings with former President Ronald Reagan and the entertainer Rod Stewart. Elaine had no real idea of what he was up to when he sent her to Italy, France and Switzerland to open bank accounts for him. It seems that he was using her mainly to launder his money and stash it away safely where the police would not be able to retrieve it without negotiating almost insurmountable banking obstacles first. At this stage in Walker's tortuous masquerade, he introduced Sheena as his teenaged daughter.

Platt was in need of employment again, so Walker set him up in a radio and TV repair shop, trading as Rutland Radio because it was situated in Rutland Road in Harrogate. It wasn't a good location, and the business proved unprofitable. It is tempting to ask whether Walker was losing a little of his financial edge at this juncture because in the past he had always had what seemed like a clear instinct for good commercial property locations.

Next, Walker offered to pay their fares to Canada, as that remained Platt's ambition. Elaine Boyes, Platt's girlfriend, wanted a return ticket so that she could attend her sister's wedding, scheduled for the following July. On February 22, 1993, Platt and Boyes flew to Calgary. It was not a successful visit. They felt that their small, detached house northwest of the city was bitterly cold; outdoor temperatures fell to well under minus-thirty degrees, and they hadn't got the proper winter clothing they so clearly needed.

When spring came, they still hadn't been able to find jobs, so they telephoned Walker for further help and advice. He suggested Vancouver might be better, but they had no success there, either. Elaine came back for her sister's wedding, as she'd planned. By this time it appeared that Davis (Walker) was finding her something of a trial, and his type of personality did not endure trials for any length of time. If people or circumstances did not suit him, he left. It was suggested that when Elaine Boyes came back to Harrogate and insisted on staying in the town despite all Walker's persuasion, it was Walker himself who decided to go: and Elaine was left with no other way to contact him than a post-office box number in London.

Understandably, she became very depressed, and sought professional medical help. By 1994, Elaine had tried a job in Italy, but that lasted only three months. Walker's exasperation with Elaine was compounded when Platt returned to the U.K. as well. Like Boyes, he was finding it very difficult to get work — and when he did land a job, he seemed to lose it after just a few weeks or months. The last Elaine heard of Platt, her erstwhile boyfriend, was in May of 1996. Subsequently, police investigators discovered that, rather suspiciously, Davis (alias Walker) had made numerous calls on his cellphone to a South Devon exchange with the routing code number 863. A local innkeeper reported that two men giving their names as Ronald and David Platt (the latter almost certainly Walker, using part of his David Davis alias) had stayed with him in July of 1996, and a local ferry operator said that he knew "a tall American or Canadian," adding that this man owned a boat moored on the River Dart.

When asked about Platt's whereabouts, Walker said that as far as he knew Ronald had gone to France. He had, in fact, gone to the bottom of the sea near Brixham in Devon, with a five-kilogram Sewester anchor tucked into his belt to accelerate his descent!

Platt's body was discovered by a fisherman named John Copik and his son Craig, known as "Bat." The date was July 28, 1996, and the two men were trawling with their boat *Malkerry* over a particularly difficult area known as "The Roughs." The seabed was rocky and dangerously uneven at this point, and the Copiks had adjusted the depth of their nets to keep them clear of the jagged rocks and so avoid damage.

When they hauled their nets up around lunchtime they found all that remained of Ronald Platt. He was fully clothed and his Rolex watch was still on his right wrist. Their profitable haul of fish was now no longer saleable, but the Copiks did their duty faithfully and well and brought the body ashore. They made all the proper routine legal reports that have to be made when a body is discovered at sea. They also commented on the small Sewester plough anchor that had been dredged up along with Platt and his Rolex. John Copik gave his opinion that the body could not have been in the water for any length of time as the eyes were still intact.

Dr. Robin Little, a police surgeon and coroner, examined Platt's body on Monday, July 30, 1996. He discovered a head wound and bruising on one hip. It looked as if Platt could have been knocked unconscious and fallen heavily to the deck before being thrown, still alive, over the side. Dr. Fernanda, a forensic pathologist, performed an autopsy and found the dead man's lungs full of water: Platt had been alive when he went into the sea — consequently, he had died of drowning. All the investigators were puzzled as to how and why the body had got so far out to sea — hardly likely if he had been struck down on shore and tipped into the nearest convenient harbour.

Platt's Rolex watch had a central part to play in the mystery. Some journalists actually nicknamed the case the "Rolex Murder." All Rolex watches are engraved with a unique identification code. Henry Hudson, the general manager of the Rolex company's operations in Kent, was able to inform the police that this particular watch, a Rolex Oyster Perpetual Chronometer, had been crafted in Geneva in 1967. It had been serviced on two occasions — in 1982 and 1986 — for its owner: Mr. Ronald Platt of Harrogate.

The next stage of the investigation was to look into local tax records and see whether they pointed to Platt — especially to dates when he had entered or left the country. It was reported that he had declared his intention of going to France and that this would mean he no longer had to pay local property taxes. He had asked for his mail to be forwarded to Little London Farmhouse in the hamlet of Woodham Walter in Essex — the same house where Walker, his teenaged daughter, Sheena, and her two small children were then living!

The next useful piece of information comes from Stephen Powl, who had been Platt's landlord. Powl recalled that he had received a tenancy reference for Platt from a Mr. David Davis (Walker's alias) — and he gave the police "Davis's" phone number. Walker, cool as a cucumber, duly kept his appointment at Chelmsford Police Station at 4:30 p.m. on August 22, 1996. He impressed the interviewing officers as being a distinguished-looking man of impeccable character (his alleged long-term success as a con artist in Canada and elsewhere would have depended on his appearance and style). He explained to the police that as far as he was aware Platt had probably gone to France, to the La Rochelle area. Things did not seem quite so bland and straightforward when Platt's luggage was found on premises that Walker rented.

Walker and Sheena were arrested on October 3, 1996. She had been known to their neighbours in Woodham Walter as Noel Platt and had been posing as Walker's wife while he was calling himself Ron Platt. This was the situation while they lived at Little London Farm.

Sheena was released and allowed to return to her mother in Canada. She flew out on December 9, 1996. The police investigators were satisfied that Sheena had had nothing to do with the murder: she had simply been a dominated victim rather than an accomplice to any of her father's alleged crimes.

When experienced RCMP investigators came over with their own well-directed enquiries to augment the good work already done by the British police, Walker refused to answer their questions. It is tempting to ask whether Walker's previous apparent ability to wrap a complex multitude of different identities, business deals, bank accounts, relationships and cover stories into one confidently coherent life bundle was finally waning. Against the brilliantly powerful cross-examination of prosecutor Charles Barton, one of the most formidable minds in the legal profession, it was apparent that Walker was totally outgunned and outclassed. If it had been a boxing match, Walker would have seemed like an inexperienced amateur mismatched with the world champion. By the end of July 2, 1998, there seemed to be very little left of the effervescent self-confidence that had always been Walker's hallmark. On July 6 he was convicted and sentenced for the murder of Ronald Joseph Platt.

Entering, exploring and analyzing the swirling, maelstrom mind of a psychopath with factitious illness, or Munchausen syndrome, means parachuting out of reality into a bewildering, kaleidoscopic montage of science fiction, fantasy and fairy tale. In spite of that, a few significant question marks still hover over the Platt murder case: did Albert Johnson Walker really kill Platt? Was murder within his capabilities? Did his psychological profile include the ability to kill?

Another very troublesome question arises over the difference between Walker's customary effectiveness and skill — however illegally and selfishly it was employed — and the amateurish, inefficient way in which the murder was allegedly carried out. If Walker had murdered Platt, it was uncharacteristically clumsy and bungled compared with his normal ingenuity. Was it so badly done that a man as effective as Walker could not possibly have made so many mistakes? Judge Butterfield, on the other hand, described the crime as "carefully planned and cunningly executed with chilling efficiency." So perhaps it was simply a series of unlucky accidents from Walker's point of view that led to his subsequent arrest and conviction.

Killing, again, is oddly out of character for Walker. One constant aspect of his inconstant life seems to have been escape and avoidance. He once said that he deplored violence, and on that occasion he sounded as if he was speaking the truth. Then there's the curious statement Walker made about having trouble with the boat and injuring himself. If he really wasn't a fighting man, perhaps those injuries he attributed to an accidental cause had been the result of a fight with Platt. If Walker had retaliated desperately in self-defence with anything that came to hand — perhaps even the fateful little Sewester anchor — he might well have tipped the unconscious Platt overboard; fighting and killing do not seem to sit lightly on what is known of Walker.

His style was to build a profitable, enjoyable fantasy, exploit people by using that fantasy and involving them in it with him — and then run away from it when it got out of control and threatened trouble. He seemed able to move from character to character, from one personality to another, as easily as most people move house. He changed identities, relationships and lifestyles as readily as most people change their clothes. An actor knows that he or she is not Lady Macbeth, Hamlet, Caesar, Cleopatra or Othello — but while on stage, or in front of the camera, the actor plays the role as if it is real. Offstage, back in the everyday world, the actor quickly reverts to being normal, happy, human John Brown or Josephine Green.

The psychopathic Munchausen personality cannot apparently discern that vital boundary where the stage play ends and the ordinary world begins. The creatively imaginative psychopath can glide effortlessly back and forth between fact and fiction, between stage and greenroom — like a nineteenth-century spectre gliding through the gas-lit wall of a séance room. For "normal" human beings, that wall is impenetrable; for some others, it is at best an almost imperceptibly flimsy curtain.

One of the gravest questions any human being has to face is the nature of his or her own identity: Who am I? What am I? We probe the external environment for feedback. Who do our families, friends, neighbours and work colleagues think we are? How accurate are their judgments? What sort of feedback do we get from them to reinforce — or contradict — our self-image? The most honest of us can never be entirely certain about our own motives. Do generous, unselfish people give their last few cents to buy a sandwich for a hungry beggar because they care about the beggar, or because they want to enjoy the feeling that they are good and unselfish people — and, as such, feel that they ought to be admired and rewarded by society? Social feedback is important, but so is introspection. Trying to assess our own motives honestly and objectively is not always easy. For the imaginative psychopath, it must be impossible.

The late Reverend Dr. W. E. Sangster, who did a tremendous amount of good work as a Methodist leader in the mid-twentieth century, wrote a little book called *A Spiritual Check-Up*. In it, he told of having given a coin he could ill afford in those days to a hungry beggar, and having felt very proud of his generosity. Suddenly, he realized that it was wrong to feel proud, because he believed that pride was a sin. He promptly repented for his pride. Next, he felt proud of having recognized his pride, and of having repented. Consequently, he felt proud of his repentance. Sangster recalled that this went on and on until finally his traditional British sense of humour came to his rescue: he was able to laugh at himself when he realized he was riding an introspective freight train made up of infinite alternatives — pride and humility represented the rough, uncomfortable wagons!

The volatile psychopath seems unable to emulate the good sense of a professional actor, or the introspective wisdom and humour of Dr. Sangster. He simply does not know who he really is, what he is trying to be, where he is trying to go, or whether the scenario he inhabits is real or imaginary.

It is not impossible that Ron Platt — a depressed and disappointed man — committed suicide.

Nor is it impossible that someone other than Walker killed him.

The trial was a very fair and balanced one; the circumstantial evidence against Walker was compelling; in the light of the evidence presented to them, the jury reached a sensible, logical verdict.

And yet the mystery lingers — was Walker away, inhabiting one of his many fantasy worlds elsewhere, when Platt either took his own life or was killed by someone else?

26

WAS JAMES HANRATTY GUILTY?

On April 4, 1962, James Hanratty was hanged for the murder of Michael John Gregsten, who died on the night of August 22, 1961. Gregsten, a thirty-six-year-old government scientist, and his girlfriend, twenty-two-year-old lab assistant Valerie Storie, were sitting together in Michael's grey Morris Minor on the edge of a cornfield at Dorney, near Slough in Buckinghamshire. At about 8:30 in the evening there was tap on the car window, and as Gregsten wound it down, a gun was pointed at him. The man who threatened Gregsten said that he was desperate and had been on the run for months. He added that if Gregsten and Valerie did as he told them they would not be harmed.

Their kidnapper ordered them to drive around in search of food and cigarettes. Gregsten secretly turned on his hazard lights, hoping to attract attention, but no one spotted them — or, if they did, they didn't think of it as anything but a careless oversight. The attacker threatened Valerie with the gun while Gregsten was ordered to get out and fetch cigarettes, milk from a vending machine, and later some gasoline. Because he was afraid that the intruder would kill her if he tried anything, Gregsten did as the man ordered and made no attempt to get help or raise the alarm. They drove for about thirty miles until they reached Deadman's Hill on the A6 motorway, where their captor ordered Gregsten to drive into a roadside picnic area. The exact details at this point are not absolutely precise. It seems, however, that while their abductor was tying Valerie's wrists, Gregsten made a desperate attempt to hit him with a duffel bag that was on the front seat. That move proved a fatal mistake: the gunman shot him twice in the head and he died instantly.

Valerie screamed abuse at Gregsten's killer and begged him to get a doctor for Michael. "Be quiet … I'm thinking," he snapped. In vitally important evidence that, rightly or wrongly, helped to convict Hanratty, Valerie remembered that the killer had pronounced "thinking" as "finking" — a treatment of the *th* sound typical of the London dialect. After a few minutes, the intruder demanded a kiss from Valerie, and as he bent forward towards her face, she got a clear look at him in the headlights of a passing car. She was then raped. After that, Gregsten's body was dragged out, and left at the rest stop.

The next part of the account is very curious indeed. Hanratty was an experienced professional thief. It is highly likely that he would have been conversant with most makes of car — especially one as popular as the Morris Minor was at the time. Professional criminals not only frequently steal cars to sell them, but to use them in robberies, ram-raids and for quick escapes. The man who had just killed Gregsten and raped Valerie didn't know how to drive the Morris Minor — and made her show him the gears and control switches. Hanratty, on the other hand, was an expert driver. (Another prime suspect, Peter Alphon, was not an experienced driver.)

At about 3:30 a.m. the killer fired his gun repeatedly into Valerie's body and kicked her after she had collapsed, as if to make certain that she was dead. He then drove off towards Luton. She was discovered in the morning — still alive, miraculously, but permanently paralyzed from the waist down. A student named John Kerr was one of the first on the scene and Valerie told him that the killer had "staring eyes": a description that supposedly tallied with Hanratty's appearance.

Gregsten's grey Morris Minor was later found abandoned at Ilford. The gun was recovered from its anonymous hiding place beneath the seat of a London bus, and two empty .38 cartridge cases turned up in a bedroom at the Vienna Hotel in Maida Vale, where both Hanratty and Peter Alphon had allegedly stayed in different rooms and — possibly — at dif-

*James Hanratty, alleged
to have shot
Michael Gregsten.*

ferent times. Their residence in the same hotel, however, seems to be either a very odd coincidence — or something more sinister.

Based on Valerie's description, an Identikit picture of the killer was widely published: but it did not jibe with a description of a man reported as having been seen driving Gregsten's car after the killing. A second picture was therefore published.

The next development came courtesy of Gregsten's widow. Following the publication of the pictures, she dramatically pointed out a man in the street and said she felt sure that he was her husband's murderer. The man she indicated was James Hanratty — even though he bore no close resemblance to either of the Identikit pictures! There is something approximating to the paranormal, or the strangely anomalous, in Mrs. Gregsten's sighting of James Hanratty. Jung would have noted it as synchronicity, or something more than coincidence.

Janet Gregsten, Michael's widow, had a brother-in-law, William Ewer, who owned an antique shop. Because of the tragedy that had overtaken Michael, William had invited Janet to stay for a few days. She was standing at the front of the antique shop, looking out through the window, when Hanratty walked past in the process of taking a suit to the cleaners. Janet then experienced what some researchers might describe as a psychic hunch and exclaimed to William: "That's the man! I've got an overpowering feeling that's him!"

Being a local shopkeeper himself, Ewer was able to check up later at the cleaners. He found that the man who had left the suit had called himself Ryan. William decided that he ought to inform the police because Janet was so sure of the weird feelings she had had about Hanratty being the killer. This lead was not followed up, largely because Hanratty bore little or no resemblance to the Identikit pictures. It was, of course, perfectly reasonable for the investigating officers to make special allowances for Janet because of the stress and grief she was going through — the kind of psychological pressure that can easily stimulate unusual feelings.

In due course, Hanratty was arrested and charged with murdering Michael Gregsten and wounding Valerie Storie. He was convicted, and hanged in Bedford Jail on April 4, 1962.

The worst problem for the defence was Hanratty's change of story about his whereabouts on the night that Gregsten was killed. He first said that he had been in Liverpool with three friends he was not willing to name — because of the professional criminal's code of secrecy. He then changed his alibi location to Rhyl in North Wales, which is barely forty miles from Liverpool. A landlady in Rhyl more or less confirmed his story, as did other guest house proprietors and neighbours to whom he had apparently applied unsuccessfully for a room that night. These included a very convincing and reliable witness named Margaret Walker, who lived in the road behind Ingledene, where Hanratty claimed he had stayed. Under fierce cross-examination, however, the Rhyl landlady broke down and admitted that she had been fully booked. Yet Hanratty had accurately described a green bath in the attic at Ingledene. How could he have known such details if he wasn't there? Or had he stayed there at some other time, and simply recalled the green bath when it was convenient to do so? If the landlady had accommodated him on an informal cash basis — without keeping the necessary records for tax purposes — would she have been worried and frightened that such facts would come out in court?

Hanratty also claimed that, while he was in Liverpool, he had gone into a candy shop in Scotland Road to ask for directions to either Carlton Road or Tarleton Road. Mrs. Olive Dinwoodie had been serving in the shop for only two days — two critical days that were vital in terms of evidence for Hanratty. She clearly recalled being there on August 21 and 22, and she also recalled that a man answering Hanratty's description had come into the shop to ask the way to Carlton, or Tarleton, Road. The prosecution countered this support for Hanratty by arguing that he had bought the alibi — that he had paid a criminal friend who looked and sounded like him to go into the shop and say something that the assistant was likely to remember because it was unusual. Was this confederate perhaps one of the three men he so resolutely refused to name? Yet how could a false alibi have been set up prior to the murder — a crime that bore several hallmarks of improvisation and spontaneity, rather than premeditation? On the other hand, if Hanratty, Alphon, and/or others had been paid — as one theory suggested — to frighten Michael and Valerie into stopping their relationship, it could well have been part of the frighteners' plan to provide an alibi for whichever member of their gang was in place at Deadman's Hill.

There are, however, other sinister theories that cast dark, conspiratorial shadows over the Hanratty case. Remembering the political and social background of the U.K. in the late 1950s and early '60s sheds useful light on the Hanratty conspiracy theories. In 1959, Harold Macmillan was prime minister, at the head of a powerful Conservative government with a majority of more than a hundred seats. Cartoonists were referring to him as "Supermac," and political journalists were calling him "unflappable." They were horrendously wrong. Mac was anything but invincible, and discontent was growing. Japan and Germany had booming economies, while the U.K.'s was struggling. The possibility of Britain entering the European Common Market was being mooted. British voters became discontented. The Conservatives lost one dramatic by-election after another. The once-unflappable Supermac did a remarkably good impersonation of a bat flapping its way out of hell. Cartoonists called him Mac the Knife after a third of his cabinet was sacked and replaced. The Labour party under Harold Wilson, an exceptionally clever and pragmatic politician, began to look like a serious threat to the Conservatives after years in the wilderness. Talent in the form of George Brown, Jim Callaghan and Denis Healey was waiting impatiently in the wings alongside Wilson.

The last thing the British establishment, and Macmillan's besieged Conservative government, wanted was a major scandal. The cold war between Russia and the West was at its sharpest and most bitter. Diplomats Guy Burgess and Donald Maclean had fled to the Soviet Union in the '50s.

In 1961, the year of Gregsten's murder, George Blake, another ex-diplomat, had been sentenced to more than forty years in prison for spying for the Soviets. Sensationally, he escaped after serving only five years!

A few months after Hanratty's execution, the Profumo scandal broke and wrecked Macmillan's chances of reelection. John Denis Profumo, educated at Harrow and Oxford, was secretary of state for war. Married to film star Valerie Hobson, Profumo had a wild, romantic affair with Christine Keeler, one of the very glamorous and available young ladies who circulated around Stephen Ward, an influential West End osteopath who moved in the very highest social circles. Ward himself was later to die in mysterious circumstances — officially suicide, but he, too, might well have had some help! The core of the scandal was not so much Profumo's relationship with Christine as her simultaneous relationship with Eugene Ivanov, the naval attaché at the Soviet embassy.

The underlying fear in the security establishment was that the sexual peccadilloes of government ministers, members of Parliament, civil service personnel, or government scientists with access to confidential information could all too easily lead to blackmail. A man who was compromised by scandal, or by the threat of scandal, thereby became a security risk — a soft target for foreign espionage agents.

Suppose that the love affair between Gregsten and Valerie had reached the ears of a senior civil servant who was worried about security. Is it possible — without the argument getting swept away in a deluge of exaggerated conspiracy theory — that someone, somewhere, wanted to break up the affair between Michael and Valerie while there was still time?

Were Hanratty, or Alphon, or both of them, plus their alibi-makers, hired as operatives? Was the sole intention at Deadman's Hill to frighten the clandestine lovers away from each other? Did the gunman really panic when Michael hit him so ineffectually with the duffel bag?

If someone was paid to do the frightening, to what extent was Peter Alphon involved? When Paul Foot investigated the Hanratty affair, he was shown Alphon's bank statements, which revealed that more than £7,000 had been deposited between October 1961 and June 1962. Seven thousand pounds was a very substantial sum in those days, when a good family-sized house could be bought for under £3,000. There were some alleged occasions on which Alphon was supposed to have said that he had killed Gregsten but that the establishment had killed Hanratty. Alphon later denied that he had said any such thing.

Various public-spirited individuals, as well as Hanratty's own family, maintained all along that he was innocent, and they did everything possible to get the case reopened so that he could be exonerated posthumously. In 1997 and 1998, after DNA testing had become established as a powerful and accurate form of identification, tests were performed on items that had allegedly been in contact with Hanratty on the night of the murder. DNA samples from his family showed a very strong probability that the forensic samples from 1961 did indeed carry Hanratty's DNA.

When he was exhumed and another DNA sample was taken directly from the remains of his body, it suggested even more strongly that his DNA was present on a handkerchief that had been found wrapped around the murder weapon, and on a fragment of Valerie's clothing. The DNA evidence seems overwhelming, until careful thought is given to the location and storage arrangements of the fragments of cloth. If, as seems possible, these had been stored near other physical exhibits pertaining to the case that did belong to Hanratty, what are the chances that the handkerchief, and the fragment of Valerie's underwear, had become contaminated from items that would definitely contain Hanratty's DNA? It is not the highly accurate, scientific DNA evidence that is in question: it is the sources of the samples which give serious cause for doubt.

Many of Hanratty's most industrious, persistent and determined supporters have also raised pointed questions about the withholding of important evidence from the defence during his trial. If their suspicions are well founded, the conspiracy theory refuses to lie down and be quiet.

27

Just How Lucky was Lord Lucan?

On November 7, 1974, the peaceful Plumber's Arms in Lower Belgrave Street in South West London received a very distressed visitor. She was Lady Lucan, the wife of Richard John Bingham, the seventh Earl of Lucan. With blood pouring from severe scalp wounds, she shouted: "Help me! He's murdered my nanny! I've only just escaped from being murdered!" The assistant manager of the pub, Derrick Whitehouse, made her comfortable and then called an ambulance and the police. When help arrived, Veronica Bingham, the Countess of Lucan, was taken to hospital, while Police Sergeant Donald Baker went to investigate the Lucan home at 46 Lower Belgrave Street. He found bloodstains and splashes that led him to the body of Mrs. Sandra Rivett, the children's nanny. She had been brutally battered to death with a length of lead pipe, which had been deliberately bound with surgical tape to change it from an innocuous pipe into a deadly cosh. Weighing about a kilogram, it would have been a lethal weapon in the hands of a strong, determined attacker.

The first intimation that Lord Lucan had vanished came from disappointed guests at a dinner party that was to be held at the luxurious

Clermont Club in Berkeley Square. Bingham had simply failed to turn up. It was only later that it transpired that he was the principal suspect in the Sandra Rivett murder case. It also seemed highly likely that Sandra was not the intended victim. It was simply her tragedy to be in the wrong place at the wrong time: Lucan's intended victim seems to have been his wife, Veronica.

Veronica had come to London, entertaining hopes of working as a model, when she was only eighteen. She started off hopefully, but never made enough to live on properly. One of her friends, Christina, married Bill Shand Kydd, and through their friendship, Veronica met Lord Bingham, who was later to inherit the Lucan title. All went well with their relationship for the first few years.

Lucan, a well-built six-footer, was moderately good at a number of sports. He was a member of the British bobsleigh team that competed at St. Moritz, and he also raced powerboats. That particular skill might have provided a clue to his later baffling disappearance: some researchers believe that the end of the Lucan mystery was simply that he took a boat out into the English Channel and jumped in.

He was a good card player, excelling at bridge, but his great love — the central thing in his life — was gambling. His skill at cards led him to achieve considerable success at the gaming tables. On one occasion he won over £20,000, a feat that inspired his nickname of "Lucky" Lucan, and he lived as a professional gambler more than anything else. Lady Lucan did her best to share his fascination with gambling, and tried to support him by accompanying him to those clubs that would admit female members or guests. Some social psychologists would have wondered whether watching his total absorption in his gambling made her feel that she was having to share him with a rival — Lady Luck!

For whatever reason, her health started to deteriorate. It was said that Veronica became tense, stressed and nervous. It was alleged that she was frequently seen and heard to contradict and humiliate him in public. Some observers felt that she might have damaged their relationship by seeming to spy on him in the gambling clubs to make sure that he wasn't forming new relationships with other girls. It was also suggested that her other apparent mistake was failing to establish a genuinely independent life of her own. Caring and concerned friends who knew Veronica well at the time often commented that she never really seemed able to relax.

Whatever Lord Lucan's faults may have been, there was no doubt in the minds of all the family members and friends who knew him well that nature had engineered him as a perfect father. He loved his three children deeply; he was devoted to them. The developing tragedy in the Bingham household was that Veronica and John — as she called him — were drifting further and further apart. On at least two occasions he was alleged to have tried to have her committed to hospital as a mental patient. Veronica steadfastly refused to have anything to do with the idea that there was anything wrong with her mental health. As their relationship began to fail, so did Lucan's luck at the gaming tables. Debts began to mount. The shadow of impending insolvency cast its drab ugliness over their lives. Things reached a climax in January of 1973: Lord Lucan left Veronica and the children in their luxury home in Lower Belgrave Street and rented a private apartment for himself in Elizabeth Street, which was not far away.

Desperate to prove that she was an unfit mother to the three children he cared so much about, Lucan employed private detectives to watch Veronica. So desperate was he to have the children with him that he somehow obtained a High Court order and snatched two of them, and their then nanny, from Green Park. By June of 1973 there was another court case, and this time Veronica got the children back.

Lucan was devastated. Friends who knew him well knew that the traditional British "stiff upper lip" philosophy was deeply ingrained in the earl, and that his hard, strong exterior concealed deep and profound emotional hemorrhage within.

In the autumn of 1974, Sandra Rivett became the children's seventh nanny. Friends and family often remarked on how much she enjoyed her work there. Some investigators commented on her similarity to Lady Lucan as far as her height and build went. It was said that in dim light, or silhouette, one could easily be mistaken for the other. It was a tragic irony that Sandra would be dead only five weeks after starting her new job.

Lucan saw his children during the weekend of November 2 and 3 in Northampton. There seemed, on reflection, to be something more than casual in his questions to eight-year-old Camilla and ten-year-old Frances about what the new nanny did, and when she had her day off. Camilla told her father that Sandra had boyfriends and went out with them; Frances said that Thursday was the nanny's day off.

It was Sandra's tragic misfortune that, during the week of the murder, her boyfriend was unable to get away on Thursday, November 7, and so she had switched her day off to Wednesday the sixth, when he was free.

"Lucky" Lord Lucan.
Where is he now?

At around 8:30 on the evening of November 7, Veronica and the children were watching TV. Sandra put the two younger ones to bed, leaving Frances upstairs with her mother. Sandra then went downstairs to make a cup of tea for Veronica and Frances. Nearly half an hour elapsed before Veronica, feeling puzzled about Sandra's prolonged absence, went downstairs to look for her. Veronica called Sandra's name, and then an attacker sprang at her from the darkness, striking savagely at her head with a lead pipe.

Lady Lucan was certain that it was her husband who had attacked her. He left a completely different account of the events before vanishing so completely and mysteriously. Allegedly, Lord Lucan phoned his mother at about the same time that the badly injured Veronica was staggering into The Plumber's Arms. He told her that he had been passing the house and arrived just in time to interrupt a terrible fight between Veronica and an intruder. He added that Veronica was badly hurt, and so was the nanny. Then he asked his mother to look after the children as a matter of the highest priority. The sprightly seventy-five-year-old dowager soon had things under control, collected all three children and took them back to her flat, accompanied by Police Constable Chris Baddick. While Baddick was still with her, her son phoned from the house of a friend in Uckfield in Sussex, nearly fifty miles away. Having reassured himself that his children were safe with his mother, Lucan told her that he'd phone again in the morning — and that he would phone the police as well. Then he hung up. Mrs. Susan Maxwell — Lucan's friend in Uckfield, from whose home he'd phoned his mother — was the last person to see him prior to his enigmatic disappearance.

After he left Uckfield, where did he go and what did he do? Before the tragedy happened, he was known to have been studying a book by Willi Frischauer entitled *Millionaires' Islands*, which contained details of exclusive, exotic hideaways favoured by the very wealthy. Had his original plan been to disable Veronica, kidnap the children and escape with them to a remote island paradise where loyal and wealthy friends would conceal and protect him from the police?

His friends in Uckfield, Ian and Susan Maxwell Scott, quickly grasped the gist of his weird story, a tale so strange that it might just have been the wildly improbable kind of truth that is often stranger than fiction. He told how he had entered the house and that an intruder had run out. He said that Veronica had accused him, as she had done more than once, of hiring a man to attack her.

Numerous researchers into the mystery of Lord Lucan's disappearance have alleged that his loyal relatives and friends closed ranks to protect him and to argue strongly that he was innocent. Some investigators have commented that their actions resembled the unbreakable Mafia code of *omerta*, which translates broadly as a vow of silence.

The search for Lucan was immense and persistent, and produced dozens of leads. He was seen painting by the roadside in Spain; he was in Bulawayo; he was in Haiti; he was driving up the M1 motorway; he was on the quay at Newhaven; he was dressed as a policeman and directing traffic in London; he was boarding a train in Edinburgh. There were hundreds of sightings — but never an arrest.

What might really have happened to the missing earl?

When someone is able to vanish as completely as Lucan did, it normally means that he's dead and that his remains have been disposed of. His body might be burnt to ashes; dismembered and fed to the dogs; or deposited somewhere remote and inaccessible — underwater, immersed in a swamp or buried deep in a wasteland far away. But a strong and resourceful man with rich and loyal friends can find a number of secure retreats, and plastic surgery can work miracles. Even his enemies never denied that Lucan was a man of honour, that he had his own strict codes of behaviour. His friends would respect him as a truthful man. If he said that by an incredible but genuine coincidence he'd been in the wrong place at the wrong time — just as poor Sandra Rivett was — they would believe him because they knew that he was too honourable to lie to them. If they knew that — improbable as it looked to the rest of the world — Lucan was really innocent, then not only would loyalty prompt them to hide him, but their sense of justice would as well.

Of all the possible alternatives, it seems that the strongest probability is that Lucan is still alive, somewhere a long way from Britain, with a new identity and a drastically changed appearance. Perhaps it's just one more very odd coincidence, but, allegedly, his name once appeared on the temporary membership list of the very exclusive Muthaiga Club in Kenya — the same club associated with Lord Erroll's death on January 24, 1941.

28

DID FREDDIE MILLS REALLY COMMIT SUICIDE?

Freddie Mills was born in Parkstone, Dorset, England, on June 26, 1919. Before his seventeenth birthday, he became a professional boxer. Freddie was a powerful fighter who punched hard, accurately and scientifically with both hands. Like many pugilists of his generation, Freddie learned his craft in the many boxing rings that were a feature of English life in those days. He learned something new about the game from every one of the hardy opponents he encountered in Devon, Cornwall and Exeter. It was a hard school, but a very effective one. Freddie served in the Royal Air Force during World War II, but even during those service days he was able to continue his promising boxing career. Having beaten Jock McAvoy, Freddie went on to defeat the formidably scientific Len Harvey by a knockout. This gave Mills recognition as the world light heavyweight champion as far as the U.K. was concerned, but to gain universal recognition of his title Freddie would have to meet the fast, powerful American Gus Lesnevich. They had a terrific bout that gave the most sophisticated fight fans a night they would never forget.

Mills had massive courage, and often took on much heavier opponents, including the British heavyweight champion Bruce Woodcock and the gigantic Joe Baksi. In 1950, Mills lost his title to Joey Maxim; he retired, became a TV personality, and owned a nightclub, the Freddie Mills Nite Spot in Goslett Yard, Soho. It was Freddie's routine to go to his club every Saturday night at around 10:30 and check on everything with his partner Andy Ho and the staff. They would look around the club, check the kitchen, and Freddie would always taste the food himself.

Freddie was in the habit of taking a nap in his car, a silver-grey Citroën. When his wife, Chrissie, reached the club rather late on the night that Freddie died, Andy Ho came across the road to greet her and told her he was very worried because he couldn't wake Freddie. Chrissie went with Andy to her husband's car and saw him — as she thought — asleep in the back with the window down. Although it was July, the weather was keen, and Freddie had recently had pneumonia. Chrissie climbed into the back of the car with him and realized that he felt very cold and rigid. She became aware of something in the car that she described as being like a long metal rod, and saw blood on his mouth. Her first thought was that the metal rod was a starting handle, and that Freddie had somehow slipped and cut his mouth on it. It was only when she realized that it was a gun that the horrendous truth dawned on her: Freddie was dead! He had either shot himself, or someone had shot him and rigged the scene to create the impression that it was suicide.

This was an epoch of organized crime and gang warfare. It was widely known that the Kray Brothers ruled north of the Thames while the Richardsons governed the south.

Mills was by nature a friendly, ebullient extrovert. He genuinely liked people, and enjoyed being the centre of admiring attention. His boxing career, however, had brought him many hefty blows to the head — especially when he had fought bigger, heavier opponents. It was possible that those repeated blows had bequeathed him a legacy of brain damage. Freddie never appeared to be punch-drunk, but those who knew him well as a centre-stage entertainer would have been very surprised to learn of his frequent dizzy spells and bouts of depression. Among the many other good things he'd done in life, Freddie had been a member of the Samaritans, counselling and helping people who felt depressed and suicidal. Helping others in that way; sharing their sadness and going down with them psychologically to try to help them climb up from the pit of their despair, can

*World Champion
boxer, Freddie Mills:
murder or suicide?*

take a lot out of the counsellors, helpers and supporters. It saddened Freddie deeply when he lost his great friend Michael Holliday.

Freddie's business acumen wasn't up to the standard of his fighting skills. In those days, Soho was a clearly defined district — bounded by Charing Cross Road, Oxford Street, Regent Street and Shaftesbury Avenue — where tourists from overseas and businessmen from the north of England came to spend money in the pubs, restaurants, massage parlours, strip clubs and thinly-disguised brothels. Those prospective businesspeople who understood the situation would wait until property became available within that well-defined, mischief-loving quadrangle. If a business was outside the boundaries — no matter how close — it just wouldn't attract the clientele. Goslett Yard wasn't quite inside the real Soho, and it was just too far away to attract all the tourists it needed to make a business pay. Freddie's fame did attract visitors, a lot of them, but never quite enough.

Freddie also had his impromptu moments of glory outside the ring and away from the TV screen. Mills was seeing Joey Maxim off at Paddington

Station after their bout, when to his amazement he encountered Winston Churchill on his way to Wales. Churchill congratulated Mills on his performance against Maxim. "Very plucky indeed!" said Churchill. "So are you, sir!" answered Freddie, and then, as an afterthought: "Sorry I'm wearing my red tie. If I'd known I was going to meet you I'd have worn my blue one!"

The mystery of Freddie's death took place at a time when London was something of a gangsters' paradise. The Messina brothers from Malta controlled most of the prostitution. Other powerful gang leaders and their lieutenants controlled drugs, gambling and protection rackets. Most nightclub owners were apparently expected to pay for protection, but the criminals who ran these schemes knew that if one operator refused to pay, others would follow. On the other hand, if the hardest and toughest of them was known to pay up without complaining, the rest would follow like lambs. Fear was an indispensable tool the racketeers relied on to maintain their street credibility. If the word on the Soho streets was that big, tough, fearless Freddie had refused to pay, and if Freddie turned up dead — shot with his own rifle — the lesser mortals would be falling over each other to toe the line and make their tribute payments, like weak Anglo-Saxon kings hurrying to pay their Danegeld before the Vikings came back in force. The message would have been all too clear: if we can stop Mills, we can stop anybody! Was Mills murdered as an example to other would-be deadbeats?

Like so many other mysterious and questionable deaths — including the real truth behind the Lord Lucan case — there seems to have been considerable confusion amongst the varying reports of what happened to Freddie, or what he had done to himself that night in Goslett Yard. When the news first broke, the police gave the press the idea that they were treating Freddie's death as a murder case; and upon reflection it seems that those first impressions were probably best. Reporters interviewed Andy Ho, Freddie's partner; Robert Deacon, a law student who worked part-time as a doorman at Freddie's club; and Henry Grant, the headwaiter. Their stories varied widely, in part because of the psychological phenomenon by which we tend to recall not the event itself, but our own first retelling of the event. When several contradictory stories are put forward — albeit with honesty and good faith — witnesses begin to wonder whether they may have been wrong about what they think they remember.

Despite the many conflicting reports and apparently false memories to the effect that Mills had been seen in or near his club early in the evening and had then driven away to some unknown rendezvous before returning after ten that night, the most reliable evidence came from Chrissie. She and the family were positive that Freddie had stayed to watch the end of "The Morecambe and Wise Show" before leaving their home in Denmark Hill to drive to Goslett Yard. Their evidence proved that he couldn't have got to his club much before 10:30 p.m.

The scenario is, then, that as he dozed in his car with a window open, someone crept up and shot him through the eye. Suicides involving guns almost invariably put the muzzle in the mouth and fire the shot upwards and backwards. Shooting oneself through an eye is very rare. On the other hand, especially when a small-calibre weapon is employed, a killer may prefer to shoot a victim through the eye so that strong bone does not deflect the round.

The murder weapon itself, and the ammunition, raise other difficult questions. It was a .22-calibre Belgian repeater, of the kind favoured by rifle-range proprietors at fairs. Mills had borrowed it from his friend, Mrs. Mary Gladys Ronaldson, who ran a rifle range at Battersea Funfair.

Mrs. Ronaldson told the inquest that Freddie had called to see her on the Tuesday before the fatal Saturday night and asked to borrow a rifle. He explained that he would be opening a fête dressed as a cowboy. She added that when he had gone she noticed that two or three pieces of ammunition had disappeared from a cluster of loose rounds on her mantelpiece. Mrs. Ronaldson explained that she would never normally lend a gun to anyone, but that she had the greatest respect and admiration for Freddie and trusted him implicitly because he had once been in the boxing ring next to her rifle range, and they had been friends a long time.

Forensic experts were not completely satisfied about the position in which Chrissie had found the rifle when she found Freddie dead. The general opinion was that if a suicide victim held a rifle to his head while sitting in the back of a car, the recoil would dislodge it — even though this rifle was only a very small-calibre weapon. The shells used on fairground rifle ranges also tended to be short in length, and low-powered compared with the rounds used in serious competitions.

Another vital factor that weighed against the suicide theory was that Freddie had left no note; nor had any of his family or close friends had any inkling that there was anything worrying or disturbing him.

Murder is far more likely than suicide in this case, but that leaves huge unanswered questions. Was it a gangland killing? If so, which gang was responsible and why? There is an ancillary mystery connected with the blood. Why did the first people who went to try to wake him fail to see it? Is it possible that Freddie was simply in a deep, heavy, but natural sleep when the first members of his staff went out to check on him? Had the killer who shot him through the eye committed the murder between the first attempt to wake Freddie and the discovery by Andy Ho that something was very seriously wrong with his business partner?

Three months after the tragedy, Chrissie, who had been employing private detectives to investigate her husband's death, had a sinister encounter with a mysterious stranger. He called at her home in Denmark Hill and asked if she was Mrs. Mills. He then warned her not to waste any more time or money on private detectives, as she couldn't really afford them, and, more importantly, he said that the investigation was disturbing certain people who had an interest in the case. Being as tough as Freddie, Chrissie refused to be warned off — but the truth about Goslett Yard has never been discovered.

29

THE CONTROVERSIAL WILBERT COFFIN CASE

It was June 5, 1953, when three rugged American outdoor adventurers — Eugene Lindsay, his son Richard, and their friend Frederick Claar — set out from Hollidaysburg, Pennsylvania, for the Gaspé Peninsula near the mouth of the great St. Lawrence River with a truck loaded with equipment. The three Americans had planned to spend two wonderful, wild, back-to-nature weeks hunting and fishing in one of the world's few remaining unspoiled areas. A month later, on July 5, when they were already long overdue back home, they were officially reported missing.

Canadian search and rescue teams went into efficient action. There were numerous abandoned prospectors' camps on the St. John River, and among these the searchers soon found the missing truck — now as abandoned as the old camps. They were assisted by Wilbert Coffin, himself a mining prospector, a practical man who knew the area well. He reported that he had helped the three Americans on June 10 when their truck had let them down. Coffin had been instrumental in getting it moving again for them. He volunteered to work with the rescuers, but the body of Eugene Lindsay had just been discovered in an area close to a stream called Camp 24. Lindsay was badly mutilated: his scalp was found on one side of the small river, and his headless body on the other — the missing head was never found. Eugene's body was mangled as though bears had worked it over. There were bullet holes in his tattered clothing, and his rifle, which lay not far away, had hair from his torn scalp adhering to the stock. As far as the tragedy could be reconstructed, the murderer had used Lindsay's own weapon to strike him down, then used it again to fire at him, leaving bullet holes through his clothing. The killer had then left him to the mercy of the bears.

It was known that Lindsay tended to carry large sums of money with him, but his wallet was empty when it was retrieved. Robbery was, therefore, a prime motive. It was also alleged that Lindsay ran a money-lending business, and it was hinted in some quarters that his clients were not always treated kindly if they had trouble keeping up their payments. It was said that he had hurt and offended a number of people in this connection, and that in so doing had made many enemies — some of whom might well be murderously vengeful.

Two miles farther on, the bodies of Lindsay's son, Richard, and their friend, Claar, were also found. Both men had been shot and left to the bears, just as Eugene had. The motive in their case, however, would seem to have been purely to silence them, in case they had seen what had happened to Eugene and could have identified his killer — or killers. Had one or more of his former loan victims followed the Lindsays and Claar from Pennsylvania and decided that the empty wilderness of Gaspé was the ideal place to dispose of their enemy?

As in so many doubtful and mysterious murder cases, Wilbert Coffin had the fatal misfortune to be, yet again, in the wrong place at the wrong time. Because he had volunteered the information about meeting the three Americans and helping to fix their truck, he was arrested — more or less for being there, as the only evidence against him was circumstantial! Coffin's lawyers allegedly prevented him from speaking in court; his only opportunity to put forward his side of the story was a statement written in prison after he had been sentenced to hang. In this testimony, Coffin referred to seeing two other Americans in a Jeep in the same vicinity as Claar and the Lindsays. He had told the police about this Jeep and its occupants before they arrested him. Other people in the area had independently confirmed his report, and later a Jeep that could well have been the one Wilbert and the other witnesses described was found abandoned near Bathurst, New Brunswick. Was this the vehicle that the hypothetical money-lending victims out for revenge had used to track down Lindsay in the wild emptiness of Gaspé?

Desperate to obtain the impartial justice that would have saved his life, Coffin broke out of prison in Quebec City, using a replica gun he had carved from a bar of soap. He went straight to his legal adviser for help — hoping against hope that the case would go to the Appeal Court. His lawyer advised him to surrender himself and go back to prison. If Coffin had decided to make a break for it and go back to the Gaspé wilderness he knew so well, he might have survived. He took his lawyer's advice, however, and returned voluntarily to the prison. It was his last and most important wish to be allowed to marry the lady who had lived with him as his common-law wife, but this was denied him. There were a few stays of execution, but the shadow of the gallows lay darkly over him, and on February 10, 1956, Wilbert Coffin was hanged.

Two years later, in 1958, Francis Gilbert Thompson, an Aboriginal Canadian, was arrested for vagrancy by the police. Surprisingly, Thompson confessed that he was the man who had killed the three Americans in Gaspé in 1953. He also reported that he'd had an accomplice named Johnny Green. This could have accounted for the two men seen in the mysterious Jeep that turned up in Bathurst. The Miami police contacted their colleagues in Quebec. Thompson's confession was examined very carefully but, despite his apparent knowledge of intimate details of the tragedy, the Quebec police refused to believe his story and declared him to be an impostor.

It never ceases to amaze experienced investigators that so many false confessions are made by publicity seekers whenever a murder takes place. It is almost as though the people who come forward with such admissions — which are often wildly inaccurate — have some deeper, convoluted, psychological motives that baffle even the best professional criminologists. It has been suggested that some of these self-deluded "confessors" may be motivated by feelings of failure and inadequacy so powerful that they would rather run the risk of being arrested, charged and convicted than face their own chronic anonymity. Thompson, charged with vagrancy, may well have belonged to this group. On the other hand, some experts feel that even the most hardened criminals are occasionally subject to repeated attacks of conscience which finally overwhelm them and lead to genuine confession. Ironically, these real confessions may not be believed

— especially in cases where the crime has apparently been solved. Francis, in view of his detailed knowledge of the Gaspé murders, may have been telling the simple truth. He stuck by his story for several days and then — when the police steadfastly refused to take it seriously — changed his tune and said that he hadn't done it after all.

If ever a verdict was what the legal experts refer to as "unsafe," it was the verdict that sent Wilbert Coffin — who was almost certainly innocent — to his tragically undeserved death on February 10, 1956.

The Gaspé murder mystery still remains open.

30

WHO REALLY KILLED LYNNE HARPER?

Tuesday, June 9, 1959, was a warm summer evening in south-western Ontario. At about 6:30, fourteen-year-old Steven Truscott went out for a ride on his bike. His parents asked him to be home by 8:30. He gave a lift on the crossbar to one of his school friends, twelve-year-old Lynne Harper. Three of their other school friends saw them together, and then one of the witnesses, Gordon Logan, saw Steven again, on his own, about five minutes later. Steve arrived home at around 8:30, as promised, seemingly perfectly normal and behaving exactly as usual. When Lynne failed to return home, her parents were naturally anxious about her. Her father called at all the houses in the neighbourhood, asking if any of her school friends had seen her. Steve immediately told him about the bike ride, and explained that after he had left her on Highway 8, at her request, he had seen her get into a car. He described it as a grey 1959 Chevrolet with a yellow licence plate. When she still failed to return after two days, there was a massive search involving more than 250 people. Her raped, strangled body was found near the edge of a small wood known locally as Lawson's

Bush. Her left leg was badly scratched, suggesting that she had been dragged to the place of concealment after being killed.

Her clothes had been neatly arranged close to the body, adding the same incongruously sinister touch that accompanied the nineteenth-century murder of old Father Gélis of Coustaussa in France. Having butchered the elderly priest with an axe, the murderer — whoever he, or she, was — had laid out the body neatly, with the arms folded piously across the chest. What sort of strange mentality mixes homicidal brutality with a fetish for compulsive neatness afterwards?

Lynne's family, and Steve's, were Royal Canadian Air Force personnel, stationed on the base at Clinton, Ontario. Like many other regular-service bases all over the world, Clinton was self-contained. It had its own family accommodations, school, shops and swimming pool. Consequently, almost everyone on the base knew everyone else. As Steve set off on his bike ride, he came across Lynne in the play area with a group of other schoolmates. They chatted for a while, and then she asked if he could give her a lift on his crossbar as she wanted to go up towards Huron Road to see a man who had some ponies — like many girls of her age, Lynne was attracted to horses. Steve readily agreed and they set off together towards Huron Road, which was also called King's Highway 8. On their trip, they encountered three school friends: Allan Oats, Douglas Oats and Gordon Logan.

One strange and disturbing aspect of the trial that Steve subsequently endured was that the prosecuting counsel, Crown Attorney H. Glenn Hays, seemed to do all he could to discredit the evidence of these vitally important young witnesses. If their testimony had been accepted impartially on a full and fair basis, it could have made all the difference to the verdict. Gordon Logan in particular was adamant that he had seen Steve by himself no more than five minutes after he had seen him cycling with Lynne. How could he possibly have reached the murder site, undressed Lynne, arranged her clothes neatly, raped her, strangled her and then concealed her body near the edge of Lawson's Bush — all in five minutes? Then he would have had to get back to his bike — appearing cool, calm, confident, nonchalant and unruffled — before Gordon saw him again.

If Hays was to prove that Steve's guilt, he had to invalidate young Gordon Logan's testimony and that of the other young witnesses. He directed one of his attacks towards twelve-year-old Douglas Oats, who had said firmly and confidently, "I was standing on the east side of the bridge."

Hays scornfully told the jury, "I suggest to you that he was too bright.… Too bright to be believed."

We can imagine that if young Douglas had been timid and quietly spoken, Hays would have said, "Gentlemen of the jury, you must have noticed how hesitant and uncertain the boy was. We can't place any reliance in anything he told us."

Royal Tax Gatherer Morton had a similar device centuries before the Truscott case. He would say that if a man was living very modestly, he must have a lot of money saved and could well afford to pay taxes. If a man spent lavishly and dressed well, then he must have the means to do so — and he too could well afford to pay taxes! The famous Catch-22 of Joseph Heller's novel was a similar double-edged sword. Heller depicts a scenario in which mental illness was sufficient grounds to declare a pilot unfit for a dangerous mission, yet anyone who asked to be excused from such a mission was showing a rational concern for his own safety, and therefore had to be sane. Such a man could only be declared fit for duty. If the pilot flew a mission, he was crazy, and didn't have to. If he didn't fly the mission, he was sane and therefore had to.

At the trial, establishing the exact time of Lynne's death became very important. If Lynne had died after 8:30, after the mysterious driver of the hypothetical car had allegedly abducted her, then Steve was totally in the clear because he had been home before that time. A tightly sealed jar containing partly digested food the pathologist had removed from Lynne's stomach during the postmortem examination was entered as evidence; medical experts considered the degree to which food had been digested as an important clue, since digestion would have stopped at death. Dr. John Llewellyn Penistan, the district pathologist, gave his expert opinion that death had probably occurred at some time between 7:00 and 7:45 p.m. on June 9. Under cross-examination by Truscott's layer, Frank Donnelly, Dr. Penistan said that levels of digestive acid in the stomach increase for up to two hours after food has been ingested. Were the contents of the jar fully digested, or only partly — or were they just beginning to be broken down? Steve's possible guilt — or probable innocence — balanced on that question, and yet, very strangely, not as much was made in court of that apparent breach in the medical evidence as one might expect. If only the forensic scientists of 1959 had had the knowledge and facilities to carry out the procedures available today: DNA testing, for example, would have established Steve's innocence or guilt beyond any reasonable doubt.

Although he was only fourteen years old, Steve was sentenced to death. In its wisdom, the government commuted the sentence to life imprisonment. In 1969, he was released. Later, under a different identity, he married and raised three children.

In April 2000, Truscott took part in a television program about the case, and consequently, vast numbers of viewers concluded that he had been given a very raw deal in 1959. The broadcast highlighted evidence that had been overlooked during the trial, and that would almost certainly have resulted in a different verdict being brought in had it been presented. Much credit is due to the meticulous researchers who went through mountains of material and turned up this new evidence. Witnesses from forty years past were traced. Whatever material was still available from the trial was examined using the latest techniques.

One of those who was contacted was an ex–air force major who had information about a psychiatric report that allegedly pointed to a soldier who had been convicted of sex offences against young girls. The researchers also discovered that a murder committed at about the same time as Lynne's had been linked to the same soldier.

Further superb work in the archives led eventually to the reopening of cases involving the murders of two other young girls who died at about the same time as Lynne. This new evidence largely corroborates Steve's account of her getting into a grey 1959 Chevrolet after he left her on Highway 8 to go and look at the ponies.

Lynne Harper's murderer has yet to be brought to justice, and after so many years it may well be that he has already gone to face infinite justice in the next world.

31

KILLED IN THE LINE OF DUTY: OFFICERS MCCURDY AND UTTLEY

February 1, 1920, was an historic day in Manitoba: it marked the inauguration of the Manitoba Provincial Police Force under its first commissioner, J. G. Rattray. One of the force's priorities was to enforce the Prohibition laws. Tragically and ironically, it was while attempting to enforce these laws that two fearless, unarmed officers of what was then known as the morality squad were killed, and a third was seriously wounded.

Although it varied from one province to another, the Prohibition Era in Canada lasted approximately ten years, from 1915 until 1925. It had been brought in thanks to the efforts of the temperance movement, which enjoyed enthusiastic support in Britain, Canada and the United States. The main arguments of the movement, begun in the nineteenth century, were that alcohol was responsible for poverty, crime and disease among the poor. Alcohol was also blamed for much of the abuse and ill treatment of women and children at that time. In 1878, as a result of pressure from the temperance groups, the Canadian Temperance Act was passed. Its main provision was that the making and selling of what was then described as "hard liquor" was banned throughout Canada.

Up until 1916, however, there were plenty of public bars in Manitoba, and beer was not subject to taxation. The 1916 Prohibition law allowed alcohol to be consumed privately at home, but not in any public places. Because of the temperance legislation, Manitoba drinkers tended for a while to bring alcohol in from Ontario. During the most extreme period of Prohibition, the government employed officers known as "spotters," who went around checking up on people to try to find anyone breaking the Prohibition laws.

Whenever there is unreasonable and unpopular legislation, there will always be determined and ingenious people who find ways around it. Such was the case with Prohibition in Manitoba. Alcohol was buried in gardens, and illicit stills were concealed in wells. There are many fascinating anecdotes describing how this was done. One moonshiner had a still hidden in the woods. He went out to inspect it one day and found it empty — with a dozen or more inebriated locals sleeping blissfully around it! His secret had got out.

Another moonshiner threw raisins into the big barrel of mash — a mixture of bran and sugar — from which the illicit alcohol was distilled. Once the alcohol had been extracted and bottled, he threw what was left over into the yard to feed his chickens. Within three hours, he went outside to investigate strange sounds — and even stranger behaviour — among his chickens. They were all staggering around like sailors on a storm-swept lugger, and the cockerel was cackling in unison with his hens.

Yet another popular old moonshiner carried his coat on a pole over his shoulder as if for comfort and convenience. His regular customers knew that the illicit booze hung in a large bottle or two below the coat.

Despite all the spotters, the enthusiastic temperance workers, and their restrictive legislation, the Stockyards Hotel in St. Boniface, at the corner of Marion and Archibald streets, was a popular drinking venue for those who were in the know. Because of its reputation, the hotel had been raided half a dozen times, but it still defiantly flew the drinkers' metaphoric flag of freedom, and did its best for its faithful regulars. Then, on Thursday, November 11, 1920, tragedy struck.

Around one o'clock in the morning, a squad of morality officers led by Alex McCurdy raided the Stockyards Hotel. They weren't carrying their revolvers, or any other weapons, because they had never encountered resistance on such anti-alcohol raids. This was in part because the penalty for alcohol offences was a fine — violators did not face the prospect of jail time.

McCurdy's team consisted of officers James Uttley, Jack Dineen, Fred Cawsey and A. W. Miller. The police party split into two groups; McCurdy and Uttley went upstairs to check on guests, while the other three went to inspect the restaurant area and the hotel staff. Apparently, Uttley and McCurdy found a naked man and woman in Room 8. With great thoughtfulness and chivalry, the two policemen withdrew politely from the room for a few moments to give the couple time to dress. When they re-entered, however, the man fired two shots at McCurdy. The first struck his arm, and brought him down. The second shot was the fatal one: it passed through McCurdy's head.

Uttley grabbed the killer and wrestled with him vigorously, but the gun went off again and Uttley was shot in the chest. The bullet passed through his left lung and struck his spine, shattering it and causing paralysis. The murderer ran from the room into the hall, where he was momentarily trapped by Dineen and Cawsey. He fired at Cawsey, but the gun mechanism failed and Cawsey raced into an adjacent bathroom to escape. The gun suddenly became operational again, and the murderer fired savagely at Dineen, who was still on the stairs. Dineen crashed down into the hall and two more shots hit him in the back. Officer Miller realized that the only possible course of action was to call for backup. He raced out in search of a telephone to summon armed police assistance.

There was apparently another criminal staying in the hotel, and he must have been woken by the shots and shouting. He now joined the killer and they forced the hotel owner to drive them away in his car before Miller's backup arrived. They drove along Marion Street and then via Tache Avenue towards the Provencher Bridge. At the bridge, the killer and his associate leapt out and disappeared into the night. Thanking his lucky stars that he had not received the same vicious treatment as the police officers, the hotelier drove to Rupert Avenue, where the police station was situated. Here he told his story to the duty officers. The car was searched and some live rounds were found, as well as three empty .38 cases. The wounded officers were taken to St. Boniface Hospital.

McCurdy, with a terrible head wound, died in a matter of hours. James Uttley fought valiantly for his life, and made vitally important statements before dying five days after the shooting that shattered his spine and wrecked one of his lungs. Despite three major bullet wounds, Jack Dineen went on to recover and resume his duties.

Relentless police investigators swung into action to bring in the man who had killed and wounded their brother officers. The woman in Room 8 turned out to be an innocent hotel employee. She knew nothing of the killer except that he had registered under the name of James Brown. The investigators ploughed on with their work.

The elusive "James Brown" was apparently none other than the notorious James Buller — a highly dangerous professional criminal. If Brown was Buller, then it went some way towards solving the hitherto inexplicable gun attack on the unarmed officers who were only looking for infringements of the alcohol laws. If Brown was Buller — wanted for a string of serious offences — it would not be hard to imagine that he thought the police were after him specifically, and not just on a random alcohol raid, and it would explain why he chose to shoot his way out of the situation.

There had been a major bank robbery in Winkler on October 13, scarcely a month before McCurdy and Uttley were murdered. It was unsolved, but there were strong suspicions that Buller was one of the robbers. A gang of five men had cut the telephone and telegraph lines to the town. They had also cut the rope attached to the town fire bell so that it could not be used to summon help. They had abducted the bank's teller and forced him to unlock the main outer door of the secure vault, but he had had no access to the inner safe. The gang blasted the safe open with dynamite, but it was a long job — requiring three heavy charges — before they got away with nearly $20,000. There was only one town policeman in Winkler. He wasn't a coward, but neither was he a fool. For one officer to have gone out alone against five desperate, heavily armed criminals would have been a demonstration of suicidal tendencies rather than of courage. His wife also insisted that he stayed at home to protect her. The town blacksmith made a valiant attempt to ring the warning bell, but the gang had left one of its number in place to guard the bell, and he blasted the blacksmith's legs with his shotgun. If Buller really was a member of the gang that robbed the Winkler bank, it would explain why he thought the police were looking for him when they came to the Stockyards Hotel.

Whoever Buller really was, he used several aliases, including Brown, Kidd, Grey and Bullard. He was deeply involved in racing, and this, along with his criminal activities, took him all over Canada and the United States. His criminal record showed that he invariably carried two revolvers and had allegedly figured in a serious gunfight in Regina. He was known to be extremely violent and dangerous.

The police lost no time in making the public aware of Buller's activities and what he was wanted for. Thousands of posters were distributed, and a $2,500 reward was offered. The vast search area included Canada, Mexico and the States. It lasted for over eleven months before justice finally appeared to catch up with the man who had gunned down McCurdy and Uttley in the Stockyards Hotel in St. Boniface, Manitoba.

Whoever he really was, Buller was clearly identified sitting beside Patrick Joyce in the back of a Ford parked on Prairie Avenue near East 24th Street in Chicago. It was four o'clock in the afternoon on October 15, 1921. Detective Sergeant Mike Grady, accompanied by Officer Ernie Daliage, caught up with Buller and his associate and dealt with them swiftly, ruthlessly and effectively. The Chicago coroner's report said that Buller had died of shock and hemorrhage following a bullet fired into his head by Mike Grady. Joyce also died from shock and hemorrhage after both policemen shot him in the chest.

The Coroner's Jury justified the police action: "From the evidence presented, we the jury believe the deceased Buller and Joyce were in hiding for the purpose of doing an unlawful act and the Police Officers fired said shots in self-defence and believing their lives were in jeopardy, and while in the performance of their duty."

The mystery remains: had Buller and Joyce been in the Stockyards Hotel together? Were they the men who forced the hotelier to drive them away after the police officers had been shot? Were they members of the gang that had blown the safe in the bank at Winkler, abducted the teller and shot the blacksmith?

32

THE MYSTERY OF WAYNE RICHARD GREAVETTE

An experienced homicide officer looks for three things: the motive, the method and the murderer. Once a victim has been identified, and the essential forensic scientific work has been conducted, detectives try to answer the question of why. When there is no answer to that question, an investigation is severely hindered from the start. Motives point to suspects. Suspects can be interrogated. Alibis can be checked. Guilt can be established. Justice can be done.

The horrific unsolved murder of friendly, helpful, hard-working family man Wayne Richard Greavette has remained unsolved largely because the best investigators in the world could not find the tiniest shred of motive.

Greavette was born on January 4, 1954. On December 12, 1996, he was killed by a bomb sent through the mail. The bomb was disguised as a flashlight. Wayne was only forty-two years old. His wife, his children, his mother and the whole of the Greavette family miss him and mourn for him.

To describe him in the most basic terms is simply to say that Wayne was an all-around good guy, a regular guy — the kind the world needs most.

Wayne Richard Greavette: mail bomb victim.

He was a skilled engineer, specializing in packaging machinery. He could install equipment that would take nutritious products safely and hygienically all the way through to the shelf in the grocery store. He serviced that machinery as well as fitting it, and he worked for food and drink companies all over Ontario — and much farther afield. In 1993, Wayne and his wife started their own business, putting his long years of experience and high levels of engineering skill to good use for the benefit of food and drink manufacturing and distributing organizations in and around Acton, Ontario. In 1996, the Greavettes decided to extend and diversify their business. They also moved to a farm in Moffat, in the township of Puslinch, where there was a great supply of pure spring water. Wayne's plan was to extract, bottle and sell this water. Meanwhile, he continued his engineering work to maintain a satisfactory cash flow.

Tragedy struck on December 12, 1996. A small parcel arrived through the mail; it contained a typewritten letter bearing the words, "May you never have to buy another flashlight." With his engineering background, and interest in all things mechanical, Wayne switched on the "flashlight."

It was packed with a deadly plastic explosive which went off in his hand, killing him instantly.

The best clue available so far has been the make of the typewriter used to comopose the note: expert analysis has shown that it was typed using a Smith-Corona typewriter with a daisywheel print head. The exact model was a 10/12 #59543. The machine had an unusual fault: each time a period, or full stop, was typed, it was followed by a backward slash, like this: .\

His widow Diane describes Wayne as a quiet, hard-working man, who was devoted to her and their son and daughter, Justin and Danielle. Diane and Wayne had been together since they were teenagers. The family had no money problems, no debts, and Wayne had never been involved in anything resembling criminal activity.

If only there was a motive for the police to work on.

Was the bomb sent to the wrong man? Was this another tragic case whose victim was in the wrong place at the wrong time? Just as there are cunning, lethally clever assassins, so there are hopelessly inefficient ones.

If there was no motive that a sane and rational investigator could possibly understand, could the bomb have been sent by an irresponsible, mentally ill murderer? If so, any logical search for motive would be meaningless.

But assuming the bomber was a sane and rational being, his or her psychological profile is that of a person who combines the unenviable characteristics of callousness and cowardice. The explosive could equally well have killed an innocent mail sorter, or mail delivery worker.

Somebody somewhere has seen that daisywheel with the odd ".\" fault on it. Somebody somewhere has access to plastic explosives. Somebody somewhere had a real or imagined grudge against a good, honest, regular guy.

Detective Inspector Coughlin of the Ontario Provincial Police has never closed the case.

One day soon, justice may yet overtake the flashlight bomber.

33

Is Jeremy Bamber Innocent?

It was Wednesday, August 7, 1985. Investigating officers of the Essex
police force in England were called to White House Farm, situated in
Tolleshunt d'Arcy. The police had been contacted by Jeremy Bamber,
who lived in Goldhanger, about four miles from White House Farm. He
had reported that he'd received a desperate phone call from his father to
the effect that his sister, with a sad history of mental illness, had a gun and
was in a highly dangerous state. Bamber added that the line then went
dead, and all his subsequent attempts to reach his father by phone were
met with a busy signal.

It was reported that three police officers, PC 1509 Stephen John Myall,
PC 1995 Saxby and Police Sergeant Bews, reached the scene shortly
before Jeremy Bamber himself arrived to see what had happened. It was
alleged that all the lights were on upstairs and downstairs. A dog could be
heard whining, and a figure was seen moving around in the upstairs bedroom. Prudently, the three officers moved away and called for backup
from the Police Tactical Firearms Unit. At 5:30 a.m., the Firearms Unit
arrived and studied the situation.

While they assessed the situation, the police discussed the matter with Jeremy, who explained the situation to them and repeated his statement about the phone call from his father. He also expressed grave anxiety about his sister Sheila Caffell's mental health. He told the officers that she had only recently come out of hospital, where he said she had been treated for paranoid schizophrenia. Jeremy added that this was not the first time she had needed therapy for that condition. He reported that there had been a family discussion the night before about having her six-year-old twins, Daniel and Nicholas, fostered locally so that she could still keep in close touch with them. It was felt that this discussion might have been traumatic for Sheila, given her delicate mental health.

Jeremy also explained to the police that after calling them he had telephoned his girlfriend, Julie Mugford, a student in London, for some moral support and helpful advice. It was alleged that Julie was at a party at the time, and that she advised Jeremy to go back to bed. Far from happy about what might be going on at White House Farm, Jeremy dressed and headed out in that direction in his car. Along the way he was overtaken by a police car which was also heading for the farm.

Jeremy helped the police as best he could by drawing a map of the farm and advising the officers about the guns that were kept there. One of these in particular was an Anschutz .22-calibre rifle which had been used the previous evening after rabbits were seen in the farmyard.

The investigating officers gained entrance to White House Farm at around 7:30 a.m. by using a sledgehammer on the back door. They found Ralph Bamber dead in the kitchen, not far from the stove. It looked as if he might have put up a struggle of some kind before being killed. His wife, June, had been shot twice — once as she lay in bed, and later, fatally, as she struggled towards the bedroom door. Tragically, the six-year-old twin boys had been fatally shot in their beds. Sheila's body lay on the floor of her parents' bedroom, with the rifle on her chest and a Bible beside her. It appeared that her own bed had not been slept in; neither was there any apparent disturbance in the lounge downstairs.

Careful examination of the premises seemed to exclude the possibility of any intruder having broken in — although access via a downstairs toilet window could not be completely ruled out. Naturally enough, the police suspected that because of Sheila's mental illness she had murdered her sons and her parents before turning the Anschutz on herself. In view of her alleged unpredictability, it seemed to be the most logical and rational conclusion.

Among the major factors that seem to have complicated the later stages of the investigation and subsequent trial was the breakdown in relations between Julie and Jeremy. After the massacre of his family, Jeremy was helped, supported and comforted by many friends, including Brett Collins — recently returned from Greece and staying with Jeremy at his cottage in Goldhanger. It was alleged that Julie was upset by this, and that she reportedly turned against her former boyfriend. It was also alleged that her friend, Liz Rimmington, had supposedly told Julie that she'd had a relationship with Jeremy during the time that he and Julie were going out together. This revelation was said to have had a traumatic effect on Julie. It was alleged that, after Liz was supposed to have given Julie this information, a statement was made to the police that Jeremy had hired a hit man to wipe out his family. Consequently, Bamber was arrested and interrogated thoroughly, but was then released. It was said that investigating officer Taff Jones had formed the opinion that Julie's story was a fabrication, generated by her deep unhappiness because of the ending of her relationship with Jeremy.

It was not in the least surprising that after all the emotional stress, interrogation and publicity that Jeremy Bamber had been through, he felt the need to take a break from it all in France. When he came back from that short holiday on September 29, 1985, he was taken into custody, where he has remained until the present day — constantly and consistently maintaining his innocence.

The case for the prosecution apparently rested on seven points. The Crown challenged the idea that there had been any discussion about fostering Sheila Caffell's twins. Forensic evidence from the swabs taken from Sheila's hands made it highly unlikely that she had handled the gun. Police evidence suggested that the disturbed state of the kitchen made it look as if a grim struggle had taken place there. Ralph Bamber was a big, powerful man, who could easily have overpowered Sheila. This disarray in the kitchen seemed to suggest that another powerful man — such as Jeremy — had done battle with him near the stove, where Ralph was eventually found dead. The phone call to Julie, argued the Crown, suggested her complicity, and her evidence suggested that she knew Bamber had paid a hit man to massacre his family. There was, said the Crown, forensic evidence that showed Jeremy had got in through the ground-floor bathroom window to carry out the murders. There was also a sound moderator, or silencer, which fitted the .22 Anschutz, and medical evidence showed that traces of blood found on it belonged to the same blood group as Sheila's. The Crown argued that since she was found upstairs, and the silencer was found downstairs, she couldn't have done the killings and then committed suicide.

The passage of time makes it increasingly difficult for additional witnesses, or new forensic evidence, to help the accused in cases such as the White House Farm massacre. However, it has been alleged that mentally ill Sheila had spoken to psychiatrists and other mental health staff about killing her family. If anyone who recalls her saying that were to come forward, it would greatly aid Jeremy's attempts to obtain his freedom — assuming that he's genuinely innocent. It is also alleged that there had been serious family discussions about fostering the six-year-old twins because Sheila wasn't really able to care for them. If a social worker, or a prospective foster parent, came forward with that evidence — and such evidence may well exist — it would also be highly significant. The evidence of the forensic swabs taken from Sheila's body is also something of a legal minefield. It has been alleged that the swabs might have been taken after her body had been cleaned in the postmortem room. If so, it would be unlikely that they would have revealed any traces of gun oil, powder burn, or anything else associated with the repeated use of an Anschutz .22 rifle.

The Crown also apparently made the point that Sheila's immaculate, glamorous fingernails were neither chipped nor broken from desperate use of the gun. But would they have been? She had been a professional model — known as Bambi — at one time. As such, she would almost certainly have been expert at applying the kind of professional cosmetic preparations that strengthened nails and kept them flexible. There is a point to be made against the Crown's argument for a struggle in the kitchen between big, powerful Ralph Bamber and whoever had the gun: what if the disturbed appearance was due to the police officers breaking in that way? Powerful, burly investigating officers are under the impression that a gunman or gunwoman is in the building. It is not the calmest of situations.

When co-author Lionel was playing the role of Captain of the Royal Guards in an episode of his TV series "Castles of Horror/Bloody Towers," the director asked him to charge as dramatically as possible through a medieval chamber door in order to protect the boy king from a potential assassin. Getting enthusiastically into the part, Lionel crashed his two hundred pounds of bodybuilder's muscle into the venerable door — which promptly came off its hinges! A dozen equally strong and determined police officers with sledgehammers might well have disarranged the White

House Farm kitchen to an extent where it would look as if a desperate struggle had taken place there earlier.

The validity of Julie Mugford's critically important evidence needs to be considered very carefully indeed. The allegations about her quarrel with Jeremy might be thought by some to have influenced her thinking. It was also alleged that she might have received a substantial payment for her story.

The evidence of entry to the house through the bathroom window does not seem conclusive — nor does it point exclusively to Jeremy, even if someone had gained access that way on the fatal night. The most difficult point for the defence to overcome is the matter of what was thought to be Sheila's blood on the silencer. If she was lying dead upstairs, there was no way that she could have put that silencer back in the cupboard — where it was found — after shooting herself in the bedroom. The first vital question is whether or not it was Sheila's blood on the silencer. It was only said to belong to her blood type. As all blood donors are widely aware, many people share blood types — which is why transfusions are able to save lives. If the blood had been Ralph's or June's, there is no problem for the defence. It is also perfectly possible that Sheila had sustained some minor injury while removing the silencer. It could have caused a little bleeding — enough to leave her blood traces on it. Imagine a scenario in which the desperate, mentally ill girl tries to fit the silencer, fails, cuts herself while trying, bleeds slightly onto the silencer, and finally gives up trying to fit it, leaving it — bloodstained — in the cupboard. She then shoots Ralph in the kitchen and runs wildly upstairs to kill June before shooting her own children. With that ultimate horror destroying her mind totally, she goes back to her parents' bedroom and takes her own life.

The seven prosecution points are well constructed, logical and closely argued — but they are not infallible. There is still a huge chasm of doubt in the Bamber case down which the truth can slide quietly and disappear.

Jeremy Bamber argues his case equally soundly, and there is something compelling about his consistent and unswerving assertion of his innocence. If only someone, somewhere, has a vital piece of evidence — that might make all the difference to his fight for liberty.

There is an extremely interesting and thought-provoking Web site (http://www.jeremybamber.com) that covers all aspects of this intriguing case in detail. It is a resource that every interested reader should study carefully at first hand before deciding on Jeremy's guilt or innocence.

34

THE CHRISTINE DEMETER GARAGE MYSTERY

Perhaps it is because garages are often built away from the main part of their owners' houses — or because they are rented separately — and stand in rows like soldiers on a parade ground at a discreet distance from the sergeant major's eye, that they have all too often become the settings for murder. Another grim correlation between garages and sudden death is the availability of heavy tools and equipment that can turn at a moment's notice into the famous "blunt instrument" of so many homicide reports. The site is relatively isolated. The weapon is at hand. The murder is facilitated.

One of the earliest recorded garage murders took place in Southampton, England, as far back as 1929. The victim, Vivian Messiter, worked for a big oil company. In his rented garage in Grove Street, he quarrelled with an associate named Billy Podmore, who killed him with a hammer that lay among the garage tools. After the murder, Podmore locked the garage and ran for it. Several weeks elapsed before Messiter's body was found. Billy was soon caught, tried and convicted.

The authors know Portland, Oregon, very well as the venue of one of the best annual Science Fiction Conventions in the world, and co-author Lionel has lectured and sung there more than once. Portland — like Southampton — is a great coastal city, and like Southampton it has sinister garage-murder associations. On January 26, 1968, an encyclopedia saleswoman called on the tall, powerfully built, freckle-faced Jerry Brudos. He lured her inside with a greeting that door-to-door salespeople very rarely hear: "Please come in. I'm keenly interested in buying encyclopedias!" Perhaps an older, more experienced salesperson would have felt instinctively that something was wrong, but Linda didn't. Jerry's next words were also slightly suspicious: "We've got people upstairs — come on down to the garage." Once inside that garage-workshop, Linda was battered to death.

For Brudos, who suffered from extreme sexual fetishism and necrophilia, the death of his victims marked the beginning of his interest in them, not the end. Like so many other serial killers with similar mental illnesses, Brudos had had a very unhappy childhood, and his relationship with his dominant mother had been particularly negative. Criminal psychologists would suggest that a transfer process within the mind of a man like Brudos would transmit and relay that specific hatred of his overpowering mother to a general hatred of all women — and a desire to punish them for what she had done to him. Linda was not Jerry's only victim. In the late 1960s Jan Witney, Karen Sprinker and Linda Salee also vanished.

On May 10, 1969, a fisherman working the Long Tom River, which flowed into the Willamette, found one of their bodies weighted down with car parts — another garage-workshop link. Less than twenty metres from the first grim retrieval, a second woman's body turned up. This one had been mutilated in much the same way that Jack the Ripper had cut his victims.

When Brudos was being questioned about the murders, he told the police about his weird sexual exploits, ranging from rape to necrophilia. To corroborate his statement, the investigating officers found dozens of women's shoes hidden in a box in the loft, and attached to the ceiling of his garage there was a sturdy hook from which he hung the bodies of his victims as he played with them.

Strangest of all, Brudos had been married for some years, and although his wife Darcie commented that some of his sexual demands seemed unusual, she testified that he had never harmed or ill-treated her in any way. She also gave evidence that he often suffered from very bad headaches and frequently shut himself away in their garage workshop for long periods.

Brudos was sentenced to life imprisonment, and although Darcie was also tried, she was acquitted.

Perhaps the best known of all garage murder incidents is the case of Christine Demeter from Mississauga, Ontario. Garages often offer both seclusion and substantial piles of junk behind which a potential murderer may hide and wait for a victim. This is what evidently happened in the Demeter case.

Christine was a beautiful Austrian girl who came to Canada with Peter Demeter, and worked very successfully as a model. She and Peter got married in Toronto in 1967. He was Hungarian, and had suffered as a boy when the Nazis occupied Budapest. In 1944, after the Red Army disposed of the Nazis, Peter made several attempts to leave Hungary for Austria, finally succeeding in 1954. He reached Canada two years later, and eventually went into the real-estate business, which prospered for him. His wealth enabled him to make frequent trips back to Vienna, where he had an on-off relationship with an Austrian girlfriend he had known before meeting Christine.

Christine did not know that this old relationship revived itself from time to time, and when she finally discovered what was going on there were furious rows between her and Peter. Their relationship deteriorated to the point that Christine actually told some of her friends and acquaintances that she thought Peter was trying to get rid of her. After Peter had a secret meeting in Montreal with his Austrian lady friend, who had came over to see him, he and Christine began to discuss divorce.

On the day of the killing, Peter had taken their house guests shopping in Toronto, some twenty miles from their luxurious home in Mississauga. Christine and their three-year-old daughter, Andrea, were quietly watching TV at home when Peter and the others left on the shopping trip, at around 7:30 p.m. When Peter and their guests returned roughly two hours later, and opened the remote-control garage doors, an ominous gleam of fresh red blood shone in the headlights. Christine lay dead on the garage floor with her skull smashed in. Little Andrea, entirely unaware that anything had happened, was still quietly watching television.

Mississauga was a quiet, peaceful place — murders were very rare — but within a matter of days, a student was raped and murdered in the Demeters' neighbourhood, and another girl simply vanished. Peter

Demeter's best defence was the theory that a psychotic serial killer was at work in the vicinity and that Christine had just been another unfortunate, random victim — yet again in the wrong place at the wrong time. In Christine's case, however, there were a number of factors that didn't quite square with that hypothesis. The autopsy revealed that death had come from seven massive blows to her skull. There was no sign of any sexual attack, and robbery didn't seem to be the motive — the house was full of expensive stuff, but nothing had been touched. Furthermore, no murder weapon was found.

In the 1929 Southampton garage murder, Podmore had used a hammer from the toolkit and left it behind when he'd finished killing Messiter. When no weapon has been left behind for forensic examination in a police laboratory, it usually suggests a professional hit man rather than a casual psychopath is at work.

The damning evidence against Peter Demeter came from an erstwhile friend of his named Csaba Szilagyi, who testified that Peter had had a lengthy discussion with him in Vienna about the most effective ways and means of disposing of Christine. It was alleged that techniques ranging from electrocution in the swimming pool to a shooting by a break-in artist were all mooted. Fearing that Peter really meant to dispose of Christine, Csaba said that he came to Canada to try to prevent it.

After Christine's murder, Csaba went to the police, who wired him with a hidden tape recorder, and asked him to talk to Demeter. He did: the fateful tape was subsequently produced at the trial. Allegedly it contained a reference to Csaba taking a lie-detector test. Peter Demeter was said to have told him not to, adding, "You're the only one who knows!"

The trial was one of the longest in Canadian legal history. At its conclusion, after a bewildering kaleidoscope of witnesses had paraded in front of a stalwart jury blessed with commendable powers of endurance, Peter Demeter was found guilty of procuring Christine's killer, and sentenced to life imprisonment in 1974.

The heart of the Demeter mystery still beats. Who actually lay in wait and struck Christine down in that sinister garage? The seven powerful blows to her head were not the work of some frantic uncontrolled maniac: they were the coldly efficient execution method of a professional contract killer making absolutely certain that his victim was dead.

35

CHRISTIE OR EVANS?

On March 24, 1953, Beresford Brown, the new occupant of 10 Rillington Place, Notting Hill, London, was looking for somewhere convenient to put up a shelf for his radio. As he tapped on a likely-looking part of the kitchen wall, he was surprised that it sounded strangely hollow. Curiosity prompted him to tear off some wallpaper, which revealed a cupboard door. A corner of the door was missing, and Beresford shone a torch through the hole to see what was inside the cupboard. The beam revealed part of a female corpse. Brown forgot all about building a shelf and promptly called the police. They in turn called the great Professor Camps, the most widely acclaimed forensic pathologist since the world-famous Sir Bernard Spilsbury. But even Camps needed all his professional skill and experience to examine the grisly contents of that cupboard. The open door of the cupboard revealed the almost-nude body of a seated woman. She was removed carefully and laid in the next room. Behind her were two more bodies. All three were women in their mid-twenties. Diligent searching uncovered another female body under the dining room floor. This turned out to be Mrs. Ethel Christie,

John Reginald Halliday Christie: serial killer.

wife of John Reginald Halliday Christie. The two of them had been the tenants of 10 Rillington Place.

Camps' analysis of the bodies revealed that all three young women had had sex shortly before or after death. More bodies were found in the garden, and more brilliant work by Camps detected carbon monoxide poisoning together with strangulation. Mrs. Christie had been under the floorboards — but where was John?

Delving into police and court records soon revealed that there had been two more deaths at 10 Rillington Place — four years before Christie had fled and Beresford Brown had discovered the silent occupants of the kitchen cupboard. These two victims were Mrs. Beryl Evans, wife of Timothy Evans, and their infant daughter Geraldine. Timothy, tragically, had the mind of a child. He was mentally as helpless as Lennie in Steinbeck's *Of Mice and Men*. It transpired that he had told Christie, with whom they were lodging, that Beryl was pregnant again. Christie, it was alleged, had convinced Evans that he was an expert abortionist and could easily put things right for them. It then seems that while Tim was out, Christie had murdered Beryl and little Geraldine. He had then advised Evans to make a run for it, as he would be suspected. Poor Tim had followed Christie's fatal advice, been apprehended quickly and easily, and had "confessed" to the murders. At one point, he told the police and the court that Christie had done it, but no one believed him. He was a bewildered, confused, inadequate young man with a very low IQ. He could not communicate effectively.

Christie, who had been gassed and blown up in World War I, had served as a War Reserve Policeman during the Second World War, and had the air of authority that went with it. He was believed — Timothy Evans was hanged.

In 1943, while still in the Reserve Police Force, Christie had lured a girl named Ruth Fuerst back to his home, claiming that he had a wonderful cure for nasal problems, catarrh and sinusitis. Having mixed friars balsam, herbs and other ingredients with boiling water, and placed a towel over her head while she inhaled the brew, he popped a gas pipe under the towel as well. As soon as Ruth lost consciousness, she was carried through to the bedroom, raped and strangled.

Muriel Eady had the misfortune to be a friend of Mrs. Christie. One day she called while her friend was away, and never came out of the house again! Mrs. Christie herself joined the list of victims in 1952. Christie's other victims included prostitutes Rita Nelson and Kathleen Maloney, who had been lured to Rillington Place in the belief that Christie was just another normal cash customer. Hectorina McLennan's boyfriend was out of work, and Christie had said that they could sleep on the floor rather than be out on the streets. In the morning, while her boyfriend was out looking for a job, Hectorina came back to Rillington Place and, like the other women, never left.

Christie's terrible mental problems may in some measure have come from his injuries in World War I, and further serious damage that resulted from a road accident in 1934. Most of his aberrations, however, were due to the cruel treatment he had received as a boy. His father was a Yorkshire carpenter who beat young John savagely on numerous occasions, and it seemed that this had left the boy scarred mentally as well as physically.

A policeman on Putney Bridge in London recognized Christie a week after he left Rillington Place. Tall, thin almost to the point of emaciation, exhausted and rather confused, Christie made no attempt to escape or resist arrest. His confession to the murders caused a sensation, and he was executed on July 15, 1953.

As well as the women's lives that he destroyed directly and murderously, Christie almost certainly seems to have been responsible for sending hapless, defenceless Tim Evans to the gallows. There can be little doubt that if anything of Christie's track record had been known or suspected, Tim Evans might well be alive today.

Murder and mystery walk together along the darker corridors of the human psyche: they lurk in unexpected places. Human curiosity about them, and fascination with them, may be one of the best defences against them. Awareness of danger is one of the surest safeguards against it.